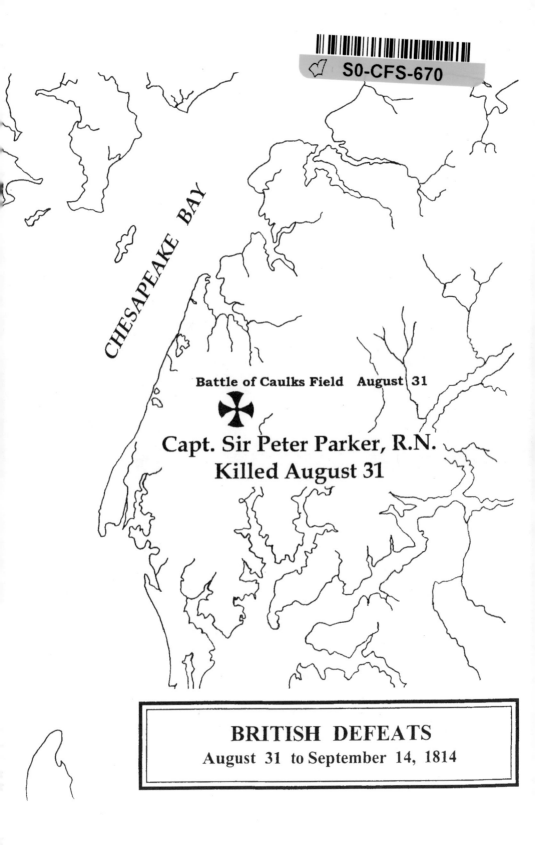

SO-CFS-670

CHESAPEAKE BAY

Battle of Caulks Field   August 31

✠

Capt. Sir Peter Parker, R.N.
Killed August 31

BRITISH DEFEATS
August 31 to September 14, 1814

Copyright © 2000 by Christopher T. George

ALL RIGHTS RESERVED—No part of this book may be reproduced in any form without permission in writing from the publisher, except by a reviewer who wishes to quote brief passages in connection with a review.

Maps by Richard J. Sherrill.

This White Mane Books publication
was printed by
Beidel Printing House, Inc.
63 West Burd Street
Shippensburg, PA 17257-0152 USA

In respect for the scholarship contained herein, the acid-free paper used in this book meets the guidelines for permanence and durability of the Committee on Production Guidelines for Book Longevity of the Council on Library Resources.

For a complete list of available publications
please write
White Mane Books
Division of White Mane Publishing Company, Inc.
P.O. Box 152
Shippensburg, PA 17257-0152 USA

Library of Congress Cataloging-in-Publication Data

George, Christopher T.
   Terror on the Chesapeake : the War of 1812 on the Bay / by Christopher T. George.
      p. cm.
   Includes bibliographical references (p.) and index.
   ISBN 1-57249-058-6 (alk. paper)
   1. United States--History--War of 1812--Naval operations. 2. United States--History--War of 1812--Campaigns. 3. Chesapeake Bay Region (Md. and Va.)--History, Naval--19th century. 4. Cockburn, George, Sir, 1772-1853. 5. Great Britain. Royal Navy--History--19th century. I. Title.

E360 .G46 2000
973.5'25--dc21

                                                    00-033384

PRINTED IN THE UNITED STATES OF AMERICA

E
360
.646
2000

022602—4470D3

To my darling Donna, for her love,
patience, and understanding

WITHDRAWN

. . . scenes of invasion and pillage . . . were witnessed all along the waters of the Chesapeake, . . . but if the fact be, as has been repeatedly asserted without contradiction, that the watchword of the day was the significant words *"beauty and booty,"* no charge would seem too atrocious for belief against the British commanders.

T. H. Palmer
*Historical Register
of the United States for 1814*
Philadelphia, 1816

Contents

v

Introduction

In the span of two weeks in 1814, the British offensive in the Chesapeake Bay ground to a halt after two key commanders were killed by American militiamen.

The first of these British commanders, Royal Navy Capt. Sir Peter Parker, was the less important. Though not in the highest echelons of command, Parker was nevertheless a cousin to Lord Byron and grandson of an admiral who carried the same name and who had bombarded Charleston during the American Revolution. Captain Parker, infused with the disdain for the "Yankees" instilled in him by his superior, Rear Adm. George Cockburn, landed on a moonlit night late in August intent on capturing a camp of militia on Maryland's Eastern Shore. Expecting little opposition, he armed his sailors with pikes to slit the tents of the despised militia. However, local militia commander Col. Philip Reed had prepared a trap for the young captain's pike-wielding sailors. American fire severed Parker's femoral artery. Parker died before he could be carried back to his ship, his invading force badly mauled.

An even greater loss for the British occurred two weeks later, when Maj. Gen. Robert Ross, victor of the Battle of Bladensburg, died trying to attack Baltimore. Ross, a daring and fearless commander, had successfully captured Washington, D.C., on August 24 at the head of a British army of approximately four thousand troops. Early in the afternoon of September 12, the general fell in a skirmish as he led his Redcoats toward Baltimore. Once more, the British underestimated the militia and misunderstood the determination of the Americans to defend their native soil.

I began to learn of these stirring events one wintry day late in 1991 as I stood gazing at a small white obelisk on Old North Point Road, southeast of Baltimore City. The monument sits on a private lawn within sight and sound of vehicles speeding by on the Baltimore Beltway, Interstate 695. An inscription on one face of the monument records that there General Ross "received his mortal wound." A few yards away, militia riflemen Pvts. Daniel Wells and Henry G. McComas died in the same skirmish. Baltimore legend says that one of these teenage boys fired the fatal bullet that killed Ross. An inscription on the obelisk says, "How beautiful is *Death* when earned by *Virtue*."

The pathos of the monument intrigued me. I started to read about the Battle of Baltimore. Through Scott S. Sheads, ranger-historian at Fort McHenry, I met Francis de C. Hamilton, a descendant of the British general's. A staff member of the World Bank, Hamilton at the time was a resident of Washington, D.C., the city that his ancestor captured and burned. With the help of Hamilton, I met another Ross descendant, Stephen Campbell, who still lived in Rostrevor, Ross's home village in County Down, Northern Ireland. In September 1992, I stood on the plinth of the general's one-hundred-foot-high granite obelisk that dominates the unspoiled shoreline of Carlingford Bay at the foot of the Mountains of Mourne. The money to build the monument came partly from British officers who had served with Ross in the Chesapeake.

At the time of my visit to Northern Ireland, all four sides of the monument had been spray-painted with the letters "PIRA" designating "Provisional Irish Republican Army." The plinth of the monument was overgrown with blackberry briars burdened with glistening blue-black fruit. A jungle of yellow-flowering prickly gorse bushes choked the path from the road.

As I write now, in the more hopeful atmosphere following the Irish peace accord of May 1998, I have learned from local historian Robert Linden that there are plans to rehabilitate the site. The local council is negotiating a 25-year lease to develop the site to make it more attractive to locals and visitors. The council hopes that the Ross monument will be a major tourist attraction on the Irish/American Folk Trail. May it come to fruition!

During my 1992 visit, however, such a happier outlook seemed a long way off and U.S. tourists were scarce. As I drove into Rostrevor, a British army patrol in black camouflage makeup and armed with automatic weapons stopped me for questioning. I got a sense of the climate of fear that then existed in Northern Ireland—fear much like the people of the Chesapeake felt during the War of 1812. Indeed, during the war, the citizens around the bay were terrorized and preyed upon almost at will by the British. The people of the bay suffered repeated scenes of invasion and plunder by the enemy conducted under the battle cry of "*Beauty and Booty!*"—a quainter way of saying "*rape and pillage.*"

The British depredations followed on the heels of a vicious sort of "warfare" in the summer of 1812 practiced by Americans themselves against fellow Americans in the streets of Baltimore. Over several days in June and again in July 1812, a Republican mob fought anti-war Federalists, spilling the first blood of the War of 1812. The mob incidents included the killing of Gen. James M. Lingan, a Revolutionary War veteran, and the torturing of another, Gen. Henry

"Light-Horse Harry" Lee, father of Robert E. Lee. Those bloody scenes, in which it is suspected that a number of militiamen participated, shocked the nation. Luckily, such sordid political divisions were healed in time to unite to fight the common enemy—the British.

Here we will tell the story of how the citizen soldiers of Maryland, Virginia, and Pennsylvania ultimately joined forces to cooperate with veteran U.S. Navy men and U.S. Marines to defeat the British peril and to save Baltimore and the Chesapeake Bay.

I thank the Deputy Keeper of Records, Public Record Office of Northern Ireland, Belfast, Northern Ireland; the Keeper of Manuscripts of the National Library of Scotland, Edinburgh, Scotland; the Keeper of Manuscripts, Public Record Office, Kew, England; Jennifer Bryan, head of the Manuscripts Division of the Maryland Historical Society, Baltimore, Maryland; and the Manuscripts Division of the Library of Congress, Washington, D.C., for permission to quote from the manuscripts in their collections.

I also wish to express gratitude to Rosemary, Viscountess Brookeborough, Brookeborough, County Fermanagh; Dr. D. S. MacNeice, FRICS, Director, and Patrick Fitzgerald of the Ulster American Folk Park, Omagh, County Tyrone; Stephen Campbell of Rostrevor, County Down; Canon D. C. L. Jameson of the Church of Ireland, Kilbroney parish, Rostrevor; Maj. John Hallam, Regimental Secretary of the Royal Regiment of Fusiliers (successors to Ross's 20th Regiment), Bury, Lancashire, England; Maj. Boris Mollo, Curator, The Shropshire Regimental Museum, Shrewsbury, England; and Col. Henry Brooke, MC.

Useful conversations that helped me to clarify issues about the War of 1812 in the Chesapeake were held with Lt. Col. J. A. Every-Clayton, USAR, Retd.; Geoffrey M. Footner; Joseph A. Whitehorne; historian and archeologist Kathy Lee Erlandson; Jim Parker, Alabama Historical Commission; and historian and archeologist Donald G. Shomette; Stanley Quick; and ranger-historian Scott S. Sheads of Fort McHenry. I also thank Paul Plamann of Fort McHenry and Walter Lord for granting me access to Mr. Lord's notes for his 1972 book on the war in the Chesapeake, *The Dawn's Early Light*, archived at the Fort McHenry.

I also thank Ann Marie Frederick, editor of the *Valley Times*; Laurel Durenburger of *The Urbanite* magazine; Brigitte Fessenden; Charles P. Ives III; Dandridge Brooke; Robert Reyes; Barbara Stewart; Ralph Eshelman; Robert Linden; Francis and Catherine de C. Hamilton; Dr. Robert J. Brugger, Ernest L. Scott, and Robert I. Cottom, editors of the *Maryland Historical Magazine*; Montgomery Phair; James Chrismer; and Beth Miller and Sally Johnston of the Star-Spangled Banner Flag House.

I express my appreciation to Richard Sherrill for creating the exceptional maps which illuminate the pages of this volume.

Finally, I thank my uncle, Douglas R. Matchett, my mother, Yoria George, and my late father, Gordon B. George.

Chapter One

Militia on the Run

On March 3, 1813, Rear Adm. George Cockburn of the British Royal Navy arrived in the Chesapeake Bay. Cockburn would be the commander who would most shape the British offensive in the bay during the War of 1812. Although he would serve under two successive Royal Navy superiors and work with British Army and Royal Marine commanders, it would be the aggressive Lowland Scots admiral who suggested and planned the attacks on major targets in the region. Cockburn, moreover, unleashed a reign of terror around the Chesapeake that has made his name live in infamy.[1]

Lord Bathurst, the secretary for war and the colonies, anticipated that the attacks in the Chesapeake would force the Americans to remove troops from the Canadian border for the protection of the capital, Washington, D.C.[2] The plan was a vital one for the British. After the loss of their 13 American colonies, Canada remained their remaining major interest in North America. They must protect their Canadian provinces at all costs.

On the surface, Bathurst's plan had merits. At its closest, the Chesapeake Bay is barely 50 miles from Washington, D.C. Yet, despite Cockburn's torching and plundering of communities around the bay, the strategy proved a failure. U.S. President James Madison, heavily in the sway of arrogant Secretary of War John Armstrong, refused to divert regulars from duties up north. In 1814, when the citizens of the southern Maryland county of St. Mary's protested to the president about repeated incursions, he allegedly replied, "It cannot be expected that I can defend every man's turnip patch."[3]

The American military response was left in the hands of the Virginia and Maryland militias and a few naval gunboats. Yet, the militia and navy were usually too stretched to do more than try to fend off the British raids and were in no position to mount any sustained offensive action. The notable exception

1

Rear Adm. Sir George Cockburn (1772–1853)

Courtesy of National Archives of Canada

was Com. Joshua Barney's July 1813 proposal to Secretary of the Navy William Jones to build a flotilla of small boats to fight the enemy. Unfortunately, it took nearly a year for Barney to recruit crews and build his flotilla. By the time his force was up and running, it proved little more than a distraction for an enemy soon to be reinforced by troops fresh from fighting the French in the Iberian Peninsula.[4]

Given the lack of real opposition from the local part-time soldiers who tried to protect the small towns he attacked, it is not surprising that Cockburn had a low opinion of the militia. Time and again, he would write in his despatches that his men chased the militia "into the woods." In fact, Cockburn had the regular's dislike of volunteer forces. The American militia no doubt reminded him of the ill-disciplined volunteers who had turned out all over England during the Napoleonic invasion scare of 10 years earlier.[5] Yet, the admiral took this dislike of volunteers to a new extreme, fired by his own haughtiness. He failed to realize that the militia could be shaped into a viable fighting force when led by capable commanders or when given backbone by U.S. Navy regulars and marines. This would prove the fatal flaw in British strategy in the Chesapeake.

A month before Cockburn arrived, on the morning of February 4, 1813, a squadron of Royal Navy warships under the command of Adm. Sir John Borlase Warren hove into position at the Chesapeake capes to begin a blockade of the bay. Implementation of the blockade followed instructions sent from London on December 26, 1812. The admiralty wanted to bottle up the privateers that since Madison's declaration of war had swarmed out of Baltimore to prey on British shipping.[6]

Warren, an elderly gentleman who headed up a Bible society in Halifax, proved tentative in command. This fact was made painfully clear four months later in the British rebuff at Craney Island, Virginia, in their half-hearted attempt to attack Norfolk. The admiral's hesitant approach may have been partly due to age but was also forced on him by problems of supply. Manpower and ships were chronically scarce on the Halifax Royal Navy station. Whatever the reason, except in implementing the blockade, Warren did not produce results. British naval historian William James, writing shortly after these events, pronounced the last word on Cockburn's superior. Instead of sending a "dashing" flag officer to punish the Americans, James concluded that the admiralty had sent "a superannuated admiral."[7]

Cockburn was held up in February from joining Warren by the need to wait for repairs to his flagship, H.M.S. *Marlborough*, at Bermuda's Ireland Island naval base. Now that he had arrived in the bay, he carried instructions from his superior to destroy trade and shipping off Baltimore, to gain intelligence on U.S. Navy gunboats in the bay, and to ascertain the situation of the U.S. Navy frigate *Constellation*. Capt. Charles Stewart, skipper of the U.S. frigate, had sought protection in Hampton Roads just as the British entered the bay. Warren ordered his subordinate to devise means to capture the warship.

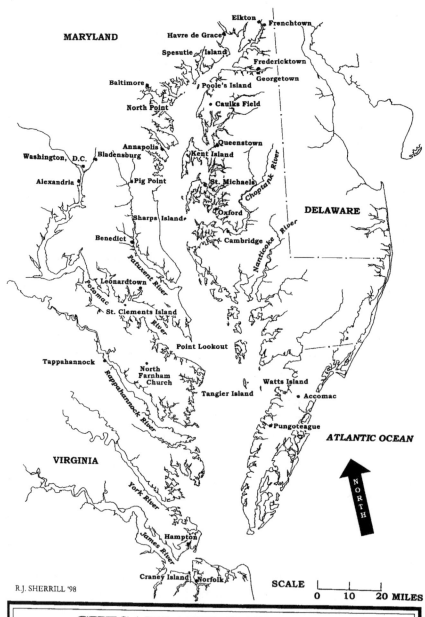

MARYLAND

Elkton
Frenchtown
Havre de Grace
Spesutie Island
Fredericktown
Georgetown
Baltimore
Poole's Island
North Point
Cauiks Field
Queenstown
Annapolis
Kent Island
Washington, D.C.
Bladensburg
Alexandria
Pig Point
St. Michaels
Choptank River
Oxford
DELAWARE
Sharps Island
Nanticoke River
Benedict
Cambridge
Patuxent River
Leonardtown
Potomac
St. Clements Island
River
Point Lookout
Tappahannock
North Farnham Church
Watts Island
Tangier Island
Accomac
Rappahannock River
Pungoteague
ATLANTIC OCEAN
VIRGINIA
NORTH
York River
James River
Hampton
R.J. SHERRILL '98
Craney Island
Norfolk

SCALE

0   10   20 MILES

CHESAPEAKE BAY ARENA
1813 - 1814

Maryland militia of 1813, fighting the British

Courtesy of Joseph W. A. Whitehorne

He should reconnoiter the defenses and "report any additional force required." Moreover, he should "procure pilots, taking black men if necessary for all Chesapeake rivers."[8]

As in the American Revolution, the British would use local African Americans to further their war effort. In the coming months, escaped slaves would act as guides for the enemy, and in 1814 some even fought in British uniform. Both of these developments followed a precedent set in the previous war.[9]

As a result of the arrival of the enemy fleet off the shores of his state, Virginia Governor James Barbour mobilized the militia of the Peninsula and the district of Norfolk. The commander of Norfolk military district, Brig. Gen. Robert B. Taylor, wrestled with the task of readying the area's defenses. Tay-

James Barbour (1775–1842), governor of Virginia

Courtesy Virginia State Archives and
Joseph W. A. Whitehorne

lor was new to the command, having only been appointed by Barbour on January 14, 1813. His headaches included dealing with an unreliable militia, lack of ammunition and supplies, as well as the problem of coordinating defense plans with the U.S. Navy.[10]

Likely British targets would be the port of Norfolk, Gosport Navy Yard, and the *Constellation*, now at anchor in the Elizabeth River. These targets were protected by a fleet of 21 gunboats and a system of forts. The gunboats were of the type proposed for coastal defense by President Thomas Jefferson in February 1807. Jefferson's "gunboat navy" proved of limited worth except in shallow waters against similarly sized small vessels. Although the strategy had been endorsed by army commanders including controversial Marylander Maj. Gen. James Wilkinson, naval men condemned it. They believed—rightly so—that the money would have been better spent constructing 74-gun ships of the line and frigates. Jefferson's gunboats, such as they were, ranged in length from 50 to 75 feet and in beam from 16 to 20 feet. Each mounted a 24- or 32-pound cannon in the bow or on a pivot and two 12-pound carronades, one on each side. The cannons had to be stowed in heavy seas, in which the boats could become unmaneuverable.[11] In fact, many of these vessels were no better than the barges the British used for operations in the bay shallows. The Royal Navy barges also were mounted with a cannon in the bow and carried as many as 50 to 75 men. What the Americans lacked at this point in the history of the young republic was the large resource of men-of-war that the British possessed, and particularly 74-gun ships of the line. At least on water, the Americans in the Chesapeake were vastly outgunned by the Royal Navy, the most powerful navy in the world.

Three fortifications added steel to the gunboat defense: (1) Fort Norfolk (30 cannons), begun before the Revolution and recently strengthened, located in the city of Norfolk on the east bank of the river; (2) Fort Nelson (39 cannons) on the west bank across from the Norfolk wharves, north of Portsmouth and the Navy Yard; and (3) an unfinished blockhouse on the southeast point of Craney Island (two 24-pounders and one 18-pounder). The latter fortification had been begun by Col. Walker Keith Armistead of the U.S. Army Corps of Engineers.[12]

Because of the plan of attack ultimately chosen by the British, low-lying Craney Island would have great strategic importance in the defense of Norfolk and the *Constellation*. In modern times, the island has been emasculated as a freestanding entity, its shape rendered unrecognizable by development as a U.S. Navy fuel depot and a U.S. Army Corps of Engineers disposal area. In 1813, the island was shaped roughly like a hotdog, running northwest to southeast, nine hundred yards long by three hundred yards wide.

On March 13, Cockburn reported to Warren that Norfolk was well defended with a force of at least three thousand men. He said the *Constellation* lay halfway up the river guarded by gunboats. The rear admiral well knew that he had his work cut out to try to capture or destroy the American frigate. In the river, as elsewhere around the bay and its tributaries, British operations were limited by numerous shoals. The British 74-gun ships of the line usually could not approach closer than four to five miles to shore, and even frigates had to be lightened to enable them to navigate the rivers. To get the *Constellation* as far up the river as they had, the American sailors had to "kedge and warp" the frigate through the shallow water, i.e., pull the ship laboriously over the shoals with rowboats and ropes. In order for Cockburn's men to approach the frigate, they would have to negotiate an intricate channel by rowing up the river in armed launches or barges. In daylight, those launches would be no match for the U.S. gunboats—so Cockburn began to plan a night attack.[13]

Although Cockburn was correct about the difficulty of the channel leading to the *Constellation*, he misread the readiness of the defenders to repel an attack. The Americans planned to use the militia to man the gunboats. Yet, both Taylor and Stewart knew the militia were not up to the task. The general wrote to Governor Barbour on March 11, "The Gun Boats are most wretchedly manned . . . and should they fall into the Enemy's hands, as they must if boarded by night, they will be turned against us."[14] Similarly, six days later, Stewart wrote to Secretary Jones that, although he had sunk four hulks in the channel, he felt pessimistic due to the unreliability of the militia. He stated that the gunboats were only "half manned" and that dependence on the local militia "has proved abortive." Indeed, he said, some of the militiamen had already deserted for fear of being ordered to man the gunboats.[15] Such reactions from militia followed precedents on the Canadian frontier. For example, on October 13, 1812, New York State militiamen refused to cross the Niagara River to Canada to fight in the Battle of Queenston Heights. They complained that they had not signed up to fight in a foreign country.[16] Yet, at this early stage in the British offensive in the Chesapeake, it seemed that the local militia could not even be relied on to defend their own land.

On the night of March 20, Cockburn ordered a barge attack on the *Constellation* under the command of Lt. George Augustus Westphal, first lieutenant of the *Marlborough*. The attack was timed to coincide with ebb tide when the U.S. frigate's stern would be presented to the attackers. One line of barges would launch an assault on the American gunboats while the other division, including two boats armed with Congreve rockets, attacked the *Constellation*'s stern. Westphal's sailors began the arduous five-mile row toward the American warship at 10:00 P.M. However, within two miles of the U.S. frigate, contrary winds and tides interfered. The attempted attack had to be canceled.[17]

Ironically, Stewart learned of the foiled British attempt to destroy the *Constellation* when Lt. Charles G. Ridgely was engaged on a diplomatic mission to Cockburn under a flag of truce. Ridgely had been sent to the enemy fleet on March 21 to escort Russian Ambassador Andrei Dashkov to Cockburn for negotiations. Dashkov was acting under orders from Czar Alexander I, who was anxious to mediate peace between the United States and Great Britain. The Russian monarch wished to keep Britain as an ally against France. At the same time, he desired to remain friendly with the United States, which he viewed correctly as an important carrier of neutral trade.[18]

Although the Russian mediation would ultimately prove unsuccessful, a letter written by Secretary of State James Monroe to Governor Barbour provides an interesting sidelight on the czar's diplomatic effort and the administration's attitude toward it:

> It is not known whether G. Britain has accepted this mediation. The President acts on motions independent of that consideration. If [Britain] accepts with a view to fair and just accommodation, it may probably lead to peace. If she declines it the responsibility will be on her government. In the meantime, no relaxation should take place in our military operations. They should on the contrary be carried on with greater vigor.[19]

The Americans realized they had experienced a close call for the *Constellation*, one of the young republic's original four U.S. Navy frigates built in 1797. For added safety, Captain Stewart moved the frigate further upriver and sank more hulks in the channel. The captain urged the federal government to strengthen Norfolk's defenses. He recommended building on Craney Island an additional strong battery "of eight or ten guns."[20] Thus, the U.S. Navy commander correctly anticipated what would be needed later when the British would attack in force.

Frustrated in his aim to destroy or capture the *Constellation*, Cockburn ordered raids up the James and Rappahannock Rivers. His sailors destroyed

Capture of the *Dolphin* on the Rappahannock River, 1813

Courtesy Mariner's Museum and Joseph W. A. Whitehorne

oyster boats and captured small craft that might be useful in the shallow waters of the tidewater. Then, on April 1, the British began to sail up the bay to have a firsthand look at Baltimore and to chart the waters of the upper Chesapeake for future operations. Late on April 2, British lookouts sighted four large schooners, the *Arab*, *Lynx*, *Racer*, and *Dolphin*, and another vessel off New Point Comfort. The American vessels fled for cover in the shallows of the Rappahannock. Cockburn ordered Capt. James Polkinghorne to chase the schooners in the small boats. In the early hours of April 3, Polkinghorne caught up with the Americans. After a fierce battle, he captured all four schooners at the cost of two killed and eleven wounded.[21]

The British thus continued to assemble an armada of light craft that would help them in their later activities. The famed Chesapeake Bay schooners, renowned for their speed and seaworthiness, would be put to good use by the enemy. On the evening of April 5, the captured vessels proved their value as the British sighted two brigs and seven schooners to the north-northeast. After hoisting the U.S. ensign, Lieutenant Westphal in the *Racer* took full advantage of the speed of the U.S.-made schooners as he led the *Dolphin* and *Lynx* in chasing the American boats. When they drew down on the U.S. vessels, the captain of a pilot boat hailed them. Assuming them to be friendly, he enquired if they needed a pilot. The British answered, "No."

The American hollered, "Have you seen anything of the Britishers?"

The British called, "Yes, they are coming up the Bay!" Then the wily Royal Navy tars hauled down the Stars and Stripes and raised the Union Jack. They fired broadsides at the astonished Americans. All the Yankee vessels were captured. Five Americans were killed and ten wounded, and one American subsequently died of his wounds. The British casualties were two killed and eleven wounded.[22] The victory proved pyrrhic, however. During the night, a gale drove several of the captured vessels ashore and destroyed them.[23]

Warren in his flagship *San Domingo* accompanied Cockburn's squadron almost to Annapolis. Then he left his aggressive subordinate to sail north to menace and perhaps attack Baltimore. Cockburn's squadron comprised his flagship *Marlborough*, the frigate *Maidstone*, the brigs *Fantome* and *Mohawk*, and the three tenders, the former American schooners, *Dolphin*, *Racer*, and *Highflyer*, which he could use to penetrate the shallow rivers in the upper bay. Cockburn had a special naval brigade of 180 seamen and two hundred Royal Marines for land operations. He also had along with some men of the Royal Artillery loaned by Brig. Gen. George Horsford, lieutenant governor of Bermuda.[24] The people of Baltimore and towns at the head of the bay might well fear what Cockburn had in mind.

Chapter Two

"A Nest of Pirates"

In the War of 1812, the British knew Baltimore to be a well of pro-war sentiment and a target well worthy of attack. With a population of approximately 50,000, the city was the third largest in the United States behind New York and Philadelphia. For decades, it had enjoyed a reputation as a haven for privateers. At the time of the Revolution, the British had labeled the city a "nest of pirates."[1] Now, with the new war, the city's privateering industry burgeoned after Congress passed an act which encouraged it. The federal government made a conscious effort to augment the infant U.S. Navy by giving sanction to unofficial armed vessels to give the United States more muscle at sea. On June 26, 1812, Congress approved an "Act Concerning Letters of Marque, Prizes, and Prize Goods." The act detailed the procedures for privateering. It also constituted somewhat of a pretense. A government-issued "letter of marque" only gave a ship's captain license to arm his merchant vessel for self-defense, but many captains set out solely to capture and destroy enemy merchantmen. Hezekiah Niles, the pro-war editor of the national periodical *Niles' Weekly Register* published in the city, wrote that by means of privateering, Americans could "distress and harass the enemy, and compel him to peace."[2]

The two most successful Baltimore privateer captains were Joshua Barney and Marblehead, Massachusetts-born Thomas Boyle. Late on the morning of July 11, Barney set sail from the city's Fell's Point wharves in the privateer schooner *Rossie* after failing to obtain a commission in the U.S. Navy. As the *Rossie* beat down the Patapsco to Fort McHenry, the future commodore began a cruise that William S. Dudley has termed "one of the most remarkable in the history of American privateering."[3] Barney had served in the Continental navy during the Revolution and, controversially, during the 1790s with the French navy. He put his experience to good use. In the first six weeks, he captured 18

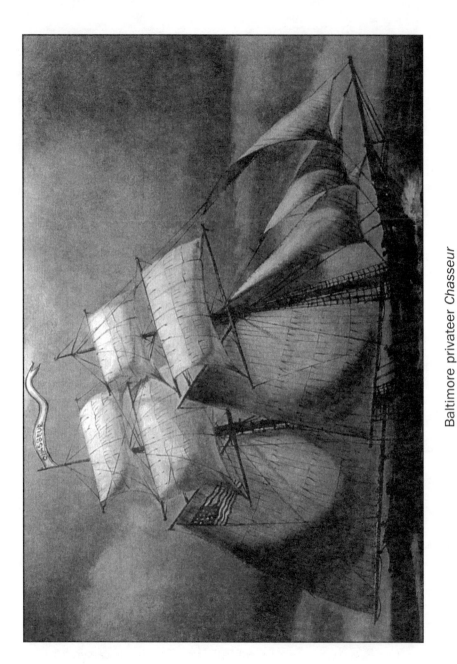

Baltimore privateer *Chasseur*

Commanded by Capt. Thomas Boyle, the *Chasseur* was one of the most successful privateers during the war.

Courtesy of Fred W. Hopkins, Jr.

vessels. By October 22, when he returned to Baltimore, he had taken 3,698 tons of British shipping worth $1.5 million and captured 217 prisoners.[4]

Boyle, captain of the *Comet* and later of the fabled privateer schooner *Chasseur*, was even more successful. After the war ended, when the *Chasseur* swept into Baltimore harbor in April 1815 after one more lucrative cruise, he had captured or destroyed more than 30 enemy vessels. An excited and by then victorious city proclaimed the *Chasseur* the "Pride of Baltimore." The British had other, less complimentary names for Boyle and his privateers. By then "Wild" Tom Boyle had escaped innumerable Royal Navy warships specifically ordered to capture him. In August 1814, Boyle even had the impertinence to lampoon the enemy blockade of the U.S. coast by declaring a blockade of Great Britain. To compound his audacity, he demanded that his proclamation be posted at Lloyd's Coffeehouse in London. Never mind that he only had the *Chasseur* with which to enforce his blockade. One ship against the hundreds of warships the British could call on. Boyle's act must have struck the British as typical of the behavior they had endured from the Americans. No wonder they thought of their former colonists as "Jonathan," the ungrateful bastard whelp of John Bull.[5]

The sailors of Baltimore were a unique, intrepid breed. Another privateer that left the city on July 28, 1812, soon after the outbreak of war, was the schooner *Sarah Ann* under Capt. Richard Moon. A month later, Moon sighted the enemy ship *Elizabeth* off Memory Rock near the Little Bahama Bank. The British vessel was bound for London from Kingston with a cargo of sugar and coffee. With his one long nine-pound swivel gun, Moon found the *Sarah Ann* outgunned by the Britishers' ten 12-pound carronades. He maneuvered out of range and took potshots with his 9-pounder. Then, ending a three-hour artillery duel, the spunky Baltimorean made a mad rush toward the enemy. His men stormed on board the British vessel and succeeded in capturing it. Among the Americans, two were wounded compared with four of the British. Moon convoyed his prize to Savannah, Georgia.[6] Once he had arranged to parcel out the spoils of victory, Moon took to sea again. However, now his luck began to wear thin. On September 13, the *Sarah Ann* was captured by the enemy frigate H.M.S. *Statira*. The British singled out six of the crew and accused them of being British subjects. Among them was George R. Roberts, a black man who later served as a gunner on board the *Chasseur*. The men were sent in irons to Jamaica. In a letter sent to the owners in Charleston, Moon said he feared the men would "be tried for their lives." He also rebutted the British charges. "[In regard to] George Robert [*sic*], a coloured man and seaman, I know him to be native born of the United States," Moon wrote. "He entered on board the *Sarah Ann* at Baltimore where he is married." *Niles' Weekly Register* reported that the owners took 12 British prisoners "and put [them] into close confinement, to be detained as hostages." The ploy worked. The episode was but one of George Roberts' many hairbreadth escapes during the war.[7]

On the morning of February 8, 1813, four days after the Royal Navy began to blockade the bay, a lookout on board the frigate H.M.S. *Maidstone* spied a sail to the northwest. The sailor had sighted the Baltimore letter-of-marque schooner *Lottery* commanded by Capt. John Southcomb. Southcomb was headed for the open sea probably unaware of the blockade, bound for Bordeaux with a cargo of coffee, sugar, and logs. The British intercepted the schooner. Two hundred Royal Navy tars led by Lt. Kelly Nazer attempted to board. Southcomb repelled Nazer's initial assault with the *Lottery*'s six 12-pound carronades, well served by his crew of 25. Fierce hand-to-hand fighting followed, but inevitably the Americans succumbed to the superior numbers of the enemy. Southcomb died of his wounds, and 19 of his men were killed or wounded. The British lost one man killed and five injured, two seriously so.[8]

Remarkably, the British blockade of the Chesapeake put a dent in the city's privateering but did not stop it. The privateers that had gone to sea before the blockade instead used as their bases the southern ports of Charleston, South Carolina, and Wilmington, North Carolina, or New York and Boston to the north. They shipped their captured goods to their investors back in Baltimore overland.[9]

As might be expected of a city that earned a living from privateering, Baltimore was overwhelmingly pro-war. In contrast to southern Maryland and New England, which favored the anti-war Federalist party, Baltimore voted solidly Republican. Madison's Republican party appealed to Baltimoreans because of its democratic emphasis and its welcoming view toward immigrants. The city had a large population of recent immigrants, notably Germans, Scots-Irish, Scots, and French. These new citizens unashamedly grasped the economic opportunities that the burgeoning port afforded them. Moreover, they stalwartly refused to bow to any foreign power now that they breathed the sweet air of freedom.[10]

In the hot summer of 1812, hostilities broke out in the streets of Baltimore between the Republican mob and Federalists who opposed the war. The disturbances arose out of a war of words between two newspapers, the *Baltimore Whig* and the *Federal Republican*, a leading Federalist paper edited by Alexander Contee Hanson.[11]

On June 20, two days after Madison's declaration of war, Hanson protested the president's action in an editorial. He pointed correctly to the military weakness of the United States. He also asserted that most of the nation opposed the war—a more questionable claim. On the night of June 22, the mob attacked the newspaper's offices at the corner of Gay and Second Streets, demolishing the building. The Federalists later accused Mayor Edward Johnson and other city officials of knowing about the planned attack beforehand and failing to stop it.[12]

Hanson devised a plan to return to the city a month later. He planned to publish the *Federal Republican* out of a fortified house at 45 Charles Street. To command the Federalist garrison, he enlisted the help of Gen. Henry "Light-Horse Harry" Lee, father of Confederate Gen. Robert E. Lee. Possibly on Lee's part this was an attempt to revive a fallen reputation. The Virginian's prestige

Gen. Henry "Light-Horse" Harry Lee

Collection of the Author

had taken a severe dive since that memorable moment in 1799 when he eulogized Washington in Congress as "First in peace, first in war, and first in the hearts of his countrymen." Recently he had speculated disastrously in western land and had spent a year in a debtor's prison. No longer either the dashing, handsome Revolutionary War cavalryman or the esteemed public figure, Lee had become a bloated, bitter, old man with extremist, reactionary views.[13]

On the evening of Sunday, July 26, approximately 30 Federalists began to fortify the house on Charles Street. Unable to obtain a printing press in the city, Hanson had printed the next day's issue of the revived *Federal Republican* in Georgetown. On Monday morning, Hanson distributed the paper. That evening, a mob gathered outside the house. The crowd grew agitated when it learned that the Federalists were moving in guns and ammunition. Young boys started to throw stones and shout obscenities. Hanson yelled back that he and his supporters were armed and would defend themselves. When the boys continued to throw stones, guns were fired from the upper story of the house, wounding several of the mob and killing one man, a Dr. Thaddeus Gale. The standoff continued until around 3:00 A.M. when the militia arrived. Thirty cavalrymen under Maj. William B. Barney, son of Joshua Barney, clattered up Charles Street. Barney had only been able to muster a third of his 90 cavalrymen. One reason for this may have been that it was known that Brig. Gen. John Stricker, commander of the City Brigade, had ordered that the militiamen be issued with blanks. Barney demanded that the Federalists surrender, a request that was flatly refused. Finally, though, they agreed to his request to allow the cavalrymen to occupy the lower floor of the house for the remainder of the night.[14]

Why did General Stricker, who only lived a few doors away, not come out to lead the militia? Stricker was a Revolutionary War veteran and an experienced militia commander. However, as historian Frank A. Cassell has written, on the night of July 27–28, he "evidenced little aggressiveness and appeared reluctant to make decisions."[15] Indeed, Stricker's indecision seems to stand in marked contrast to his decisiveness in leading the militia at the Battle of North Point two years later.

We have to recognize, though, that Stricker knew which way the political wind blew. To lead citizen militiamen intent on saving Baltimore from a vengeful enemy was one thing. Trying to curb a mob infused with the war lust that gripped the city was another matter. It would be neighbor against neighbor. At 6:00 A.M., when Stricker and Mayor Johnson finally appeared, the Federalists asked him why he had not called out the entire City Brigade. The general reportedly pointed to the crowd and said, "There is the Brigade."[16]

Stricker and Johnson urged the Federalists to surrender and be lodged in the city jail for safekeeping. Hanson protested vehemently: "To jail! For what? For protecting my house and property against a mob who assailed both for three hours without being fired upon, when we could have killed numbers of them!" He then said truthfully and prophetically, "You cannot protect us [on the way] to jail, or after we are in jail!"[17]

Brig. Gen. John Stricker

Lossing's *Field Book of the War of 1812*

General Lee, however, realized the defenders' position was hopeless. No doubt trusting Stricker's word as a fellow military man that they would be protected, he recommended surrender. At 7:00 A.M., the militia formed a hollow square to protect the Federalists during the journey to the jail. Hanson and his men were allowed to keep some pistols and knives but had to surrender their muskets. As the procession moved off, the mob set about tearing down the house. Other rioters surrounded the moving procession, whistling the "Rogue's March." Although the jail was only a mile away by the Jones Falls, the procession took two hours to get there. Along the way, the mob pelted the Federalists and militiamen alike with rocks. General Stricker was among those wounded— he almost lost an eye.[18]

The Federalists were placed in a sparsely furnished cell. If Hanson and the others thought they would be allowed to go free, they were soon disappointed. A judge arrived on the scene and refused to grant them bail. During the afternoon, rumors ran rampant that the mob intended to attack the jail that night. Stricker called out the 5th Regiment of militia in response to the renewed threats of mob violence. Of a thousand troops ordered out, only 40 infantry and a half dozen cavalrymen reported, along with a number of artillerymen. Major Barney later wrote that though the militiamen were willing to sacrifice their lives for their country, they drew the line at "traitors and disorganizers."[19] Stricker was faced with the decision of whether to try to defend the jail with these meager troops or to disband them. Finally, he ordered that the militiamen be told to go home. Thus, by nightfall, the Federalists were left without protection.[20]

After the militia dispersed, the assault on the jail began. The rioters forced open the outer door, then a second door. Finally, they broke into the room that held the prisoners. Two young Federalists threatened to shoot the rioters with the pistols they had been allowed to keep. However, Hanson said it would only provoke the mob to further violence. In the confusion, some Federalists managed to escape, but not Hanson and Lee and the others. The mob knocked down John Thompson as he ran for the door, tarred and feathered him, and hauled him 'round the streets in a cart. They beat Hanson, Lee, and Georgetown tobacco merchant Gen. James M. Lingan, an aging Revolutionary War veteran who had fought at the Battles of Long Island and Fort Washington. After this pummeling, the rioters threw the Federalists down the steep flight of stairs at the front of the jail. There they lay in a heap for three hours subject to additional beatings and torture in a horrific scene that even today defies belief. A Federalist account that was never contradicted states that the mob "torture[d] their mangled bodies . . . sticking pen-knives into their faces and hands, and opening their eyes and dropping hot candle-grease into them." Lingan begged for mercy. He reminded them "that he had fought for their liberties throughout the Revolutionary war." One of the rioters stamped on him and cried out, "The damned old rascal is hardest dying of all of them!" From this beating, the old

"The Conspiracy Against Baltimore or War Dance at Montgomery Court House" (detail).

Republican cartoon lampooning the Federalists. Gen. "Light-Horse" Harry Lee wears the chapeau de bras (*center left*).

Collection of the Author

veteran died. Others stabbed Lee around the face with knives, almost blinding him in his right eye.[21]

Hanson, the chief target of the mob, managed to survive. The mob bickered among themselves whether to castrate the victims, tar and feather them, or hurl them into the Jones Falls. As the victims pleaded for mercy, women screamed, "Kill the Tories!" Small boys skipped for joy. The rioters even had a bizarre song they sang over the bodies: "We'll feather and tar every damned British Tory! And this is the way for American glory!"—with each verse followed by cheers for Jefferson, Madison, and other Republican heroes. Fortunately, Dr. Richard Hall, the attending physician at the jail, intervened. In order to save them, he pronounced all the Federalists dead. One rioter, knowing corpses were sometimes needed for dissection, remarked that the bodies "would be very good Tory skeletons." With this, the mob handed over the pathetic pile of bodies to the doctor. Hall moved quickly to set up a temporary hospital in the jail. Friends helped some of the less badly wounded Federalists to leave town. Lee was conveyed to the city hospital along with Thompson.[22]

After his beating by the Baltimore mob, Lee lived in constant pain, his face permanently scarred. He left his family in Virginia and sailed to the West Indies. There, he made an attempt to mediate with the British to end the war. Finally, he died on March 25, 1818, on Cumberland Island, Georgia.[23]

The two days of rioting at the end of July 1812 shocked Baltimore and the nation. When a mob descended on the post office in the belief that copies of the *Federal Republican* were deposited there, Stricker called out the whole City Brigade. He ordered a cavalry charge to disperse the rioters. For days afterward, armed militia patrolled the city to restore order. However, nothing could disguise the fact that law and order had broken down and not enough had been done to protect citizens' lives.[24]

Fresh waves of criticism ensued when some of the alleged rioters were tried and acquitted. Meanwhile, Hanson and 22 of the Federalists were acquitted of the murder of Dr. Gale. Although the Republicans held onto power in Baltimore, elsewhere in Maryland, revulsion over the scenes in Baltimore caused a Federalist landslide in the fall elections. In Montgomery County, Alexander Contee Hanson was elected to Congress, and Levin Winder became Federalist governor of Maryland.[25]

While Republicans and Federalists went for each other's throats in Baltimore, other area men, knowing their country was at war, enlisted to fight the real enemy: the British.

Among those who took U.S. Army commissions after the June 18 declaration of war was Col. William H. Winder, a brilliant lawyer and nephew of future governor Levin Winder. Many men from Baltimore and the counties north of the city joined the new regular army unit paid for in part by the city and led by the former lawyer.[26]

Another noted Baltimore area enlistee in the regular army was artilleryman Capt. Nathan Towson. The careers of Winder and Towson could not have been more different. Winder's record will forever be besmirched by his loss at Bladensburg. Even his record on the Canadian border is undistinguished. By contrast, Towson's War of 1812 record remains unimpeachable. He constantly received accolades for his servicing of the U.S. artillery at Chippawa, Lundy's Lane, and Fort Erie.[27]

In August 1814, when the British tried to recapture Fort Erie, Towson won praise from two generals. Brig. Gen. Edmund P. Gaines wrote that "Towson's battery emitted a constant sheet of fire." Brig. Gen. Eleazar W. Ripley waxed even more enthusiastic. Ripley doubted "that there is an artillery officer in any service superior to [Towson] in the knowledge and performance of his duty." The British had their own name for Towson's battery at Fort Erie. They called it "the Lighthouse" from the constant blaze of light emitting from his cannon.[28]

If Towson had commanded the American artillery at Bladensburg, the battle might have turned out differently. If a skilled, proven commander such as Brig. Gen. Winfield Scott had led the American army instead of Winder, Washington might not have been burned. The British could have been sent scuttling back to their ships.

Yet, in both 1813 and 1814, the experienced regulars were kept on the Canadian border, not ordered to the Chesapeake arena. As Cockburn's squadron came up the bay to threaten Baltimore in April 1813, the city had to rely for defense on its militia and on one gunboat. Nine other gunboats belonging to the Baltimore U.S. Navy station had been sent to Norfolk and Washington.[29]

Fortunately, the militia of Baltimore were led by a formidable man, United States senator and major general of Maryland militia, Samuel Smith. Smith was a wealthy Baltimore merchant who had much to lose if the British sacked the city. He was also a Revolutionary War hero. He took leave of his legislative duties in Washington to concentrate on the single-minded purpose of defending Baltimore. If Madison and his cronies in the District of Columbia were prepared to sacrifice the nation's capital to the rapacious British, Smith was determined that such a fate would not befall his native city.[30]

Chapter Three

Cockburn Menaces Baltimore

On Easter Saturday, April 16, 1813, Cockburn's squadron hove into view at the mouth of the Patapsco and threatened Baltimore. The British narrowly missed capturing the city's one gunboat, *No. 138*, commanded by Capt. Charles Gordon, chief of the city's U.S. Navy station. The boat was positioned, Cockburn later reported, within cannonshot of Fort McHenry at the entrance to the harbor. He bragged that the gunboat scuttled for the safety of the harbor along with some schooners and small vessels. The British sloop *Hornet* chased the gunboat, and the American batteries responded with a hail of gunfire. They failed to hit the British boats, which captured a few small vessels Cockburn stated contemptuously were unworthy "for sending into an English port."[1]

Gordon wrote to Secretary of the Navy Jones to tell him of the city's nervousness at the appearance of the British. Gordon said there existed "a want of confidence" from General Smith "on down to the Citizen Soldier on post upon the ramparts." He reported that "[daily] the alarm increases to such a degree that the Citizens are packing up their valuables. . . ."[2]

Smith told Secretary of War Armstrong that "On the alarm gun being fired 4,000 men assembled." Unfortunately, up to a third of these men lacked weapons. Smith had been working tirelessly in the last month to requisition supplies and matériel.[3]

There can be no doubt that Smith was the right man to energize Baltimore. In April 1781, as a colonel of militia, he had likewise been in charge of the defenses of the city when a British attack was threatened. He had commanded the Baltimore militia since the Revolution. A wealthy grain merchant and partner in the shipping firm of Smith and Buchanan, he had a share in numerous vessels that prior to the British blockade sailed out of the port. Moreover,

22

Maj. Gen. Samuel Smith
(1752–1839)

Painting by Rembrandt Peale, 1816,
courtesy Star-Spangled Banner Flag House

as a United States senator, he had the connections in Washington to get the supplies Baltimore needed.[4]

Fort McHenry had been strengthened by the addition of 56 cannons from the French 74-gun *L'Eole*, which had been wrecked off the coast years earlier, stripped of her guns, condemned, and sold. The cannons had been loaned to fort commander Maj. Lloyd Beall by the French consul in the city and mounted in the outer (water) batteries. Somehow Cockburn knew of this new armament. When he sent a boat with a flag of truce that approached within four miles of the city, his officer asked if the French guns had been mounted at the fort. He was told that the heaviest guns had been installed.[5]

Baltimoreans thought afterwards that this information discouraged Cockburn from mounting an attack. However, it is likely that he had no thought of launching a major attack on the city. Cockburn lacked the manpower. He merely wanted to get an initial peek at the fort and harbor and to chart the tricky shoals of the Patapsco. When he wrote to Admiral Warren on April 19, he enclosed an intercepted letter which he said told of the panic "our appearance here has had at Baltimore and of the Precautions taken." He added, "should it appear practicable to annoy their Fort or Vessels above it with Rockets &c. I shall not hesitate in attempting it."[6] In other words, if he engaged in any military action it would be only a "demonstration" to induce further panic, rather than an all-out attack aimed at capturing the city.

In the same way that at Norfolk Cockburn had to consider the shoals in the Elizabeth River in planning an attack, the shoals of the Patapsco also greatly limited his offensive options. In March, Gordon had written to Secretary Jones noting that "no heavy ship can enter the Patapsco without lightening more than is usual in such cases." That is, any enemy frigate would have to be stripped of guns and ballast to get close to the fort. Gordon reported that his only fear would be the approach of gunboats or bomb vessels, which could be beaten off with "well fitted & manned" boats. The captain said he did not anticipate an attack on Baltimore, although he believed "the Enemy may without much difficulty distress Annapolis."[7]

Nevertheless, as at Norfolk, the appearance of the British served notice that more needed to be done to strengthen the defenses. Thus, Jones gave Gordon permission to lease four privateer schooners to add to his one gunboat. The four vessels were the *Wasp, Revenge, Patapsco,* and Capt. Thomas Boyle's *Comet.* On March 17, Boyle had successfully slipped past the British blockade during a thick fog. From April until the first week of September, the privateers were in the service of the U.S. Navy, mostly running down the bay to monitor the movements of the enemy fleet. Gordon fitted out the schooners with heavy guns to make them a match for the British.[8]

Meanwhile, Smith worked on problems at Fort McHenry. It is probable that improvements to the fort were in progress when Cockburn's squadron appeared. Weeks earlier, Smith had written to Secretary of War Armstrong that the fort was "not in a condition to repel a serious attack from a formidable British fleet." He asserted, for example, that the double-pine gates of the sally port "may be knocked down by a few strokes of an ax." Col. Decius Wadsworth of the U.S. Army Corps of Ordnance recommended an earthen ravelin be constructed to protect the sally port. The ravelin, a triangular structure of brick and earth still to be seen today, was completed in the summer of 1813. Col. Joseph G. Swift of the Corps of Engineers advised the addition of platforms for the lower gun batteries, construction of three hot shot furnaces, and the digging of a five-foot ditch around the fort. He also suggested filling in the earthen embrasures within the bastions to allow the cannons to fire over the ramparts en barbette.[9]

Smith was also unhappy because he knew that, in addition to command of Fort McHenry, Major Beall's appointment included supervision of the Tenth Military District. Besides Fort McHenry, the district included Forts Madison and Severn in Annapolis and Fort Washington on the Potomac. In a letter of April 21 to Secretary of War Armstrong, Smith said the 61-year-old major was "sorely afflicted with the gout" and not equal to the task of defending the fort. He also complained that Beall was unwilling to allow militia artillerymen inside the fort on a regular basis. Although militiamen were allowed to drill in the fort in daytime, they were evicted at night. The fort had barracks to accommodate 350, Smith noted, while Beall only had 52 regulars. Smith's point was that the enemy could sneak up on the fort during the night and overwhelm the garrison. He was also perturbed that the major insisted on allowing his soldiers to have their wives and children in the fort.[10]

Smith wrote to Governor Winder to ask for clarification of his authority in relation to the fort. Winder reiterated that Smith had command over the militia but not over other troops at the fort. In the governor's view, Fort McHenry should remain under the jurisdiction of the War Department.[11]

The dispute was resolved to Smith's satisfaction on June 27 when Armstrong appointed Maj. George Armistead to command the fort. The new commander was a man Sam Smith knew and trusted. Armistead had been second in command at the fort from 1807 to 1812. He had since been engaged on the Canadian frontier, where he had been promoted to major and distinguished himself in the capture of Fort George.[12]

After his arrival, Armistead moved fast to assess the condition of the fort and to approve the erection of a six-cannon sod fort on Lazaretto Point across the channel from the fort. He also wrote to Smith to advise the need for a large flag to remind the British that Fort McHenry—the Star Fort—remained defiantly in the hands of the Americans:

> We, Sir, are ready at Fort McHenry to defend Baltimore against invading by the enemy. That is to say, we are ready except that we have no suitable ensign to display over the Star Fort, and it is my desire to have a flag so large that the British will have no difficulty in seeing it from a distance.[13]

That summer, General Stricker, Commodore Barney, and Lt. Col. William McDonald of the 6th Regiment of Maryland militia called on flag maker Mary Young Pickersgill at her home at the corner of Pratt and Albemarle Streets. They requested that Mrs. Pickersgill provide the fort with a huge garrison flag 30 feet by 42 feet. Making use of the floor of a nearby brewery, Mrs. Pickersgill and her 13-year-old daughter Caroline made the flag out of some four hundred yards of bunting. The giant flag would have 15 stripes (eight red stripes and seven white stripes), representing the 15 states, and 15 white stars, each star two feet wide from point to point.[14]

Smith, meanwhile, was convinced that if the British were to attack the city by land, they would land at North Point at the end of Patapsco Neck, 15 miles southeast of the city. Old Roads Bay had afforded deep water anchorage for deep draft vessels since the seventeenth century. Smith arranged with Captain Gordon to set up a system of signals from the cupola of the Ridgely house near North Point. Maj. William B. Barney and his cavalry troop were ordered to reconnoiter the peninsula. Barney determined that the area of the Bouldin farm near Bear Creek would provide the militia with a superior defensive position. The peninsula narrowed and an advancing army would have to traverse open ground. A year later, this area would be the battleground of North Point. Further down the peninsula, a defensive trench was begun from Humphrey's Creek to Back River.[15]

To aid General Smith in readying the city to face an attack, the city of Baltimore created a Committee of Public Supply. This committee had the job of providing funds and supplies for the militia and of building defenses. The committee also raised and funded two companies of U.S. Sea Fencibles for the defense of the port and harbor in accordance with a congressional act of July 26, 1813 creating such fencibles. The men recruited for this corps were largely seamen who had served aboard privateers.[16]

But, in spring 1813, the city remained safe. After striking fear in the citizens of Baltimore, Cockburn sailed into the upper bay and began the reign of terror for which he is justly famous.

Maj. George Armistead,
commander of Fort McHenry,
(1780–1818)

Painting by Rembrandt Peale, 1816,
courtesy Star-Spangled Banner Flag House

Mary Pickersgill, flagmaker
of the 15-star flag that flew
over Fort McHenry

Courtesy Star-Spangled Banner Flag House

Mary Pickersgill *(seated, right center)* sews the Star-Spangled Banner while looking on are Com. Joshua Barney and Maj. George Armistead *(left)* along with Brig. Gen. John Stricker *(right)*.

Painting by R. McGill Mackall,
courtesy Star-Spangled Banner Flag House

Chapter Four
Cockburn's Terror

On April 23, 1813, Cockburn's sailors occupied Specutie Island near the head of the bay. The British carried off cattle and hogs. The inhabitants fled, but on being assured they would not be molested, they returned to their homes.[1]

On the night of April 28–29, Cockburn ordered a raid on Frenchtown on the Elk River, having learned of a depot of military stores there. At midnight, boats commanded by Lieutenant Westphal with 150 Royal Marines and five Royal Artillerymen under Lt. Frederick Robertson rowed away from the fleet. In the darkness, the raiding party lost its way up the Bohemia River, a tributary of the Elk. The delay led to the attack beginning not at dawn as planned but later in the morning.

The militia reportedly fled but a few stage drivers and others greeted Westphal with fire from a battery of three 4-pounders. The Americans proved no match for the British veterans. While cannons from the British launches pounded the battery, Westphal and his seamen stormed the U.S. right flank. The Americans retreated. Westphal ordered his men to torch the town along with the stores. Five vessels were burned, the American guns spiked.[2]

Cockburn's *modus operandi* was that if a town offered resistance, it would be considered a fortified post and the male inhabitants as soldiers. Then the town was free to be destroyed, its property confiscated, the cattle and stock taken. At the time, the accepted law of the sea was that if you were an enemy, your property could be condemned and taken. Cockburn adopted a similar code while on land in the Chesapeake. As he stated to Warren, "should resistance be made, I shall consider [what I take] as a prize of war."[3]

Many of the British who served in the Chesapeake viewed Cockburn as a hero. To 15-year-old midshipman Robert J. Barrett, the admiral was a gallant sailor with "sun-burnt visage, and . . . rusty gold-laced hat." He was, the young

27

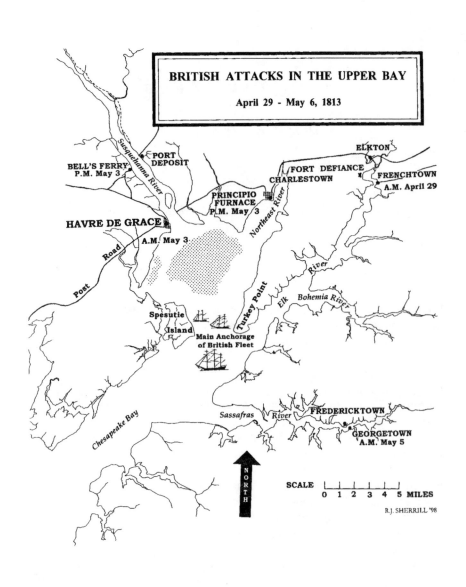

BRITISH ATTACKS IN THE UPPER BAY

April 29 - May 6, 1813

ELKTON

PORT DEPOSIT

BELL'S FERRY
P.M. May 3

FORT DEFIANCE
CHARLESTOWN

FRENCHTOWN
A.M. April 29

Susquehanna River

PRINCIPIO
FURNACE
P.M. May 3

Northeast River

HAVRE DE GRACE

A.M. May 3

Post Road

Turkey Point

Elk River

Bohemia River

Spesutie
Island

Main Anchorage
of British Fleet

Sassafras River

FREDERICKTOWN

GEORGETOWN
A.M. May 5

Chesapeake Bay

NORTH

SCALE
0 1 2 3 4 5 MILES

R.J. SHERRILL '98

man said, "an officer who never spared himself, either day or night, but shared on every occasion, the same toil, danger, and privation of the [lowliest sailor] under his command."[4] Others, though, disliked Cockburn's brand of warfare. Midshipman Frederick Chamier of the *Menelaus*, who observed the admiral in the summer of 1814, wrote:

> If by any stretch of argument we could establish the owner of a house, cottage, hut, &c. to be a militia-man, that house we burnt, because we found arms therein; that is to say, we found a duck gun, or a rifle. It so happens, that in America every man must belong to the militia; and, consequently, every man's house was food for a bonfire. . . .[5]

As Chamier sarcastically but accurately put it, the Americans were punished for "the unnatural sin of protecting their own country."[6]

Defenders of Cockburn have pointed out that if an American was deemed not to be hostile, the admiral paid for what he took. Cockburn wrote that if an American was friendly, "I shall give the owner bills on the Victualling Office for the fair value of whatsoever is taken."[7] Cockburn's biographer, James Pack, remarks, "Nothing could be fairer."[8] Chamier, though, revealed the truth of the "deals" the admiral offered the people of the bay:

> A bullock was estimated at five dollars, although it was worth twenty; and sheep had the high price of a dollar attached to them, they being in reality worth six at least. . . . But supposing, and I have seen it one hundred times, that the farmer refused the money for his stock; why then we drove sheep, bullocks, and geese away, and left the money for the good man to take afterwards.[9]

Successful at Frenchtown, the British nevertheless experienced a reverse immediately afterward. The attack force attempted to penetrate up the Elk River toward Elk Landing and Elkton. However, they were repulsed by the militia at Fort Defiance, which saved Elkton and 30 bay craft.[10]

Four days after the British operations on the Elk River, it was the turn of Havre de Grace at the mouth of the Susquehanna River to feel the wrath of Cockburn. Originally known by the less than exotic name of Susquehanna Lower Ferry, the town reputedly received its name from the lips of the Marquise de Lafayette. The French aristocrat, in passing through in the 1780s, is said to have extolled the beauty of the area. It was, he said, "Le Havre de Grace" or "The Harbor of Mercy."[11] Unfortunately, on the morning of May 3 when Cockburn attacked, the admiral was short on mercy.

Cockburn reported to Warren that he planned the attack on Havre de Grace after he "observed Guns fired and American Colours hoisted."[12] Prior to that, he said, he had given the place no thought. Soundings of the water in the direction of the town showed the water was too shallow to allow the approach of his larger vessels. Therefore, Cockburn devised a similar plan to the one used at Frenchtown. Westphal with the Royal Marines and artillerymen rowed away from the squadron at midnight in some 15 launches and a rocket boat.

As the admiral later described it, the raiders "proceeded towards Havre [de Grace] to take up under cover of the Night the necessary Positions for Commencing the Attack at dawn of day."[13]

Thus, while folk in the riverside town of some 60 two-story wood and brick houses were asleep, the enemy crept up on them. Not that they had not had warning that an attack was coming. Historian Jared Sparks, who witnessed the burning of the town, later wrote that the militia had been on alert for some days. A deserter had given them word that an attack might be imminent. However, this information did the Americans little good. Sparks said that, prior to the attack, "all of the cavalry and some of the infantry," amounting to 250 men, had been allowed to return to their homes. Those that remained, he said, "became uneasy and disorderly"—a state no doubt encouraged because their "officers were often absent." Indeed, Sparks reported, "Even at the time of the attack, the commanding officer [Lt. Col. William Smith] was several miles from town." Smith did not arrive back until "after the work of destruction was accomplished. . . ."[14]

On the fatal morning, only a skeleton garrison remained in the town's main battery on Concord Point. At first light, Westphal poured grapeshot and rockets into the battery. For some minutes, the militiamen bravely exchanged fire with the attackers. Cockburn stated that his men began "a warm fire . . . from our Launches and Rocket Boat, which was smartly returned from the Battery for a short time."[15]

The Americans stood their ground until a citizen named Webster was hit on the head by a Congreve rocket and instantly killed. The militiamen of the Chesapeake were being subjected to something new to warfare on the North American continent. Congreve rockets, cast iron cylinders three feet long and four inches wide, and packed with high explosive, could be launched either from the rocket barge or from on land. (A larger version of the Congreve rocket would be used by the Royal Navy the following year during the bombardment of Fort McHenry.) With an infernal shriek that rent the morning air, the rockets proved frightening to the untested soldiers, even if, as they did, they often wandered off target.[16]

The sole militiaman to make a stand was 2d Lt. John O'Neill. O'Neill, an elderly immigrant from the west of Ireland, was owner of the town's nail factory. At the time of the attack, he manned a gun emplacement called the "Potato Battery" closer to the town than the Concord Point fort. His battery was armed with two 6-pounders and one 9-pounder, while the main fortification mounted an 18-pounder and two 9-pounders. O'Neill later wrote:

> After firing a few shots [the other militiamen] retreated *and left me alone in the battery.* The grape-shot flew very thick about me. I loaded the gun myself, without any one to serve the vent, which you know is very dangerous, and fired her, when she recoiled and ran over my thigh. I retreated down to town, and joined Mr. Barnes, of the nail manufactory, with a musket, and fired on the barges while we had ammunition, and then retreated

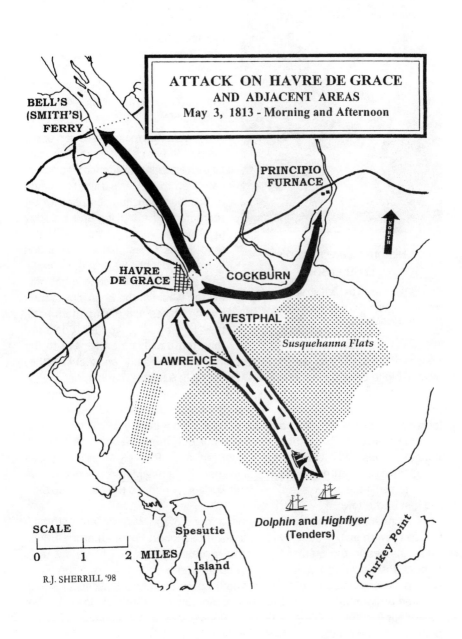

ATTACK ON HAVRE DE GRACE
AND ADJACENT AREAS
May 3, 1813 - Morning and Afternoon

BELL'S
(SMITH'S)
FERRY

PRINCIPIO
FURNACE

NORTH

HAVRE
DE GRACE

COCKBURN

WESTPHAL

Susquehanna Flats

LAWRENCE

SCALE

0   1   2   MILES

R.J. SHERRILL '98

Spesutie

Island

Dolphin and Highflyer
(Tenders)

Turkey Point

Historian Jared Sparks
(1789–1866)

Sparks witnessed the British sack of Havre de Grace while serving as a tutor to the Pringle household.

Collection of the Author

to the common, where I kept waving my hat to the militia who had run away, to come to our assistance, but they proved cowardly and would not come back. At the same time an English officer on horseback, followed by the marines, rode up and took me [prisoner] with two muskets in my hand.[17]

Westphal took possession of the main battery and turned the cannons on the retreating militiamen. The Americans fled to the far side of town, and as Cockburn haughtily described it, they "commenced a teazing and irritating fire from behind their Houses, Walls, [and] Trees." Westphal was wounded in the hand while leading the pursuit. All the same, he succeeded in "dislodging the whole of the Enemy from their lurking Places and driving them [into] the Neighbouring Woods." Cockburn reported that his men set fire to the houses of the town "to cause the Proprietors . . . to understand and feel what they were liable to bring upon themselves" by acting in a hostile manner.[18]

Cockburn came ashore to superintend the incendiarism. Sparks said that of the 60 houses of the town, 40 were torched, but not until they were first looted. The sailors, he said, carried hatchets in their belts to break open wardrobes and bureaus.[19] Cockburn himself reportedly made off with a fine coach, though he was told it belonged to a poor ferryman. Possibly all of the houses would have been burned, but several women, including Minerva Rodgers, wife of Havre de Grace native son Com. John Rodgers, implored the admiral to save the rest of the town.[20]

Architect Benjamin Henry Latrobe, a friend of the Rodgers family (though not an eyewitness), wrote on May 4 to inventor Robert Fulton, that the British "killed horses in the stables."[21] Another account states that "They cut hogs through the back, and some partly through, and then left them to run."[22] Although citizens persuaded an officer not to burn St. John's Episcopal Church, his men apparently destroyed the pews, the pulpit, and the windows, so that "every pane in the building [was] broken by stones and brickbats.[23] (See appendix 2 for a discussion of these and other alleged British outrages.)

Cockburn counted the raid a success. Apart from the wound to Westphal's hand, he could report no other casualty. The Americans had one killed in battle and a number wounded. After destroying approximately 130 stand of small

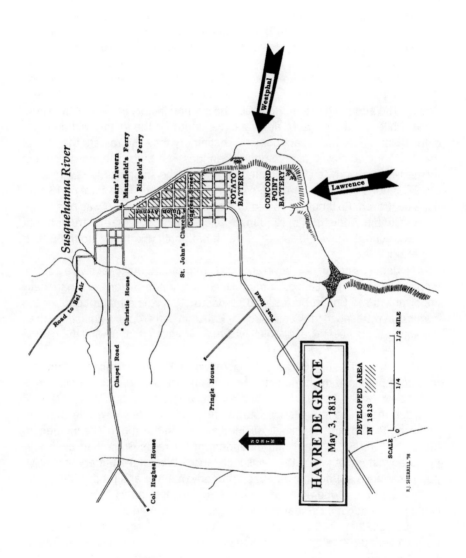

Susquehanna River

Westphal

Lawrence

Sears' Tavern
Mansfield's Ferry
Ringold's Ferry

Union Avenue
Congress Street
POTATO BATTERY
CONCORD POINT BATTERY

St. John's Church

Road to Bel Air

Christie House

Chapel Road

Post Road

Pringle House

Col. Hughes House

NORTH

HAVRE DE GRACE
May 3, 1813

DEVELOPED AREA IN 1813

SCALE

0   1/4   1/2 MILE

R.J. SHERRILL '98

arms, he took away with him the six captured cannons. O'Neill and two other citizens of Havre de Grace were taken on board H.M.S. *Maidstone*. The British reportedly accused O'Neill of being a subject of His Majesty George III and threatened him with death for taking up arms against his king. Fortunately, on receiving an appeal for mercy from the magistrates of Havre de Grace, they released him on parole. If the British had followed through with their threat, Brig. Gen. Henry Miller vowed to hang two British subjects in reprisal.[24]

After devastating Havre de Grace and sending a detachment up the Susquehanna to burn a warehouse at Smith's Ferry (present-day Lapidum), Cockburn proceeded by boat several miles northeast to Principio Creek in Cecil County. The admiral had learned about the cannon factory at the Principio Ironworks while he was in Havre de Grace. He captured the factory without difficulty. Destruction of the cannons and machinery took the raiders the rest of the day. They destroyed five 24-pound cannons in a battery meant to protect the ironworks, twenty-eight 32-pounders ready to be shipped, along with eight other cannons and four carronades of different calibers, for a total of 46 cannons destroyed. Cockburn reported to Warren that the factory "was one of the most valuable Works of [its] Kind in America." He added that he trusted that the destruction of it would "prove of much national Importance" to the British war effort.[25]

Indeed, as one of only several cannon manufacturers to receive a government contract in the 1790s, Samuel Hughes' cannon factory was nationally important to the United States, and its destruction was a major coup for the admiral. In retrospect, the destruction of Principio had greater significance than the action at Havre de Grace, which was more important for cowing the people of the Chesapeake.[26]

Successful though Cockburn's operations at Havre de Grace and Principio may have been, we might question how much luck played a part. Cockburn's biographer James Pack praises him as an expert at amphibious warfare.[27] However, there was little planning to the attacks on either Havre de Grace or Principio. The admiral seemingly decided almost on the spur of the moment to attack both targets. What if the defenders of Havre de Grace had been fully prepared instead of letting their vigilance lapse? What if the battery of five 24-pound cannons at Principio had been properly manned and ready for the raiders? Such a heavy armament, far greater than the British attack force possessed, could have made mincemeat of the admiral and his men.

Lt. Col. Charles Napier, who would shortly join the admiral for the attacks on Norfolk and Hampton, later wrote a damning critique of Cockburn's impetuous attacking style. Napier noted that the admiral insisted on attacking when he had incomplete knowledge of local conditions:

> Local knowledge is very hard to gain, yet we might gain more than we do. . . . Cockburn . . . has no idea of military arrangements; and he is so impetuous that he won't give time for others to do for him what he cannot, or will not do himself. If he had the conducting of any military operation

British burning of Havre de Grace

Contemporary print by William Charles, Maryland Historical Society

before an active enemy he would get his people cut to pieces. . . . Cockburn trusts all to luck, and makes no provision for failure: this may do with sailors, but not on shore, where hard fighting avails nothing if not directed by mind, and most accurate calculation.[28]

In truth, Cockburn's success to date could be attributed to the fact that he was attacking small communities where the militia was ill prepared. Writing of the raids in the upper bay, Secretary of the Navy Jones wrote that the British "had never attempted any thing by Land where they would not have been beaten by two hundred men."[29]

On the morning of May 6, Cockburn attacked the Eastern Shore towns of Fredericktown and Georgetown which faced each other on opposite banks of the Sassafras River. The planned amphibious attack went awry once more. Cockburn's plan, as usual, was to attack at daybreak. However, the boats, under the command of Capt. Henry D. Byng (in place of the wounded Westphal) were delayed. Cockburn wrote that the delay was caused "by the Intricacy of the River, our total want of local Knowledge in it, [and] the darkness of the Night." The admiral decided to send word ahead via two Americans. He warned the townspeople that if they acted "in the same rash manner" as the people of Havre de Grace, they would suffer a similar fate. But Lt. Col. Thomas W. Veazey, commander of the 49th Regiment of Maryland militia, was determined not to give up without a fight. Cockburn reported heavy musket fire from both sides of the river along with cannon fire from a small fort in Fredericktown. The rocket boat and launches bombarded the U.S. positions. Cockburn himself landed with the Royal Marines, who charged ashore with fixed bayonets. Veazey retreated. The British lost five wounded, one of them seriously, against at least one American seriously wounded. Although beaten, Veazey had made the British pay. The invaders burned houses, four vessels in the river, and stores of sugar, lumber, and other merchandise.[30]

A brick dwelling in Georgetown on the hill overlooking the scene of devastation was saved by Kitty Knight, who repeatedly put out the flames as Cockburn's men lit them. Impressed by her courage, one of the admiral's officers spared her house and that next door.[31]

After laying waste most of the twin towns, Cockburn entertained a delegation from Charlestown on the North East River. The delegation assured him that the town was at his mercy and that guns and militiamen would not be tolerated in their town. The admiral wrote to Warren that there remained in the upper Chesapeake Bay "neither public Property, Vessels, nor Warlike Stores . . ." He proposed therefore to return to the lower bay.[32] Of course, his claim of no further opposition in the upper Chesapeake contained some untruth. Cockburn's men were rebuffed at Fort Defiance on the Elk River. Moreover, Fort Hollingsworth, a second fort further upriver built to protect the town of Elkton, had not even been tested. And the British detachment that raided Smith's Ferry (Lapidum) had refrained from crossing the Susquehanna to attack the battery at Creswell's Ferry (Port Deposit).[33]

All the same, Cockburn's depredations had a severe effect on the commerce of the region, not to mention actual loss in property destroyed. Property losses at Havre de Grace alone were estimated to have been $50,000 in 1813 prices.[34]

British ships not only blockaded the entrance of the bay in order to intercept and prevent international and coastal trade. They actively intercepted waterborne trade between the eastern and western shores of Maryland and Virginia, including military supplies destined for Eastern Shore militia. Thus, Lt. Col. Philip Reed of the 21st Maryland Militia of Kent County on the Eastern Shore of Maryland observed that, "When in the spring of 1813 the Enemy first appeared in the waters of the upper Chesapeake, that part of the state which lies on the Eastern Shore was totally cut off from the Government. The County was left to depend on its own resources and Patriotism."[35]

As Secretary Jones had indicated, the enemy had so far desisted from attacking any large community such as Baltimore, Washington, or Norfolk. However, even so, Secretary Jones wrote that the enemy operations were causing "great loss and inconvenience to our Cities."[36]

An important aspect of this economic disruption comprised the British transportation out of escaped slaves, which constituted a severe blow to the plantation economy of the region. Cassell has estimated that three thousand to five thousand slaves from Virginia and Maryland fled to the British in the War of 1812 and were transported to British possessions, notably Nova Scotia, Bermuda, and the West Indies. Some former slaves later donned the scarlet uniforms of "Colonial Marines" to fight for the British. Blacks also helped the enemy by serving as guides.[37]

The free black man Charles Ball described an instance in spring 1813 in which the enemy took slaves from a southern Maryland plantation. The British, he said, "carried off more than twenty slaves, which were never again restored to their owner; although, on the following day, he went on board the ship, with a flag of truce, and offered a large ransom for [them]."[38]

In May 1813, the *National Intelligencer* reported that several blacks had deserted to the British and "became pilots for them in plundering." The same Washington-based newspaper assured its readers that the slaves were basically patriotic. Indeed, the slaves performed their labor, the *Intelligencer* said, "not as a task enforced by fear . . . but rather under the influence of an instinct which impels them to the voluntary performance of what they are conscious is their duty."[39]

As might be expected, Cockburn's reign of terror led to the American press heaping abuse on him. *Niles' Weekly Register* reported that "a certain James O'Boyle, a naturalized Irishman," offered a reward of $1,000 for the "head of the notorious incendiary and infamous scoundrel" Cockburn, or $500 "for each of his ears on delivery."[40]

Surprisingly, London was not pleased with Cockburn either. Secretary of the Admiralty John W. Croker wrote to Admiral Warren complaining about the way the rear admiral was conducting the war in the bay. Croker slapped

Collection of the Author

"The Yankey Torpedo"

A contemporary cartoon lampooning British fears of American torpedoes.

both admirals' wrists for getting involved in a Russian effort to mediate peace between Britain and the United States. Cockburn was also specifically reprimanded for allowing the American packet to continue to carry mail and passengers between Norfolk and Northampton. Being permissive, Croker said, could "be of the greatest injury and danger to our Military operations." As soon as the admirals had ascertained the *Constellation* was beyond reach of attack, Croker told them, they should have restricted themselves to blockade duty.[41]

Obviously, Cockburn's attacks around the bay did not have the full backing of London. Moreover, Croker's admonishment to the admirals appears to indicate British confusion about what their war aims should be in the Chesapeake.

Not only had Cockburn and Warren received a warning from London, they now had the additional worry of hostile action by Americans using torpedoes to attack individual ships. In March, Congress passed what became known as the "Torpedo Act." Under the terms of this act, the federal government promised to pay any citizen who burned, sank, or destroyed a British warship a bounty worth half the value of the vessel plus half "the value of her guns, tackle, and apparel."[42]

The "torpedo" had been pioneered by American inventor Robert Fulton. In the era of the War of 1812, such a device was what we would call today a mine or floating bomb rather than the propelled underwater projectile we now term a torpedo.[43]

On June 25, off New London, Connecticut, a schooner loaded with explosives blew up killing one British naval officer and 10 seamen belonging to the 74-gun ship of the line *Ramillies*. Following this incident, Warren stated in his general orders of July 19 that "the Enemy are disposed to make use of every unfair and Cowardly mode of Warfare, such as Torpedoes."[44]

In the Chesapeake, an American named Elijah Mix tried to attack Cockburn's squadron using torpedoes. In a confidential memo of May 7, Secretary Jones instructed Captain Gordon in Baltimore, "You will furnish [Mix] with 500 lbs. of powder, a Boat, or Boats, and Six men."[45]

Mix, described by Jones as an "intrepid Zealous" man, never succeeded in sinking or damaging a British ship, but it was not for lack of trying. During the summer, he made several attempts to destroy H.M.S. *Plantagenet*, one of the blockade ships guarding the entrance of the bay stationed near Cape Henry. On July 24, Mix almost succeeded in damaging the vessel, but his torpedo exploded prematurely. The explosion merely deluged the deck of the ship with water.[46]

By that time, however, the British had suffered a serious reversal in a renewed attempt to attack Norfolk. Moreover, French troops in the employ of the British were accused of committing atrocities at Hampton, Virginia.

Chapter Five

Norfolk Attacked, Hampton Ravished!

On June 22, 1813, the British made a fresh attempt to attack Norfolk, the frigate *Constellation*, and Gosport Navy Yard. The attack was made possible because Adm. Sir John Warren had received reinforcements of Royal Marines and six hundred soldiers under Col. Sir Thomas Sidney Beckwith, a Peninsular War veteran regarded as one of the finest leaders of light troops. Altogether, the force comprised of 2,400 men, including two battalions of Royal Marines (each with its own Congreve rocket unit), three hundred infantry of the 102nd Regiment, and three hundred troops ambiguously labeled "Canadian Chasseurs." The latter troops, shortly to be the center of a heated controversy, were *not* Canadian. Also termed Independent Companies of Foreigners, they were actually French prisoners of war who preferred fighting for the British to rotting in jail in England.[1]

The British should have anticipated that this motley bunch of Frenchmen would cause trouble once they reached the U.S. mainland. In the aftermath of the scandal they would cause by going amok after the attack on Hampton, Virginia, Beckwith confessed to Warren that he knew of their mutinous behavior on Bermuda prior to their arrival in the Chesapeake. He admitted that they acted "so perfectly insubordinate," repeated court-martials had to be held. One soldier was actually shot for mutiny. The colonel devised the name "Canadian Chasseurs" for the troops in the mistaken belief they would stay in line if given the chance of being sent to Canada after their present service.[2]

Second in command to Beckwith was Lt. Col. Charles Napier. Like Beckwith, Napier was a Peninsular War veteran. He later became a successful general in India, where he received the backing of fellow Irishman, Arthur Wellesley, the Duke of Wellington. As with the unfortunately named "Canadian Chasseurs," Napier's troops, the 102nd Regiment, also had a reputation for

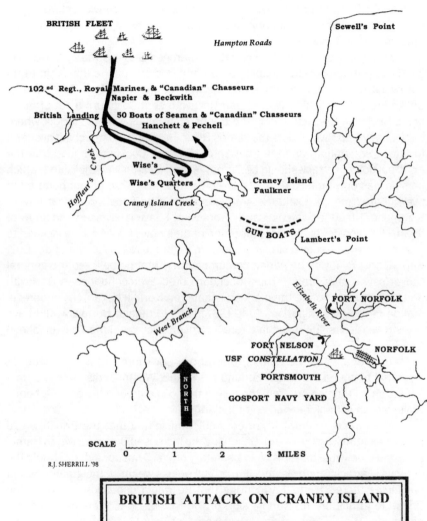

BRITISH FLEET

Hampton Roads

Sewell's Point

102 ad Regt., Royal Marines, & "Canadian" Chasseurs
Napier & Beckwith

British Landing   50 Boats of Seamen & "Canadian" Chasseurs
Hanchett & Pechell

Hoffleur's Creek

Wise's

Wise's Quarters

Craney Island Creek

Craney Island
Faulkner

GUN BOATS   Lambert's Point

Elizabeth River

FORT NORFOLK

West Branch

FORT NELSON
USF CONSTELLATION

PORTSMOUTH

GOSPORT NAVY YARD

NORTH

NORFOLK

SCALE
0   1   2   3 MILES

R.J. SHERRILL '98

BRITISH ATTACK ON CRANEY ISLAND

JUNE 22, 1813

indiscipline. Raised in 1789 as the New South Wales Fencibles, the regiment had been sent out to garrison the penal colony in Botany Bay, Australia. In 1808, the regiment's officers had mutinied against Capt. Edmund Bligh, famous for the mutiny on the *Bounty* some years earlier. The unit returned from Botany Bay in 1811 demoralized from its sojourn in the convict colony. Since joining the regiment in January 1812, Napier had been working to drill the officers and men into soldiers.[3]

An outspoken officer, Napier later disparaged British strategy at Norfolk, contending that too many people had a hand in planning the attack. In truth, however, the final plan of attack was the work of one man—Rear Adm. George Cockburn. Weeks earlier, Warren and Beckwith sent Cockburn a set of questions. Beckwith favored landing the troops eight miles west of Norfolk where the Nansemond River meets the James River. He proposed marching overland to attack Portsmouth and the Navy Yard. However, Cockburn argued that the principal point of attack should be Craney Island. By attacking the island, which he said was only protected by a "tolerably numerous" force of four hundred to five hundred men, he said the Americans would be forced to retreat toward Richmond. He added sarcastically, "From what I have lately seen and know of them, I have no doubt a larger proportion of their *now Heroes* will be inclined to take advantage of such a circumstance." In regard to Norfolk commander Brig. Gen. Robert B. Taylor, he added contemptuously that he believed the general "never saw a shot fired."[4] Thus, Cockburn bred overconfidence in Beckwith and Warren even before the planned assault on Norfolk began. His underestimation of the determination of the U.S. forces to defend Norfolk would have disastrous results and result in a rare American success in the Chesapeake in 1813.

To prepare for the coming operation, Cockburn ordered Lieutenant Westphal to sound the waters around the island. Westphal discovered a dangerous shoal running out from the island that could ground the assault boats. Obviously any attack needed careful planning.[5]

Meanwhile, General Taylor correctly anticipated that the British would focus their attack on the island. Observing the increased British activity in Hampton Roads, he wrote on June 18 to Secretary of War Armstrong that "should the enemy . . . attack Craney Island, it must fall unless we throw the greater part of our forces there." He told Armstrong that he would endeavor "to invite" the British to attack on the Norfolk side of the island. He did this by ordering a deception. The soldiers on the island were instructed to strike their rear tents during the night and pitch them in front, to give the impression the garrison was being reinforced from Norfolk.[6]

When Warren arrived on June 19, Cockburn submitted the findings of his survey of the island. He also offered to coordinate the attack. Warren turned him down. This blow must have struck the haughty Scots admiral like a slap in the face with a wet flounder. Warren informed him that he and Beckwith had already finalized the plans for the assault. Capt. Samuel J. Pechell, commander

Lt. Col. Charles Napier
(1782–1853), shown later in life
Collection of the Author

Brig. Gen. Robert B. Taylor
(1774–1834), the American
commander at Norfolk
Courtesy Virginia Historical Society and
Joseph W. A. Whitehorne

of Warren's flagship H.M.S. *San Domingo*, would lead the attack. Warren told Cockburn to transfer his flag from *Marlborough* to the frigate *Barrossa* in order to sail close enough to bombard the island's defenses.[7]

Just as the British were preparing to attack, they received a shock when the U.S. Navy gunboats took the offensive for the first time. Capt. John Cassin of the Gosport Navy Yard had learned that the enemy frigate *Junon* lay becalmed at the mouth of the river, three miles from the rest of the British fleet. He ordered Capt. Joseph Tarbell, temporary commander of the *Constellation*, to attack the lone frigate on the night of June 19–20. Tarbell devised a plan to attack using 15 gunboats manned with his own officers, midshipmen, and sailors, along with 50 riflemen loaned by General Taylor from the garrison on Craney Island.[8]

Cockburn had instructed Capt. James Sanders of *Junon* to keep watch on the activity of the U.S. gunboats. Sanders anchored in the channel on the evening of June 19. At 11:00 P.M., under the cover of darkness, Tarbell's gunboats moved down the river to attack the frigate. However, adverse winds and heavy squalls prevented the would-be attackers from approaching their target until the early hours of the morning. At 2:30 A.M., the British sailors on board the *Junon* spotted the U.S. boats—too late.

The gunboats, Cassin said, "commenced a heavy gawling fire." The commanders of two nearby British frigates, seeing the *Junon* under attack, came to

Sanders' aid. The *Narcissus* and the *Barrossa* fired broadsides at the attackers as Sanders fought to get the *Junon* under sail. The action continued for an hour and a half with the Americans hearing their shots strike the *Junon*. Cassin believed that if the calm had continued for a half hour more the frigate "[would] have fallen into our hands or been destroyed, [but] she slipped her mooring" and escaped.

Sanders reported one Royal Marine killed and three seamen wounded, as well as a sailor killed by an exploding gun after the Americans withdrew. The *Junon* had taken approximately four shots in her hull and suffered damage to her rigging. On board gunboat *No. 139*, Master's Mate Thomas Allinson of the *Constellation* was killed early in the action when an 18-pound shot passed through him and lodged in the mast. Additionally, two men were injured by splinters, and the gunboats sustained various minor damage.[9]

As author John M. Hallahan terms it, the action was no more than "a terrier's bite on the ankle."[10] However, it provided a morale booster at a critical moment. With hope that events might go their way after all, Taylor and the naval commanders prepared the defenses for the coming onslaught.

Tarbell agreed with the general's assessment that the island would be the point of attack. He loaned Lt. Col. Henry Beatty, commander of the island garrison, 150 sailors and marines, much as Taylor had loaned the 50 riflemen for the naval assault on the *Junon*. Thirty regulars were also requisitioned from Fort Norfolk, along with 15 militiamen from Col. Armistead Thompson's regiment and 15 Isle of Wight riflemen. Beatty could thus call on a total of 767 soldiers, sailors, and marines, including 91 artillerymen under the command of Maj. James Faulkner.[11]

Faulkner established a battery of seven cannons behind a small breastwork in the northwest quadrant of the island. This was the opposite end of the island to the unfinished fort established by Colonel Armistead. The four cannons on the right side of the battery would be four 6-pounders of Capt. Arthur Emmerson's Portsmouth Light Artillery, to be worked by militia gunners. These lighter guns would command the channel leading to the river. The three heavier guns on the left, two 24-pounders and one 18-pounder, were dragged from the unfinished fort by a work crew led by Capt. Thomas Rourk, master of the merchant ship *Manhattan* blockaded in the river. The heavy guns would be trained on a farm on the mainland to the northwest called Wise's Quarters in case of an attempted British land attack from that direction. A strip of water known as the Thoroughfare, fordable at low tide, lay between the island and Wise's Quarters. The guns could also be turned to cover a small wooden footbridge that connected the island to another farm to the west if the British attempted to cross the bridge. The 18-pounder would be worked by seamen under Lt. Benedict I. Neale of gunboat *No. 152*. The 24-pounder on the far left would be commanded by Captain Emmerson and the other 24-pounder by Rourk and Lt. Thomas Godwin. These two guns would be worked largely by the naval ratings. The militia infantry, including the 50 riflemen, were positioned behind the breastwork.[12]

Captain Cassin stationed the gunboats in the shape of an arc, in the channel between the southeast tip of the island and Lambert's Point. He reinforced the crews with levies of officers and men from the *Constellation* and the Navy Yard. This eliminated the anticipated weakness of manning the boats largely with inexperienced militia. The gunboats would guard the channel in case the Royal Navy forced a way past Faulkner's battery.[13]

Around midnight on the night of June 21–22, a sentry thought he saw a boat moving in the Thoroughfare. He challenged it. Receiving no answer, he fired his musket. The troops were called to arms and remained that way throughout the night, though the "boat" turned out to be a floating bush. At dawn, Lieutenant Colonel Beatty ordered the men to stand down. Then a cavalryman on picket duty on the mainland galloped across the Thoroughfare to report that the British were landing at Hoffler's Creek two and a half miles west.[14] Napier wrote that the troops had entered the boats at midnight, "pulled on shore by moonlight, and landed in tolerable confusion at daybreak without opposition."[15]

From Hoffler's Creek, the British marched toward the island with the intention of wading across the Thoroughfare to attack the Americans. The troops were divided into two brigades. Beckwith had command of one brigade, comprising one company of Frenchmen and one company of Royal Marines. The second brigade, under Napier, was made up of the 102nd Regiment and the other company of Royal Marines under Lt. Col. Richard Williams. Meanwhile, 50 armed boats under Captain Pechell, manned by seamen and the second company of Frenchmen, rowed toward the island in two columns to attempt an amphibious assault.[16]

The defenders could see the enemy troops in the distance, marching toward them, moving inland. They could make out the British Army soldiers and Royal Marines in their scarlet uniforms and the Frenchmen, the so-called "Canadian Chasseurs," in their green uniforms. However, the troops were soon lost to view in the tall pines and underbrush of Wise's Quarters. As the enemy approached, the Americans realized they did not have the Stars and Stripes flying. Some of the men ran to get a long pole. They *nailed* the flag to it and rammed it into the ground behind the heavy guns. The Americans recognized the nailing of the flag to the pole to be a singularly symbolic act. Whatever happened, they intended to hold the island.[17]

As the British troops marched toward the island, Beckwith lost by desertion an advanced party of 25 Frenchmen. Moreover, the colonel soon realized the water in the Thoroughfare was too deep to ford and the battery on the island too far away for musket fire. Lieutenant Robertson later recalled, "A man in coloured clothes, calling himself a deserter, offered to guide the troops to a wooden bridge, . . . but Beckwith, doubtful of his faith, soon returned."[18] Perhaps Beckwith thought his men would be too exposed to fire if they tried to cross the bridge. He ordered the Royal Marine artillery to open up with Congreve rockets from behind the farmhouse, to draw attention from Pechell's 50 barges. The marines started to send their diabolic rockets screaming toward the U.S. battery. The rockets, though, served only to draw the American fire.[19]

Faulkner ordered his men to open up on Napier's brigade as it appeared in sight near the house. Napier wrote, "The first shot, enfilading the road, killed a sergeant who was with me." He commanded the men to take cover in the woods. The men of the 102nd followed his order, but, he said, "The marines could not do it before the battery threw three rounds into the thick of them." He stated that eight or nine marines were killed or wounded, along with two sergeants of the 102nd. One sergeant recovered, but "the other was killed, both his legs being shot off close to his body," Napier wrote. "Good God! what a horrid sight it was!"[20]

When Beckwith realized that Napier's brigade had come under such heavy fire from grape and roundshot, the British commander sent word for Napier to withdraw. The officer he despatched to tell Napier to get out of the firing zone, stopping himself short of danger, shouted, "You are to retire! You are to retreat!" A contemptuous Napier yelled back, "Come and tell us so!"[21]

Yet it seemed nothing could be effected: the Thoroughfare at the moment was obviously too deep to ford. For all of Cockburn's "planning" they had come at the wrong time, when the tide was in. As Beckwith's troops retreated, Pechell's two columns of barges closed in on the island. The planned land-sea attack had gone badly awry.

The southern line of barges, that closest to shore, was led by Capt. John M. Hanchett of the H.M.S. *Diadem*. Hanchett, an illegitimate son of King George III, sat in the stern of the *Centipede*, Warren's 52-foot-long green barge. He held an open umbrella over his head to demonstrate his disdain for the Yankees. The barge, crammed with 75 men, was propelled by 24 oars. It mounted a brass 3-pounder "grasshopper" cannon in the bow.[22]

The bombardment directed at the British troops on the mainland had dislodged two of the U.S. cannons from their carriages. One of Emmerson's 6-pounders and Rourk and Godwin's 24-pounder were out of commission. The Americans were down to only five functioning cannons. The artillerymen adjusted the elevation to train their still serviceable guns on the barges, loading the hot muzzles with grapeshot and canister.

As the 50 barges grew nearer, the Americans sweated in the early morning sun. Emmerson, standing

Maj. James Faulkner (1776–1817)

Lossing's *Field Book of the War of 1812*

next to Faulkner at the one remaining 24-pounder, asked anxiously, "Are they close enough for our fire?"

"No, sir," Faulkner told him, "let them approach a little nearer."[23]

Shortly, Faulkner gave the order to fire, and the artillerymen lit the touch holes of the five cannons. A hail of canister and grapeshot greeted the barges. Yet the British kept right on coming. As the Yankee missiles landed around him, Hanchett, umbrella still held high, yelled encouragement to the oarsmen, oblivious of his safety.[24]

In the bow of the lead boat of the north line of barges, Capt. Samuel Romilly of the Royal Engineers stood sounding the water with a boathook. Suddenly, three hundred yards from shore, Romilly's barge ground to a halt on the shoal. They had hit the shoal that Westphal had detected in his survey of the island. Romilly reported that the boathook indicated "three or four feet of slimy mud" below the barge. Pechell did not like the sound of that. His men could not wade ashore in four feet of *mud*.[25]

Some of the artillerymen switched to roundshot. Hanchett ordered his oarsmen to row toward the north line of boats, which brought the *Centipede* broadside to the American battery. Suddenly, a roundshot crashed into her stern, or after-thwart, wounding several of the Frenchmen, cutting the legs off one Frenchman, and striking Hanchett in the thigh. In a few short moments, three of the largest of the British barges had been disabled. Men swam for the safety of the other barges, cascades of water from the cannonballs showering all around them. Sailors loaded the severely wounded Hanchett into a nearby barge. Pechell ordered a general retreat: the day was lost.

The British later insisted that of the remaining men in the *Centipede*, 30 Frenchmen were massacred by the U.S. sailors and militiamen who waded out to capture the prize, a charge denied by General Taylor. Beatty's report stated that "twenty-two prisoners" plus the (evidently unfired) brass 3-pounder and "a number of small arms, pistols, and cutlasses" were captured in the *Centipede*.[26]

Napier recalled, "A sharp cannonade . . . cost us seventy-one men, without returning a shot! We lost some boats also, and re-embarked in the evening with about as much confusion as at landing." As if to recognize the expertise with which the Americans had beaten off the attack, he added, "We despise the Yankees too much."[27]

Craney Island proved an embarrassing defeat for the British, although Warren in his official report attempted to minimize it. He told Secretary of the Admiralty Croker, "I am happy to say the Loss . . . has not been considerable." The naval losses were limited, he said, "two Boats Sunk," 1 officer (Hanchett) severely "but not Dangerously" wounded, 7 sailors wounded, and 10 missing. Beckwith filed a report showing that among the marines and soldiers under his command, there were 3 dead, 8 wounded, and 52 missing, with 45 of the missing being the Frenchmen he insisted on calling "Canadian Chasseurs." The Americans, by contrast, reported no casualties whatsoever. Beatty reported, "The only weapon made use of by the enemy in the course of the day were Congreve rockets, a few of which fell in our encampment, though without injury."[28]

The British barges scuttled back to the fleet, and Cockburn from his vantage point on board the *Barrossa* could tell that the assault had failed badly. Now there would be no opportunity for him to sail the *Barrossa* in close to shore to bombard the American defenses. He must have been furious. He had been excluded from taking any part in the action—and the planned attack had been defeated by the amateurish Yankees! Note though that at Craney Island, the British faced a mix of seasoned naval men and militiamen. The defenders were not the raw, poorly led militia that Cockburn had been chasing into the woods elsewhere around the bay. This should have served as a lesson for the future.

Cockburn's biographer, James Pack, states that in choosing Pechell to lead the attack, Warren "had erred badly . . . when an expeditionary force might have made a real impact on the course of this unfortunate war."[29]

To Taylor's relief, his plan to concentrate his forces at Craney Island had succeeded beyond his brightest hopes. The British were beaten off by the artillery bombardment from Faulkner's battery alone. The gunboats and the river forts were not tested. Perhaps because the gunboats did not venture from their station southeast of the island, they were hardly engaged. Only gunboat *No. 67* fired a couple of roundshot toward the enemy troops at Wise's Quarters, without apparent effect.[30]

There would be no renewed attack on Norfolk. Instead, in the words of a contemporary commentator, "The British again turned their attention to the easier duties of laying waste unprotected villages."[31] On the morning of June 25, they attacked Hampton, on the north shore of Newport News, in a joint sea and land attack using 30 to 40 boats under Cockburn and troops led by Napier and Williams of the Royal Marines.

Four days earlier, Hampton militia commander Maj. Stapleton Crutchfield wrote to Governor Barbour about the town's perilous position. The major had, he said, "not more than five hundred men . . . many of whom are in the Hospital."[32] Indeed, Crutchfield's effective force, by his later account, amounted to 436 men or 349 infantry and riflemen, 62 artillerymen, and 25 cavalrymen. In the early morning hours of June 25, as the British crept up on them at Newport News, these troops were encamped on the Little England estate southwest of Hampton, divided from the town by a creek. The camp was defended by two batteries including four long 12-pounders and three 6-pounders under Capt. B. W. Pryor.[33]

Crutchfield's men gave a good account of themselves if we consider the overwhelming force the British hurled against them—possibly 2,400 men in total. The troops landed two miles west of the town, half an hour before daylight, and marched along Celey's Road toward the American camp. Beckwith later wrote, "Cockburn, to engage the Enemy's attention, ordered the armed launches and rocket boats to commence a fire upon their batteries."[34]

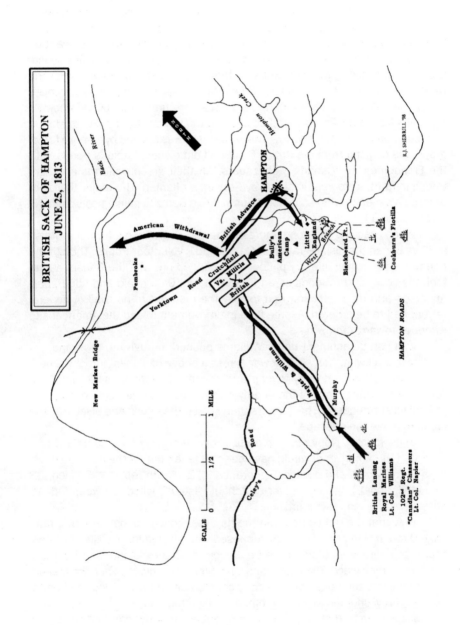

BRITISH SACK OF HAMPTON
JUNE 25, 1813

NORTH

Back River

Hampton Creek

HAMPTON

American Withdrawal

British Advance

Pembroke

Crutchfield

Yorktown Road

Va. Militia

British

Bully's American Camp

Little England

West Branch

Blackbeard Pt.

Cockburn's Flotilla

HAMPTON ROADS

New Market Bridge

Napier & Williams

Murphy

Celey's Road

SCALE

0   1/2   1 MILE

British Landing
Royal Marines
Lt. Col. Williams

102nd Regt.
"Canadian" Chasseurs
Lt. Col. Napier

R.J. SHERRILL '98

Crutchfield reported that Cockburn's attack "was repelled by our batteries under the command of Capt. B. W. Pryor in a manner worthy of veteran troops."[35] The barges withdrew behind the point throwing rockets and cannon-balls at the American camp. The standoff, he said, lasted three quarters of an hour. Meanwhile, he despatched the rifle company under Capt. R. Servant up the road to harass the approaching enemy troops from the cover of a wood. Crutchfield, banking that the British intended to make no landing from the barges, led his infantry in support of the riflemen. As the Americans advanced in column toward Celey's Road, he said, "We were fired upon by the enemy's musketry from a thick wood" and he ordered the troops "to wheel to the left in line and march upon the enemy." This movement was spoiled by a sharp fire of grape and canister from the British 6-pound field pieces. Napier's troops, with the Frenchmen, or "Canadian Chasseurs," in their green uniforms and light troops in front, were kept in check by Servant's riflemen. The major therefore ordered his men to wheel again in column into a defile to gain a position in the woods behind the riflemen.[36]

When reaching the wood, more discharges of grapeshot from the British artillery began the disintegration of Crutchfield's volunteer troops. Though the riflemen and leading infantry platoons exchanged fire with the British, others took the cover of the woods as an excuse to run. Crutchfield and Adj. Robert Anderson and other officers tried to rally the men but to no avail. A general retreat had to be ordered. A large flanking movement forced the Americans to withdraw toward Yorktown.

A British detachment under Williams pushed through the town and, according to Beckwith, "forced their way across a bridge of planks" into the American camp, still defended by Pryor's artillerymen. Crutchfield said that Pryor "after slaughtering many of the enemy with the field-pieces, remained on the ground till surrounded." The gunners then spiked their guns and dived into the creek to make their escape.

In his journal, Napier gave a perfunctory summary of the battle. He concluded, "[The Americans] would have been all taken but for the extreme thickness of the wood, and our local ignorance."[37] Beckwith reported 5 killed, 33 wounded, and 10 missing. Major Crutchfield listed 7 killed, 12 wounded, 11 missing, and 1 man taken prisoner.[38]

Now that the British had won the day, the French troops went on a rampage through Hampton. This was supposedly in revenge for the alleged "massacre" of their compatriots in the *Centipede* off Craney Island. Murder, rape, and looting took place. The Americans later cited one incident when the Frenchmen broke into the house of an elderly couple named Kirby, killed the bedridden Mr. Kirby, shot his wife in the hip, and killed their dog.[39]

Napier wrote that one Frenchman robbed an American and then shot him in cold blood:

> One robbed a poor Yankee and pretended all sorts of anxiety for him: it was the custom of war he said to rob a prisoner, but he was sorry for him.

When he had thus coaxed the man into confidence he told him to walk on before, as he must go to the general; the poor wretch obeyed, and when his back was turned the musket was fired into his brains.[40]

Captain Robertson of the Royal Artillery complained, "They even shot an officer after taking off his epaulettes."[41] Napier wrote, "[Beckwith] ought to have hanged several villains . . . had he so done the Americans would not have complained; but every horror was committed, rape, murder, pillage: and not a man was punished!"[42]

We might wonder why Napier himself did not punish the men. This after all is the man who years later in India abolished the custom of *suttee*, the burning of widows on the funeral pyres of their husbands, and who insisted on hanging any men guilty of killing women.[43] Of Hampton, where he was Beckwith's junior, he wrote somewhat lamely, "Much [as] I wished to shoot some [of the Frenchmen] . . . I had no opportunity."[44] Possibly he had his hands full trying to keep his own troublesome troops, the 102nd Regiment, from joining in the rampage. He admitted, "[the 102nd] almost mutinied at my preventing them joining in the sack of that unfortunate town."[45]

General Taylor was outraged at the news of the atrocities at Hampton. In a letter of protest of June 29 to Warren, he wrote, "I have heard with grief and astonishment of the excesses both to property and persons committed by the land troops who took possession of Hampton." He noted, "The world will suppose those acts to have been approved. . . ."[46]

Beckwith promised Taylor's aide, Capt. John Myers, that the Frenchmen would not be employed on the U.S. coast again. Possibly the colonel hoped the problem would disappear of its own accord, but Taylor's persistence would not let the abuses go unnoticed.[47]

Repulsed at Norfolk, the British had done their worst at Hampton. Less than a month later, they made their first menacing moves to attack the capital, Washington, D.C. However, Com. Joshua Barney proposed a plan to stop British incursions: a "flying squadron" of armed barges, or row-galleys, to defend the Chesapeake.[48]

Chapter Six

Commodore Barney's Plan to Defend the Bay

Joshua Barney returned to Baltimore on November 23, 1812, after his second successful cruise in the privateer *Rossie*. Although he received numerous offers from privateering syndicates, he refused to make another cruise and instead retired to his farm at Elkridge, south of Baltimore. He still desired a command in the U.S. Navy. However, his loss of seniority and tenure because of his service in the French navy—not to mention the ill will in naval circles he had caused by his stint with the French—again meant that he failed in his quest. Through spring and early summer of 1813, like many Marylanders, the old sailor felt outrage at the enemy insults to the bay. Yet, rather than merely venting his fury, Barney came up a workable plan to fight the British.[1]

On July 4—Independence Day—Barney sat down and penned a letter to Secretary of the Navy Jones that he titled "Defense of [the] Chesapeake Bay."[2] As was his way, the old sea dog scribbled his ideas with numerous underlinings for emphasis. He began by estimating the potential land forces the British could throw at the region. He feared they might soon be able to land a force of "upwards of 8000 men" in the bay. He estimated that the British could presently muster approximately four thousand Royal Marines from "11 ships of the line, 33 frigates, [and] 38 Sloops of war" already off the coast. Added to those troops, he said, two additional battalions of Royal Marines (2,000 men), two battalions of Royal Artillery (1,000 men), and two battalions of seamen (1,200 men) might be expected to arrive from England. His guess about the troops already on station in the bay would appear to be an overestimate, given that Warren and Beckwith only had some 2,400 troops in the attacks on Norfolk and Hampton. But even so, Barney offered some idea of the scope of the dilemma that might soon face the people of the bay.

52

Com. Joshua Barney

Courtesy Franklin D. Roosevelt Library,
Hyde Park, New York

Barney predicted that, among other targets, the British intended to destroy Washington. "The <u>Avowed</u> object of the Enemy," he wrote, "is, the distruction [*sic*] of the <u>City & Navy yard</u>, at Washington, the <u>City & Navy yard</u> at Norfolk, and the City of <u>Baltimore</u>. . . ."[3]

In his plainspoken way, Barney stated what many in Madison's administration did not want to believe—that the British meant to target the capital. However, he was preaching to the converted. Quite opposite to the thinking of Secretary of War John Armstrong and others in the administration, Jones thought Washington *was* open to attack. In February 1813, Jones had established a Potomac flotilla. The flotilla was meant to cooperate with Fort Washington, 14 miles below the city, to block the Potomac in case the British tried to force a passage toward Washington.[4] In contrast to the Potomac flotilla, which was purely defensive, Barney proposed a new flotilla that not only would have defensive duties but also would have the potential to go on the offensive against the enemy. Indeed, Barney said, the new flotilla might even have the capability to drive the British from the bay. Barney wrote:

> the only defence we have in our power, is a Kind of <u>Barge</u> or <u>Row-galley</u>, so constructed, as to draw a small draft of water, to carry <u>Oars</u>, light sails, and <u>One heavy long gun</u> [e.g., a 24- or 32-pound cannon]. . . . Let as many of such Barges be built as can be mann'd, form them into a <u>flying Squadron</u>, have them continually watching & annoying the enemy in our waters, where we have the advantage of <u>shoals & flats</u> throughout the Chesepeake Bay. . . . [Such a squadron when combined with fire ships] might oblige the Enemy to quit our waters, for during the <u>summer</u> months, they could harrass them at <u>Night</u>: by getting near the ships of War, and keeping up a constant fire upon them. . . .[5]

Jones recognized the brilliance in Barney's proposal. The secretary saw that Barney was using *same strategy* the enemy had adopted to attack the bay area targets. Because the British could not get close to land with their 74-gun ships of the line or even their 38-gun frigates, they were obliged to use row barges to mount their attacks. Barney proposed using the same type of shallow draft vessel to drive them from the Chesapeake.

Barney's plan had an added attraction. The secretary knew the owners of the four privateer schooners, leased to Captain Gordon at Baltimore, would

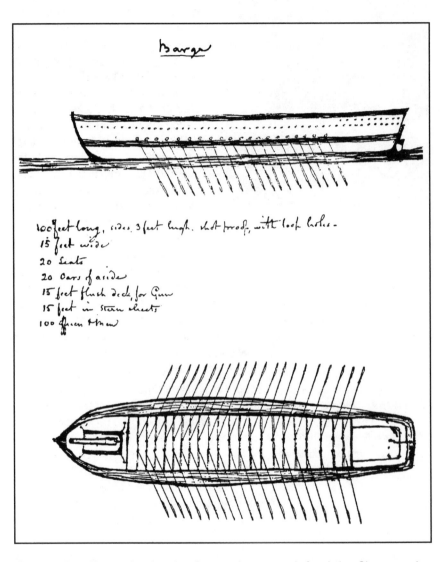

Commodore Barney's sketch of a row barge to defend the Chesapeake

Courtesy National Archives and Record Service

sooner or later want their vessels back. If Gordon lost the use of these schooners, the Chesapeake would be even more open to British attack. In April, Jones had recommended the leasing of the schooners to President Madison as a means of providing "a cheap prompt and efficient force."[6] Barney's plan gave him something even better to suggest to Madison: a force specifically designed to battle the British menace—and at a budget cost! As Barney put it, "<u>50 Barges</u> will not cost more than <u>One half</u> the price of <u>One frigate</u>. . . ."[7] What could appeal to the bureaucrats in Washington more? The prospect of results *and* a cost savings!

Within weeks, Jones appointed Barney "Acting Master Commandant" in the U.S. Navy with the officers immediately subordinate to him having the title of sailing master.[8] Barney hurried to Washington where Jones assured him that he was being given a command separate from the naval establishment. Because he would be answerable only to the government, he thus would not be subject to orders from naval men with greater seniority. Barney was delighted.[9]

While in the capital, however, he heard that his enemies in Baltimore were trying to discredit him with the Navy Department. Lemuel Taylor, a leading Baltimore merchant and onetime friend of Barney's, had written a letter characterizing Barney as "a most abandoned rascal . . . despised by $^9/_{10}$ of all that have taken an active part in the defence of Baltimore. . . ."[10]

Enraged, Barney challenged Taylor to a duel. Taylor accepted the challenge of a duel with pistols in Virginia. In the duel, Barney shot Taylor, leaving him with a severe wound in the chest. Feeling that his honor had been upheld, Barney left for Baltimore to superintend the building of his flotilla. The task would take all autumn and winter, and into the spring of 1814.[11]

While Secretary Jones had been mulling over the plans for Barney's flotilla, the British continued their raids. Approximately a week after Barney wrote his Independence Day letter, on the morning of July 12, Cockburn and Napier attacked Ocracoke, North Carolina. Their aim was to injure inland navigation with Norfolk. This time they instructed the troops that any man getting out of line would be punished. The British wanted no repeat of the behavior at Hampton. The troops easily took possession of the North Carolina ports of Ocracoke and Portsmouth. The biggest coup was the capture of the American privateer brig *Anaconda*, which Cockburn described as a "most beautiful Vessel," copper bottomed and mounting eighteen 9-pound cannons. They also took the Philadelphia letter of marque schooner *Atlas* of 10 guns. Under British colors and rechristened the *St. Lawrence*, the schooner would have a prime role to play in battling Barney's flotilla on the Patuxent the following year.[12]

Warren meanwhile was active in the Potomac, menacing the federal capital. On July 14, British cutters from the sloop *Contest* and the brig *Mohawk* went in chase of the schooner *Asp* and the sloop *Scorpion*, two vessels of the Potomac flotilla. The American commanders had been ordered to reconnoiter the mouth of the river. Their arrival coincided with that of Warren's squadron. The *Scorpion* escaped, and would later become Commmodore Barney's flagship. The

British engaged the *Asp* in a brisk action, killing her commander, Midshipman James B. Sigourney. Out of the crew of 21, the Americans had 10 killed, wounded, and missing, and the schooner was destroyed. The British reported two men killed and six wounded, including one man severely injured.[13]

Warren ordered Capt. William H. Shirreff of H.M.S. *Barrossa* to lead a squadron of five light vessels as far up the river as possible. The squadron comprised *Barrossa*, the sixth rate *Laurestinus*, the brigs *Conflict* and *Mohawk*, and the schooner *High Flyer*. Shirreff's ships had on board six hundred Royal Marines and the 102nd Regiment under Beckwith. Warren noted that he wanted "to create an alarm in Washington and to embarrass the Enemy . . . during the setting of Congress in that City." Weeks earlier, he had written that he knew the river to be navigable and defended by only two batteries. After carrying the batteries, the capital would "be open to insult"—in which case the Americans would be forced "to withdraw a proportion of [their] regular force from the Canadas."[14]

The move caused the anticipated alarm but (unfortunately for British objectives) not a resultant withdrawal of U.S. Army troops from the border with Canada. Virginia and Maryland militia units along the Potomac were mobilized. Secretary Armstrong hurried to Fort Washington to superintend the deployment of the militia and six hundred regulars of the 36th and 38th Regiments that were hastily assembled at the fort. The regulars comprised raw recruits in two regiments that had only been recently formed.[15]

Secretary of State James Monroe rode even further down the river into St. Mary's County with a party of "gentleman volunteers" to reconnoiter the enemy. They found three or four hundred British troops digging wells on Blakiston (St. Clement's) Island. Monroe sent word back to Armstrong requesting 350 regulars to help them capture the British detachment. The secretary of war refused to part with more than half of the regulars, which he said would be needed for the defense of the capital. He told Monroe the operation was a job for the local militia. Yet Monroe had already informed Armstrong that the militia had no firearms.[16]

The British squadron made it up the river as far as 40 miles below Fort Washington. The treacherous shoals of the river had proved difficult. Warren reported to London that the ships could not proceed further "in consequence of the Shoals between Cedar & Maryland Points. . . ."[17] Warren was not prepared to order a lightening of the ships by offloading their cannons. The sailors spent their time sounding the tricky Kettle Bottom shoals.[18] The information would prove valuable a year later when the British would again attempt to sail up the Potomac.

Given this incontrovertible proof that the British *were* interested in Washington as a target, it seems incredible that Madison did not order the necessary precautions to defend the capital. Despite his zeal in coming down to Fort Washington to lead the troops, Armstrong quickly reverted to his usual imperturbable state. In summer 1814, when indications were even stronger that the

British intended to attack the capital, he was denying that they would want to attack the place. Armstrong detested the low-lying spit of land that had been chosen in 1793 as the nation's capital. He called the place a "sheep walk."[19]

Maj. Gen. James Wilkinson, in his largely self-serving *Memoirs of My Own Times* (1816), states that apart from the outfitting of Barney's flotilla, during the intervening twelve months,

> President Madison and his counsellors did not take a single precautionary measure for the defence of the national capital; notwithstanding the so-licitude of its patriotic inhabitants, manifested by repeated applications to the Secretary of War, and to the President personally.[20]

At the time, Wilkinson was under fire for his own failure to capture Montreal earlier in 1813. After the war, he faced a court-martial on charges of neglect of duty and drunkenness. Scandal also tainted him. He had been linked with former Vice President Aaron Burr in a scheme to separate the western territories from the United States, and modern historians have proved that he was in the pay of Spain. The controversial general had no reason to like either Armstrong or Madison. Nevertheless, he accurately saw that the little president was domi-nated by the arrogant New Yorker. "I had long known that the poor President was a nose of wax in his fingers," Wilkinson sniffed, "and that in military affairs [Armstrong] is a mere writer and talker, not an actor." So proclaimed the com-mander who, it was alleged, stayed drunk in his cabin on the St. Lawrence while the Americans went down to defeat at Crysler's Farm on November 11, 1813, and then blamed everybody but himself for his failure to take Montreal.[21]

Armstrong was a Revolutionary War veteran and the son of Maj. Gen. John Armstong, Sr.[22] In 1783, he played a controversial role as a leader in the Newburgh conspiracy. He was the author of an anonymous series of letters to the officer corps that seemingly urged a revolt against civilian authority. As a brevet lieutenant colonel and aide to Gen. Horatio Gates, he became the mouth-piece for a cadre of officers unhappy with congressional intransigence over giving the army its back pay.[23]

After the Revolution, Armstrong settled into a life of politics and writing. In 1800, he was elected as a Republican U.S. senator for New York State. Named by Jefferson as U.S. minister to France, he served in that capacity from 1804 to 1810.[24] In 1812, he wrote a book entitled *Hints to Young Generals*. In this 71-page book, which he signed "By an Old Soldier," Armstrong borrowed exten-sively from the French military writer Maj. Gen. Antoine Jomini. The book sold well and helped to introduce Jomini's concepts, which would influence Ameri-can military thought over the next 50 years. Armstrong boasted to his wife that "This work did not employ me above three or four days."[25] When the president offered him the position of secretary of war on January 14, 1813, he was not Madison's first choice.[26]

Inheriting a war office that had fallen into disgrace after the military fail-ures of 1812, Armstrong chose to organize the meager resources given him by

Secy. of War John Armstrong

Courtesy National Portrait Gallery,
Smithsonian Institution

Congress by concentrating the U.S. military effort on the Canadian border. Skeen says that because of this policy, "practically the entire coast lay open and unprotected from incursions of the enemy"—thus the exposed situation of the Chesapeake Bay. Skeen adds, though, that Congress, by failing to provide adequate funds for the war effort, "must bear the major responsibility for the ill-fed, poorly clothed, inadequately equipped condition of the troops."[27] Armstrong's overriding focus on the northern frontier led to him resisting suggestions that the defenses of Washington be improved. Maj. Gen. John P. Van Ness, commander of the District of Columbia militia, later testified that he frequently asked the secretary to improve the defenses. He said it was evident that Fort Washington alone was insufficient for the defense of the capital. Even the secretary acknowledged "the incompetency" of the fortification, he said. Throughout 1813, Armstrong forestalled the general with promises that he had a project in hand. Yet he never produced the plans. Van Ness said the secretary mostly "appeared rather indifferent, and expressed an opinion that the enemy would not come, or even seriously attempt to come, to the District."[28]

Early in May 1813, a deputation from Washington, Alexandria, and Georgetown urged the secretary to strengthen the fort. Armstrong ordered Col. Decius Wadsworth to examine the fort. On May 28, the colonel reported that "an additional number of heavy guns . . . and an additional fort in the neighborhood, are both to be considered unnecessary."[29]

In his *Memoirs*, in which he had the advantage of hindsight, Wilkinson rendered the opinion, "Fort Washington [was] a mere water battery, of twelve or fifteen guns" that could easily be knocked out either by the guns of a frigate or taken by a force at night from the back.[30]

Wilkinson insisted that if Warren had shown more persistence in July 1813, the capital could have fallen then. He is possibly correct. By not attacking Washington, the admiral displayed the same lack of will he had shown three weeks earlier in not pressing an attack on Norfolk after the rebuff at Craney Island. Perhaps the British commander felt that the land force of 2,400 available to him was insufficient for the job of attacking the U.S. capital. However, Van Ness admitted that his militiamen were not prepared to face an attack.

He cited "the great want of preparation by the Government, in respect to arms, ammunition, camp equipage [*sic*], provisions, and the consequent delays and confusion. . . ."[31]

Why did Madison not insist on having a strong army to protect the nation's capital? To answer this question, we must consider the roots of the beginnings of the American system of government. We need to remember the ingrained distrust of a standing army manifested not only by Madison but by George Washington and other leaders. During Washington's presidency, the United States had started to put its faith in levies of militia. Washington had reversed himself on his earlier criticisms of militia and said that a large professional army would be a danger to democracy, expensive, and unnecessary. He proposed a small

Maj. Gen. James Wilkinson
(1757–1825)

Courtesy National Portrait Gallery,
Smithsonian Institution

regular army of some 2,600 soldiers, to be mainly used for frontier defense, that would be backed with militia. As first envisioned by him, the militia would be under federal supervision and made up of able-bodied men aged 18 to 50 years commanded by officers trained at a national military academy. The president's proposal was adopted in the Militia Law of 1792, though with the vital caveat—federal control—eliminated. As enacted by Congress, the law stated that all able-bodied white males aged 18 to 45 years were to enroll in their state militias and training was to be left to the states.[32]

It is likely Madison never forgot the precept against a standing army in the *Declaration of Rights* drafted by George Mason for the 1776 Virginia Convention, to which he was a young delegate from Orange County. The declaration stated, "That a well regulated militia, composed of the body of the people trained to arms is the proper, natural, and safe defence of a free state. . . ." By contrast, it decreed, "standing armies, in time of peace, should be avoided, as dangerous to liberty. . . ."[33]

Undoubtedly, the president also remembered an incident in June 1783 when mutinous soldiers threatened the government. Madison had been shocked by the appearance in the streets of Philadelphia of soldiers demanding pay. In a memorandum of June 21, 1783, he wrote, "Mutinous soldiers presented themselves, drawn up in the Street. . . ." Drunken soldiers, he wrote, were "uttering offensive words and wantonly pointing their muskets to the windows of Congress."[34]

The great irony is that because Madison did not arrange for the necessary forces to repel the British invasion of 1814, it was the enemy who pointed their muskets at the windows of Congress. The British shot them out after General Ross's horse was killed, along with several of the general's men. Not only this, but the presidential mansion was "grossly insulted" by the enemy, not to mention looted by rowdy Americans.

But we are getting ahead of our story. For now, the capital enjoyed a reprieve—because Admiral Warren chose to pull his punches. Washington socialite Margaret Bayard Smith, wife of Samuel Harrison Smith, founder of the pro-administration *National Intelligencer,* wrote to her sister expressing confidence in the city's safety:

> It is generally believed impossible for the English to reach the city, not so much from our force at [Fort Washington], tho' that is very large, as from the natural impediments; the river being very difficult to navigate. . . . There is so little apprehension of danger in the city, that not a single removal of person or goods has taken place. . . . Every precaution has been taken. . . . We go on regularly with our every day occupations. . . .[35]

Significantly, though, Mrs. Smith mentioned the generally held fear of a slave insurrection: "As for our enemy *at home* I have no doubt they will if possible join the British. . . . [but] the few scatter'd slaves about our neighbourhood, could not muster enough force to venture on an attack."[36]

In southern Maryland, the British were carrying on with their usual practice of looting the countryside, carrying off slaves, cattle, and property. Indeed, the southern Maryland counties of St. Mary's and Calvert would be preyed upon by the enemy so many times during 1813 and 1814 that the consequences of their raids can still be felt down to our day in terms of population lost to emigration west forced by the depredations.[37]

Warren reported that after the return of Shirreff's light squadron, the troops under Beckwith were landed "to protect the Party Employed in procuring Cattle and Forage for the use of the Squadron. . . ." The British took with them "120 head of Cattle and 100 Sheep" and sailed for the upper bay.[38]

Once more Baltimore was threatened. On August 8, a squadron of 15 vessels hove in sight of Baltimore. General Smith put the regulars and militia on alert. Since the previous British approach in April, Fort McHenry had been strengthened in terms of personnel, works, and armament. For example, the firepower of the fort had been boosted by the addition of Capt. George Stiles' Marine Artillery. Stiles' 36 cannons on naval carriages had been mounted in the fort's water battery. Incidentally, the Marine Artillery Company should not be confused with the U.S. Marines. The unit was made up of out-of-work merchant seamen such as Captain Stiles himself.[39]

On the Ferry Branch, a mile and a half west of the fort, an earthen battery had been constructed armed with six French 18-pounders. This redoubt was alternately named the Six-Gun Battery, or Fort Babcock, after Capt. Samuel Babcock, who supervised its construction for the city. The batteries of Fort

Covington and Spring Garden stood further west. East of the fort, across the channel, another battery stood opposite the fort on Lazaretto Point. In case the British tried to force the channel, General Smith ordered barges armed with 32-pound cannons in the bow and stern to be stationed in the channel between the Lazaretto and Fort McHenry. The garrison at Fort McHenry was also reinforced with a detachment from the 38th Regiment of the U.S. Army.[40]

Smith still anticipated that any British landing would be made at North Point. Thus, he ordered Maj. William Jamison's 7th Regiment from the Baltimore County 11th Brigade to march down the North Point road to Bear Creek. Additionally, if, as he anticipated, the enemy did attack from the east, Smith ordered 40 pieces of artillery to be collected on Hampstead Hill (present-day Patterson Park). Thus, the city stood ready to repel the invaders. Although few expected that an attack would be attempted given the small size of Warren's fleet, General Smith and his officers took the mobilization seriously.[41]

Again no attack on Baltimore came. Instead, the British sailed south toward Annapolis, to threaten Maryland's capital. On August 12, Secretary Jones ordered Capt. Charles Morris and the crew of the frigate *Adams* to Annapolis to serve as artillerists at Forts Severn and Madison. Morris's 220 seamen and one hundred marines, backed by local militia, stood ready to repulse the British if necessary. However, by August 29, Jones decided that no attack would be forthcoming on Baltimore, Annapolis, *or* Washington. He disagreed with Brig. Gen. Joseph Bloomfield, commander of the 4th Military District, who feared the British might attempt to land at Herring Bay, south of Annapolis, and by a forced march try to destroy the capital. Jones told Morris, "I do not . . . believe that the enemy is at all prepared, or disposed, for so bold and vigorous an enterprise."[42]

Warren reported to London that he and Beckwith discussed the possibility of attacking Annapolis and Baltimore but that they felt the odds were against them being able to successfully attack either place. He said "upwards of Eleven Thousand Troops" had been assembled at Baltimore and "Five Thousand men were around Annapolis and others expected from Washington." He told London that Beckwith agreed that attacks with the forces available "would prove very doubtful."[43]

The admiral contented himself with easily attainable goals. Thus, there was more of the usual depredations. They settled for continued disruption of the commercial life of the bay and attacks on easy targets. On July 28, for example, he ordered Shirreff to sail his light squadron up the bay to try to capture Gordon's Baltimore flotilla. One of the British brigs grounded on a shoal off Annapolis in chasing the schooners *Active* and *Patapsco* (one of Gordon's leased vessels). The brig was hauled off the shoal by a British frigate.[44] Cockburn reportedly later boasted to an American that he told Warren that "should a gun be fired [on the stranded brig], he would sack [Annapolis] in half an hour."[45]

The British established a temporary base on Kent Island with the aid of three companies of the 102nd Regiment and the Royal Marines who easily rounded up the weak militia force on the island. Warren described Kent Island as a "valuable & beaut[iful] Island which is half the size of the Isle of Wight. . . ." He said his troops and crews "so long Embarked and living upon Salt Provisions" could look forward to enjoying the cattle, stock, and vegetables on the island. And, indeed, the British, suffering from scurvy and fever, badly needed the fresh supplies.[46]

Early on the morning of August 13, Beckwith and Napier led 1,500 men in an attempt to surprise a camp of militia at nearby Queenstown on the Chester River just east of Kent Island. While the Redcoats crept up on the town in the early morning darkness, a detachment in 45 barges approached the town to attack it from the river. Again, the British adopted a land-sea attack as at Craney Island and Hampton. However, the barges lost their way. Then, Beckwith lost the element of surprise when an American scouting party spotted the Redcoats tramping along the darkened road toward town. Capt. Benjamin Massey and 18 men had been scouting in the direction of Kent Island. The militiamen fired several times at the approaching column with telling effect, particularly as the panicked British started to shoot each other in an incident of friendly fire. Royal Artilleryman Robertson wrote, "The reverberating sounds seemed to spread all around them, [and the troops] fired right and left, shooting each other." He said that although Beckwith ordered the band to play and resumed the march, "At every turn the American picquets fired and the panic returned." Beckwith's horse was shot, and Napier was thus dangerously exposed as the only mounted man. Robertson tried to get the colonel to dismount, but he refused to do so.[47]

Having wreaked havoc in the British ranks, Massey retreated to join the main body of three hundred militia under Maj. William H. Nicholson. In the face of the superior British forces, Nicholson judiciously retreated to Centreville without losing a man. The British, lacking cavalry, could not pursue them.[48]

The British had been dealt a serious blow in morale. The Queenstown debacle added to the British miseries caused by the intense Chesapeake August heat and the mosquitoes that plagued the tidewater. Indeed, the Baltimore-published *Niles' Weekly Register* exulted that while they were on Kent Island "'the long month of August' will slay hundreds of them." Niles added gleefully, "The mosquito . . . in countless multitudes, will fasten on them, and, assisted by disease, terminate the life of 'many a fine, tall fellow' not used [to] them."[49]

Still, the British did not yet scale down their raids. On August 10 and again on August 26, in a minor and easily repelled raid, they attacked St. Michaels on the Miles River. It is logical to think that the British targeted the town because they knew it to be a shipbuilding center for the construction of privateers. However, Warren's orders of August 7 to Cockburn say nothing about the town being a shipbuilding center. The admiral ordered Cockburn to capture or destroy some armed vessels rumored to be at the town. Cockburn was also directed to destroy the "small Battery" erected for the defense of the town.[50]

There seems to have been a glaring failure in British intelligence gathering in regard to St. Michaels that endured for the whole campaign in the Chesapeake. How else can we explain that there is no mention of shipbuilding at the town in the commanders' correspondence? Apparently Warren and Cockburn were both ignorant of the fact that St. Michaels was an important target because of its shipbuilding industry. It is thought that at least two vessels were under construction in the town at the time of the attack: the privateer *Surprise* and the schooner *George Washington*. And, if they were to but know it, Spencer's Shipyard at St. Michaels would shortly receive a contract to build barges for Barney's flotilla.[51]

The enemy attacked from barges in the river while the troops marched toward the town from the land side. Lieutenant Polkinghorne led eleven barges manned by Royal Marines and sailors while Beckwith with the soldiers and marines landed four miles from the town. However, as at Craney Island and at Queenstown, the combined land and sea attack failed to go as planned. The morning of August 10 proved rainy, dark, and miserable. Beckwith was delayed in a futile attempt to attack what he thought was a camp of militia but that proved to be only a picket. In the end, he and his troops never reached St. Michaels and only the amphibious forces were engaged.[52]

Local commander Brig. Gen. Perry Benson, aware that a British attack might be imminent, had assembled at St. Michaels a force of five hundred Talbot County militiamen. A boom was thrown across the entrance of the harbor, between Parrott's Point and Three Cedar Point, where batteries were also erected. Polkinghorne found that the boom blocked his passage, and ordered his men to row toward Parrott's Point, which was defended by a battery with two 9-pounders manned by 15 men under Lt. Henry Dodson. Because of the dark, rainy conditions, the raiders were not detected until they leaped from their barges. Dodson's artillerymen were suddenly alerted. When the enemy sailors and marines got within 30 yards, Dodson ordered his men to open up with grape and canister. Although momentarily checked, the enemy soon began to mass around the battery. Realizing his situation was hopeless, Dodson ordered his men to join the main force in the town.[53]

Polkinghorne ordered his men to spike the guns, split the carriages, and destroy the ammunition and stores. Because Beckwith's troops had not arrived to support him, he knew he had to retreat quickly or risk capture by the militia. The landing party came under a well-directed fire from two field pieces operated by the Easton Artillery under Lt. Clement Vickers. Polkinghorne retreated to the barges under protecting fire from a carronade in a launch commanded by the aptly named acting Lt. Charles Blood. According to Polkinghorne, his only casualties were two men wounded. General Benson reported, "Some of the houses were perforated, but no injury [occurred] to any human being."[54]

Due to the failure of the land-sea attack and their need for a hasty departure, the British raiding party failed to locate or strike a blow against St. Michaels' shipbuilding industry. Polkinghorne reported, "Not a vessel to be seen, I deemed the object of the enterprize fulfilled. . . ." He reported the loss of only two wounded.[55]

The time of year that the British called "the sickly season" had arrived: the time in climates such as that found in the Chesapeake when they believed typhus would be rife. Additionally, hurricane season was beginning. Mindful also of desertions in the army, poor discipline among the marines, and illness aboard the ships, Warren brought the expedition to a close. Along with Beckwith and the troops, Warren sailed for Halifax, Nova Scotia. Cockburn went to Bermuda for the winter, as biographer Pack terms it, "for a well earned break." Capt. Robert Barrie of the H.M.S. *Dragon* with a small squadron remained in the bay on blockade duty.[56]

Beckwith's expedition had achieved nothing of consequence. Napier wrote, "We were five months cruising along that hostile coast, acting with so much absurdity, and so like buccaneers . . . that we did no good to English fame, no real injury to America."[57] Realizing their lack of success, the future general said he came up with a grand scheme to resolve the stalemate. He suggested using the slaves who were fleeing to the British to build a vast army to defeat the Americans. Napier claimed his proposal could have brought the war to a speedy conclusion and abolished slavery at the same time.[58] (See appendix 3, "Napier's Plan to Use Ex-Slaves to Win the War for the British.") Napier's proposal had its harebrained aspects. Yet what he suggested in terms of using former slaves in the British forces did come about, if not on the grand scale he envisioned. In spring 1814, the British started to train able-bodied male former slaves in the use of arms at a base on Tangier Island. Whether this development stemmed from Napier's suggestion or independently is hard to know. The induction of Chesapeake Bay blacks into the British forces in spring 1814 would be part of a new offensive by the British under a new commander in chief determined to punish the Americans.

Chapter Seven
The Gathering Storm

In spring 1814, as Barney continued to wrestle with the problems of getting his flotilla shipshape, a significant change occurred in the British command. Aged, ineffective Admiral Warren was replaced as commander in chief in North American waters by Vice Adm. Sir Alexander Cochrane. Cochrane had an inveterate hatred of Americans, possibly because his elder brother had been killed at Yorktown. He contemptuously referred to Americans as "spaniels" who needed a "good drubbing."[1]

Although the admiralty in May 1813 had reprimanded Cockburn for conducting raids in the Chesapeake instead of restricting himself to blockade duty, Cochrane gave Cockburn complete license to wreak havoc:

> You are at perfect liberty as soon as you can muster a sufficient force, to act with the utmost hostility against the shores of the United States. . . . Their sea port towns in ashes and the country invaded will be some sort of retaliation for their savage conduct in Canada where they have destroyed our towns. . . . It is therefore but just that retaliation be made near to the seat of government from whence these orders were enacted. . . .[2]

The new commander was giving Cockburn permission to retaliate for the April 1813 burning of the government buildings of York (present-day Toronto), capital of Upper Canada. Thus, fears expressed by Navy Secretary Jones that the British offensive of 1814 would prove fiercer than that of the previous summer were fully justified. Because of those fears, Jones had ordered Barney in December to contract for 10 more vessels to increase the size of the Chesapeake flotilla by a third.[3]

On April 2, Cochrane issued a proclamation aimed at anti-war whites and at the slaves who continued to flock to the British:

65

[you] will have [the] choice of either entering into His Majesty's sea or land forces, or of being sent as free settlers to the British possessions in North America or the West Indies, where [you] will meet with all due encouragement.[4]

Cockburn distributed the proclamation, and U.S. newspapers obligingly printed it. Cochrane's intent was partly to supplement his available forces with able-bodied blacks. The new British commander, though, had unrealistic ideas about the possibilities of using the former slaves. He wrote to Lord Bathurst:

Vice Adm. Sir Alexander Cochrane
(1758–1832)

Brenton's Naval History,
Courtesy Library of Congress

The Blacks are all good horsemen. Thousands will join upon their masters' horses, and they will only require to be clothed and accoutered to be as good Cossacks as any in the European army, and I believe more terrific to the Americans than any troops that could be brought forward.[5]

He prophesied to Cockburn that "With [the former slaves] properly armed and backed with 20,000 British troops, Mr. Maddison [*sic*] will be hurled from his throne."[6] The admirals knew events were rapidly unfolding in Europe. The Duke of Wellington was pushing Napoleon's forces out of Spain and back into France. They anticipated that a huge force of 20,000 soldiers might soon be available to enable them to finish off the Yankees. They had already been assured that a battalion of Royal Marines was on the way. Four days after Cochrane's proclamation, Napoleon abdicated. With the Bourbon monarchy restored, the British high command began to discuss sending veteran troops to North America.[7]

Until the marines and the soldiers arrived, the admirals had to work with what manpower they had available. The training of able-bodied male former slaves in the use of arms was one solution. However, Cockburn recognized the paradox of his superior's proclamation. He warned Cochrane that given "the option of being sent as free settlers to British settlements . . . they will most certainly all prefer [that] to the danger and fatigue of joining us in arms."[8]

All the same, he followed Cochrane's orders and set about recruiting a "Corps of Colonial Marines" that would "be formed, drilled, and brought forward for service."[9] Each recruit would receive a bounty of $20 and the same red uniform as the Royal Marines. Cochrane believed the "gay" red uniform "may act as an inducement" for other blacks to join the corps. The former

Map of British Fort Albion on Tangier Island

The map shows two redoubts at bottom, officers' quarters and parade ground at center, and privates' huts used by "Colonial Marines" at top.

Courtesy National Library of Scotland

slaves would be trained in arms at a fort to be constructed on Tangier Island. This fort, shortly to become the stronghold of the British in the bay, was christened by Cockburn "Fort Albion." It was located at the southern end of the island near a deep water anchorage and had two redoubts three hundred yards apart. Within its protective ramparts, there were officers' quarters, huts for the privates, a parade ground, and a hospital.[10]

Because Cochrane's proclamation openly stated that the British would *arm* ex-slaves, it renewed American fears of a slave insurrection. In response, Barney decided to ready his flotilla to mount a surprise attack on Tangier Island. He aimed not only to destroy Fort Albion but to wreck a barge fleet the enemy were rumored to be building on the island. Only two-thirds of his planned vessels were ready to sail and even those that were seaworthy were undermanned. Nevertheless, on May 24, Barney sailed from Baltimore with 18 vessels. One of these vessels, gunboat *No. 137*, was used as a supply boat with a month's supplies on board. Several merchant vessels accompanied the flotilla in an effort to try to sneak past the British blockade.[11]

Incredible as it seems, Cockburn apparently remained ignorant of Barney's plans until this moment even though building and recruiting for the flotilla had been widely reported in the press.[12] It says something about the poor quality of his intelligence gathering. He told Cochrane that on May 30 he had been told by one of the islanders of an "extensive and formidable" flotilla that had been fitted out from Baltimore "at great expence [*sic*]" and that it "had actually sailed under the Command of Commodore Barney."[13]

Ironically, on the morning of May 30, the Tangier Island-trained former slaves, the "Colonial Marines," saw their first action when the British attacked Pungoteague, Virginia. The rear admiral had heard that a battery had been erected on Pungoteague Creek, opposite Tangier Island. A raiding party under Capt. Charles Ross engaged the Virginia militia under Maj. John Finney. Ross's men captured a small caliber field piece and burned two pine plank barracks before they were driven off. Cockburn praised "the Conduct of . . . the Colonial Marines, who were for the <u>first</u> time, employed in Arms against their old Masters, and behaved to the admiration of every Body."[14]

After the action at Pungoteague, Cockburn had intended to attack another battery at Cherrystone, Virginia. But having learned of the flotilla—if blissfully unaware that the commodore's target was his base at Fort Albion—he swiftly changed his plans. He directed Capt. Robert Barrie of the H.M.S. *Dragon* to seek out the flotilla and either capture or destroy it. Barrie took the schooner *St. Lawrence* (the former *Atlas* captured at Ocracoke, North Carolina) along with some small boats. He began to scour the inlets along the western shore as far north as the Patuxent.[15]

Around May 31, Barney anchored near Drum Point at the mouth of the Patuxent to await favorable tides and winds to make the journey across the bay to attack Fort Albion. He intended to make an eastward sprint to Hooper's Straits at the top of the archipelago comprising Bloodsworth, Smith, and Tangier Islands and then sail down to Tangier.[16]

Colonial Marines

Former Chesapeake Bay slaves being trained by the British on Tangier Island.

Sketch by the Author

Early on the morning of June 1, Captain Barrie's search party was slowly working its way up Maryland's western shore. At approximately 9:00 A.M., a British lookout spied strange sails to the north. Barrie had located the flotilla. However, he quickly realized it comprised a more powerful force than he commanded. In all, he counted 24 vessels.[17]

The British commander ordered signals hoisted and guns fired to gather his scattered boats. The cannons would also alert his 74-gun ship-of-the-line H.M.S. *Dragon*, many miles to the south at the mouth of the Potomac. Then he collected his boats and retreated toward the Potomac. This presented a golden opportunity for Barney and the Chesapeake flotilla to strike a meaningful blow against the British invaders. With men at action stations, Barney closed in for the kill.[18]

At that moment, a sudden squall came up, threatening to swamp the flotilla. The H.M.S. *Dragon*, under full sail, swept in toward Point Lookout to deny Barney access to the Potomac. The Americans, fighting to control their vessels in the turbulent seas and rainy, deteriorating conditions, found themselves headed toward the guns of the big 74. The tables had completely turned. Barney was forced to retreat, closely pursued by the *St. Lawrence*, the British tenders, and the *Dragon*. The British succeeded in destroying a schooner, probably one of the merchant vessels accompanying the flotilla. When Barrie attempted to cut off gunboat *No. 137*, Barney anchored his flagship, the block sloop *Scorpion*, and made a fight of it. The British barges, the *St. Lawrence*, and the tenders from *Dragon* were driven off under heavy fire. The Battle of Cedar Point ended in a stalemate. The commodore led his flotilla into the Patuxent and anchored three miles upriver. Barrie blockaded the river mouth and waited for Cockburn to send more vessels so he could better fight this troublesome Yankee flotilla.[19]

On June 6, Cockburn sent Barrie the sloop-of-war brig *Jaseur* and the frigate *Loire*. Barrie entered the Patuxent on the evening of June 7. After transferring his flag to the *Loire*, he made plans to attack Barney the following morning. But, just as Barrie got ready to launch the attack at 7:00 A.M., he saw the flotilla about to enter shallow St. Leonard's Creek, an inlet on the northern shore of the river. He ordered the *St. Lawrence* and *Jaseur* to give chase, along with *Loire* and seven barges. He well knew that the shoals in the creek would not permit his larger boats to enter. As the *St. Lawrence* closed in on the receding U.S. vessels, she ground to a halt on a shoal. The Americans had escaped.[20]

This began a stand off that would last for almost three weeks. Two-mile-long St. Leonard's Creek, in the words of Donald G. Shomette, although "an admirable defensive position . . . was also a closet" with no easy escape for the flotilla.[21]

At noon on June 7, Barrie led a barge attack into the creek. Barney arranged his vessels in three fighting divisions, the red division under his own command, and white and blue, respectively, under Lt. Solomon Rutter and Lt. Solomon Frazier. The commodore skippered one barge while his son, cavalryman Maj. William B. Barney, took command of his father's flagship, *Scorpion*.

The British opened the engagement by firing their infernal Congreve rockets. Barrie aimed to lure Barney down the creek to engage him at close quarters. But the commodore refused to rise to the bait. He fired back with his long guns, forcing Barrie to retreat—another stalemate. Later that afternoon, Barrie tried again with additional barges. Once more his attack failed, although one Congreve rocket slammed into a barge, passing through the body of a flotillaman. Flames ignited a barrel of gunpowder and another of musket cartridges, the explosions hurling sailors into the creek. Three men were wounded, one of them badly burned. Major Barney received permission from his father to take charge of the burning vessel. The cavalryman vaulted over the gunnels and doused the fires, astonishing his father with his bravery.[22]

To combat an expected British offensive on June 10, Barney conceived a smart counterattack. Streamlining the flotilla, he removed the masts, to rely on oars only. He gambled that the additional speed this modification would facilitate would enable him to catch the British off guard. His front line force comprised 13 barges manned by five hundred sailors.[23]

At 2:00 P.M. on a fine sunny day, 21 British barges, a rocket boat, and two schooners moved up the creek with six hundred to seven hundred Royal Marines aboard. A favorable wind blew from the north. A band played and pennants streamed in the breeze.[24]

The British ascended the creek in three lines. No doubt Barrie was confident that this time he would succeed in carrying out Cockburn's orders to

The Battle of St. Leonard's Creek

Courtesy Calvert Marine Museum

destroy the flotilla. Barges towed the two British schooners, both of which were armed with 32-pound carronades. With less than a thousand feet separating the forces, Barney's men opened with a barrage of cannonfire. The British responded with rockets and cannons. The Americans poured in a heavy, galling fire, causing Barrie to retreat. The U.S. vessels chased the British toward the *Loire, Jaseur,* and *St. Lawrence.* Barney's gunners poured fire into the *St. Lawrence.* As the British tried to get out of the way, the schooner ran aground again. *Jaseur* and *Loire* fired broadsides to stop Barney capturing the schooner. Then Barrie landed Royal Marines to drive the commodore back up the creek. By evening, the battle was over. The British had suffered grievous losses in vessels and men killed.[25]

Barney later reported,

> [*St. Lawrence*] was nearly destroyed, having several shot through her at the water's edge; her deck torn up, gun dismounted, and mainmast nearly cut off about half way up, and rendered unserviceable. [Barrie's armed gig] was cut in two; a shot went through the rocket boat; one of the small schooners carrying the two thirty-two-pounders had a shot which raked her from aft foreward; [their barges] generally suffered. . . .[26]

Barney did not escape from the trap, but he had badly mauled his tormentors. The usually unflappable Cockburn was plainly disturbed. At last he had encountered a Yankee to reckon with. He became even more upset when a reign of terror unleashed by Barrie on the country around the creek failed to lure Barney from his hiding place. He wrote to Cochrane that Barney "has . . . occasioned me much anxiety and difficulty. . . ." He added that he would wait for the expected reinforcements of marines and soldiers to enable him to finish Barney off.[27]

Indeed, the soldiers to which he alluded were on their way from Europe at that very moment. An army under Maj. Gen. Robert Ross had sailed from Bordeaux on May 30 with sealed orders. It was not, however, the grand army for which Cockburn and Cochrane had anticipated. Instead of the 10,000 to 20,000 soldiers the admirals expected, Ross would bring with him just under four thousand men. Yet, most of them *were* veterans. Three out of the four regiments sent with Ross had seen service in the Peninsula. They were experienced regiments chosen by Wellington himself.[28]

Many in Britain had thought that Arthur Wellesley, the Duke of Wellington, should be the man to "give Jonathan one good thrashing" and bring the unpopular American war to a conclusion. Yet the Iron Duke refused to go unless the high command absolutely ordered him to go. Moreover, he indicated he would only take charge if given the freedom to negotiate with Madison's government.[29]

He chose Ross, a fellow Irishman, to lead the expedition to the Chesapeake. A brilliant if not well-known officer, Ross had been a major general for only a year, having achieved that rank on June 4, 1813.[30]

Ross had made his name as a colonel in the 20th or East Devonshire Regiment. He always led his troops from the front, sharing danger with his men thereby winning his men's affection. On July 4, 1806, at the Battle of Maida in southern Italy, Colonel Ross led his men into battle at a decisive moment to ensure a British victory. The battle reversed a succession of French land victories which won Ross the first of four gold medals he was to be awarded.[31]

Ross's hunger to be in the thick of the fighting led to him being severely wounded on February 27, 1814, at the beginning of the Battle of Orthes. The neck wound would see him invalided out until he was sent on the expedition against the United States.[32]

A modern military analyst, Maj. Gen. G. N. Wood, has noted that the severity of the general's wound would have been such that, in a modern

Maj. Gen. Robert Ross
(1766–1814)

Courtesy Bury Regimental Museum, Bury, England, and Francis de C. Hamilton

army, it would probably have precluded him from a return so soon to active service. Ross and his aides were indeed what might be termed "walking wounded." Capt. Harry Smith, Ross's deputy adjutant general, was recovering from a wound in the ankle, while Lt. George de Lacy Evans, his deputy quartermaster general, had been wounded twice at Toulouse. Wood concluded that Ross and his two aides "would hardly have passed medically fit" when they were sent on the American trip.[33]

With the French war seemingly over, it must have been a stunning blow for Ross's wife Elizabeth to have her husband sent on the expedition. However, it was a duty and an honor he could not refuse. His letters to her written on board ship and during his time in the Chesapeake were full of words attempting to mollify her fears for his safety. He promised her that this would be his last campaign.[34]

Another man with a hard parting to make was Ross's aide, 26-year-old Capt. Harry Smith, of the 95th Regiment, or Rifle Corps. Two years earlier, the young rifleman had wed a young Spanish girl in a drumhead wedding attended by Wellington. The then 14-year-old Juana Maria de los Dolores de Leon and her sister had fled the debauchery following the storming of Badajoz when British troops wrecked their house. The young women sought the protection of the British officers with blood trickling down their necks caused by drunken soldiers wrenching their earrings off.[35]

Now her beloved "Enrique" was to be torn from her bosom and sent to America, half a world away. Smith, disappointed that his service in the Peninsula had not earned him a majority, grasped the chance of further service in America knowing it might lead to the advancement he craved. Smith wrote later of the anguish of leaving her:

> I left her insensible and in a faint. God only knows the number of staggering and appalling dangers I had faced; but, thank the Almighty, I never was unmanned until now, and I leaped on my horse by that impulse which guides the soldier to do his duty.[36]

Meanwhile, as Smith was departing from his young wife, a young unmarried Scotsman, 2d Lt. George Robert Gleig, penned a letter to his "Dearest Father"—the Bishop of Brechin—in Stirling, Scotland, from the camp of the 85th Regiment (or Young Bucks) near St. Jean de Luz in southern France. "I am sorry to inform you," he said, "that all my hopes of seeing you soon are for a time at least, blown in the air, for instead of returning to England, our regiment marches tomorrow to embark at Bordeaux for America." He told his father that after whatever action the regiment might be required to fight, he feared he might have to do *ten years* of garrison duty. An eternity for a young man of 18 years! He hoped his return from America would be immediate or that he might be able to quit the army after the action. Gleig, later to become chaplain-general to the British army as well as a widely published author, would write two books based on his experiences in America. In many respects, however, his diary and letters are more authentic. In them, he reported his activities and feelings at the time he experienced them.[37]

George Robert Gleig
(1796–1888)

Lossing's *Field Book of the War of 1812*

The blue flag of Adm. Pulteney Malcolm flew from the stern of the lead ship of the convoy, H.M.S. *Royal Oak*. Malcolm's flagship would serve as home for Ross and his staff for the voyage across the Atlantic. Six summers previously, in July 1808, the handsome admiral, as captain of the H.M.S. *Donegal*, had similarly escorted the future duke of Wellington, Lt. Gen. Sir Arthur Wellesley, and his troops to Portugal.[38]

Less well appointed were the enlisted men and junior officers of the expeditionary force: the 4th, 44th, and

85th Regiments, dispersed among the crowded troopships and frigates. Lieutenant Gleig, aboard the H.M.S. *Diadem*, noted in his diary, "There are 40 of us in our cabin; so the crowd is immense." He wrote to his mother, "We are so crowded that some of us [have] to sleep upon deck and the rest of us . . . upon the cabin floor."[39]

By comparison, Capt. Richard Gubbins of the 85th felt lucky. He wrote home saying, "The first Lieutenant has been kind enough to give me half his cabin—and I assure you that two in a cabin is somewhat preferable to 40 in a cabin." Within a few days, Gubbins changed his tune. *Diadem* was, he said, "a miserable old tub." In his opinion, it sailed "worse than a collier."[40]

Gubbins must have looked longingly at the H.M.S. *Menelaus*, 36 guns, captained by Lord Byron's 29-year-old cousin, Sir Peter Parker, baronet, with its spanking white sails, white yards, and white deadeyes. Parker, described by one of his officers as "the handsomest man in the navy," often came on board *Diadem* to dine with the captain or drink through the night with the officers of the 85th. An Irishman who had served for several months in 1810 as a member of Parliament for Wexford, Parker was the scion of a Royal Navy family. His grandfather, Adm. Sir Peter Parker, had bombarded Sullivan's Island, Charleston, in June 1776—and was roundly defeated by the Patriots. No doubt young Parker longed for the glory fighting the Yankees that had eluded his grandfather.[41]

In the opening weeks of June, as the British fleet approached the Azores, Gleig and his fellow officers whittled away the hours playing cards. Meanwhile, in the Chesapeake, Commodore Barney wrestled with the problem of getting out of St. Leonard's Creek.

In a belated response to Barney's plea for troops to help protect his flanks, the 36th U.S. Infantry under Col. Henry Carberry arrived on June 14. Relations between Barney and Carberry proved to be poor, and the colonel's troops proved ill disciplined and not inclined to fight. Shomette notes, "Carberry cared little for Barney, and less for his boats, and felt he and his regiment could be put to better use elsewhere, perhaps in the Canadian theater where they might earn honor and accolades."[42]

However, we might question if dreams of glory danced in the colonel's head if we consider both his past and his conduct in the following weeks. In June 1783, as a supernumary captain in the Third Pennsylvania Regiment, Carberry had been one of the leaders of the army mutiny in Philadelphia that disturbed future President James Madison. Carberry fled to England, returning in 1784 to his native Maryland. Arrested and put in jail in Annapolis, he pleaded guilty and threw himself on the mercy of the court but apparently went unpunished.[43]

When the British began raids upriver, Carberry left Barney. Although he had supposedly gone to stop the raids, he only shadowed the marauders. The commodore, deprived of the army's protection, only had the U.S. Marines to provide a weak defense for the flotilla's flanks.[44]

Secretary Jones suggested a way to free the flotilla. Perhaps the commodore could dismantle his barges and haul them overland to the Chesapeake. Barney found the idea preposterous: the British would learn of the plan and be waiting out in the bay. Moreover, where his men would have to reconstruct the vessels, there was no handy creek to provide protection. Jones grew furious when Barney did not follow his suggestion. Then, on June 20, Barney received an order from the secretary to destroy the flotilla. The order so stunned the commodore he at first hid it. Finally, worn down with arguing with Jones he began the work of dismantling his little fleet. Six of the 13 barges were dismantled and moveable parts hauled ashore. At that moment he received another despatch from Jones countermanding the original order. The commodore, no doubt cursing Jones to hell and back, ordered his men to restore the flotilla to the creek.[45]

Col. Decius Wadsworth suggested a plan to Jones that might enable the flotilla to bust out of its trap. If batteries could be mounted on the bluffs at the mouth of St. Leonard's Creek, the British ships might be driven back sufficiently to allow the commodore to escape. Jones approved the proposal. Wadsworth hurried to St. Leonard's with two 18-pounders, three field pieces, and a traveling furnace to heat the shot. The second battalion of the 38th U.S. Infantry was ordered down from Baltimore. Carberry was told to bring his 36th Infantry back from upriver. Then Barney received an additional one hundred U.S. Marines under Capt. Samuel Miller, along with three 12-pound cannons.[46]

On June 24, Wadsworth, Miller, and Barney held a council of war. On the north bluff overlooking the creek, they would erect an earth fort and install the furnace to heat the shot. The fort had to be constructed in secrecy, in case the British learned about it. One of Barney's men, Sailing Master John Geoghegan, would command flotilla cannoneers who would operate Wadsworth's two 18-pounders. Miller's marines would service their three 12-pounders in concert with Geoghegan's battery. Carberry's soldiers would be placed behind the batteries on an open plan protected by the three field-pieces. It was agreed that on the morning of Sunday, June 26, before daylight, the batteries would open up on the British blockade vessels, while the flotilla would simultaneously launch an attack along the creek.[47]

On Saturday evening, as work on the fort continued at a frantic pace, 260 soldiers of the 38th Infantry under Maj. George Keyser arrived after a forced march from Friendship. These raw recruits were added to the equally inexperienced 36th Infantry, under the command of Carberry. The scene was set for the second battle of St. Leonard's Creek.[48]

On Sunday morning at 4:00 A.M., the hidden U.S. batteries opened up on the warships some six hundred yards out in the river. The British, under the command of Capt. Thomas Brown in Barrie's absence, were completely taken by surprise, shocked by the point-blank barrage. But the combined attack went wrong due to miscommunication between Barney and Wadsworth. Barney had received a note from Wadsworth indicating that the gun batteries might not be ready on time. When the artillerymen opened the engagement, the flotilla was not in position to attack. Because of the mix-up, the flotilla was a full 45 minutes late in joining in the battle. Hearing the booming of the American and British artillery, the flotillamen rowed down the darkened creek so that the flotilla "seemed to fly under the rapid strokes of the oar." At the mouth of the creek, Barney ordered his men to open up with their carronades. The enemy, only four hundred yards away, got their second surprise of the morning. The U.S. cannonballs slammed into the *Loire*. The frigate was hulled in at least fifteen places and her mizzen topmast was shot away. The *Narcissus* also received hits that threatened to sink her. The small craft around the frigates were also badly damaged. The British returned Barney's fire. Grapeshot rained down on the flotillamen, who were unprotected by bulwarks. Barney later described it as "a scene to appall the inexperienced and the faint hearted." Captain Brown, shocked by the sudden onslaught and the damage the Yankees had inflicted, withdrew his vessels and dropped down the Patuxent to lick his wounds. This was the moment for which Barney had so long awaited. He took his flotilla out of St. Leonard's Creek and moved up the Patuxent to Benedict. Wadsworth's plan had worked.[49]

The battle had lasted nearly two hours. Of the flotillamen, around nine had been injured and one man, a midshipman named Asquith, killed. A number of men at the batteries on the bluff were injured, and one man accidentally had both arms blown off when loading the hot shot. Two American gunboats were destroyed. On the British side, despite his abject failure to keep Barney blockaded, Capt. Brown minimized the affair. It was yet another example of British "damage control" and obfuscation. Brown reported to Cockburn, "I am happy to say, the only person wounded is the boatswain of the *Narcissus* who has lost a leg."[50]

During the battle, Carberry's infantrymen and the light artillery had beaten a retreat when they came under fire from the river. Wadsworth groused that they had evacuated the scene "without my orders before they had lost a single man killed or wounded" and that he had been forced to spike the guns. Charges and countercharges in regard to the American blunders in the battle flew back and forth in the press for weeks afterward.[51]

Cockburn must have been shocked at the turn of events. Nevertheless, he wrote to Cochrane assuring him that arrival of the troops would enable him to destroy the flotilla.[52]

At that moment, the troopships bringing Ross's army were several days at sea after stopping in the Azores. By June 30, the crowded conditions on the *Diadem* led to an outbreak of typhus. Admiral Malcolm and Col. William Thornton, commander of the 85th Regiment, sought to remedy the situation by isolating the sick on board a rocket ship. Divine service on Sunday, July 3, was cancelled, and the sea grew turbulent. U.S. Independence Day, Monday, July 4, was spent knocking down the standing berths and whitewashing. The men were made to sleep in hammocks. These measures seemed to work—the epidemic tailed off, though time was lost in the Atlantic crossing.[53]

While the British were dealing with their typhus outbreak, rumors of imminent invasion ran rampant in the United States. President Madison's government made arrangements to deal with the expected onslaught. Brig. Gen. William H. Winder was appointed commander of the 10th Military District. The general had recently been exchanged after being captured on June 6, 1813, at the Battle of Stoney Creek, Canada, in a confused night contest—his first major battle. The appointment was purely political. Madison thought that by choosing the nephew of Maryland's Federalist governor, Levin Winder, the governor would be more likely to release militiamen for the defense of the capital. On paper, the new commander could call on a total of 93,500 militiamen from 15 states. In practical terms, however, the general found he only had

Brig. Gen. William H. Winder (1775–1824), commander of the U.S. 10th Military District

Lossing's *Field Book of the War of 1812*

authority to draft three thousand men from Maryland plus a few thousand from Virginia and Pennsylvania. Moreover, Secretary of War Armstrong proved uncooperative in providing arms and supplies or even advice. The stubborn New Yorker disagreed with the choice of Winder as commander.[54]

In the following weeks, Winder showed himself to be a whirlwind. In the court-martial that exonerated him of responsibility for subsequent events, everyone testified to his great energy. Unfortunately, however, his boundless energy was misdirected, and he proved unable to focus on the problem at hand. He spent more time shuffling paper and rushing from place to place than in training men and putting them in the field to face the invaders. By contrast, Maj. Gen. Samuel Smith in Baltimore prepared and drilled his men, built defensive works, and was ready when the British attacked. Not so for Winder. Granted, the brigadier general only had weeks to prepare compared with more than a year as Smith had. However, as Walter Lord has commented, "Weeks rolled by, yet Winder developed no over-all plan. . . . The capital had no fortifications, nor did he devise any."[55]

In the face of a massive British invasion, Winder showed that he was the wrong man for the job of resisting the enemy. He was a man who fretted over inconsequential details. He was not the type of leader who grasped the big picture and was able to implement a plan of action. For instance, he developed a fixation on the forts of Annapolis, Forts Severn and Madison. He decided that if the British captured Fort Madison, the guns of that fort "might be turned with success on Fort Severn." He recommended that Fort Madison be dismantled and blown up. A week later, he reversed himself. He had decided that to dismantle Fort Madison might alarm the population, and that he would prefer to risk it in case of attack.[56]

While Winder fussed and wrote endless letters, on July 15, Cockburn received the first reinforcements he had been expecting. The troops comprised a Royal Marine Artillery company and the 3rd Battalion, Royal Marines, commanded by Maj. George Lewis. Armed with this additional manpower, he ordered a series of lightning raids up the Patuxent. Between July 16 and 21, a succession of communities, including Calverton and the Calvert County capital, Prince Frederick, were raided by Capt. Joseph Nourse.[57]

The day after these raids began, July 17, Cockburn wrote a secret memorandum to Cochrane detailing his plan to capture the capital. On the basis of the detailed mapping of the Patuxent that Nourse had been carrying out, he urged that Benedict be the place to land the troops. He stated,

> I consider the town . . . to offer us advantages for [landing] beyond any spot within the United States. It is, I am informed only 44 or 45 miles from Washington, and there is a high road between the two places which tho' hilly is good. . . . I most firmly believe therefore, that within 48 hours after [our army's] arrival in the Patuxent . . . , the city of Washington might be possessed without difficulty or opposition. . . . The facility and rapidity with which an army by landing at Benedict might possess itself of the Capitol, always so great a blow to the government of a country . . . must strongly urge the propriety of the plan. . . .[58]

Contrary to Winder's fretting over the forts of Annapolis, Cockburn rejected the Maryland capital as a staging point for such an attack. Annapolis was, he said, "tolerably well fortified" and difficult to approach with the larger British ships. He believed valuable time could be lost trying to take the town, thus allowing the Americans to gather forces for the defense of Washington. The Patuxent would be deep enough for frigates and the water was smooth. He told Cochrane that at Benedict the troops would find good quarters. The rich country around the Patuxent village would yield food "and as many horses as might be wanted to transport cannon" and other supplies.[59]

To distract American attention from his true plan to use the Patuxent to seize the capital, Cockburn conducted a series of raids along the Potomac. First hit were towns along the Maryland shore, beginning with Leonardtown on July 19. Eleven days later, at dawn on July 30, Cockburn carried out a raid on Chaptico on the Wicomico River. His men allegedly desecrated Christ Episcopal Church. The Americans later claimed the British stabled horses in the nave of the church, broke tiles, robbed tombs, and even forced women to strip naked for the delectation of officers. In the nation's capital, the anti-Cockburn *National Intelligencer* ran a despatch from a shocked visitor to Chaptico after the British raid who blustered, "Their conduct would have disgraced Cannibals."[60]

Cockburn's raids created panic in the district. As usual, Winder dithered, unable to decide what the twin thrusts meant. Although the District militia were encamped at the Wood Yard near Upper Marlboro, the general proved unable to decide whether he should create a show of force. Instead, he did nothing. On July 26, Secretary Jones sent an urgent note to Barney to ask him to abandon the flotilla and rush two hundred sailors to Washington to defend the capital. The seamen were needed, he said, to crew barges and schooners. However, shortly thereafter, with the threat of attack diminishing, Jones rescinded the order.[61]

Not all was confusion among the Americans. On the morning of August 3, Cockburn's raiding party of 20 barges received a welcoming blast from a battery on Mundy's Point on the Yeocomico River manned by the 47th Regiment of Virginia militia under Capt. William Henderson. A Royal Marine in a lead boat commanded by Cockburn's aide, Lieutenant Scott, was beheaded by a cannonball. Another salvo wounded two men. Then, when the boat reached the shore, two more men were killed. Having expended their ammunition except for two rounds of grapeshot, Henderson and his men retreated as the remainder of the British detachment of approximately three hundred men charged ashore. Brig. Gen. John R. Hungerford, encamped nearby at Kinsale, wrote to Virginia Governor Barbour to describe the looting and burning which followed the action, as well as further destruction when the enemy bombarded Kinsale itself that afternoon.[62]

Hungerford had been unable to stop Cockburn burning Nomini Church and carrying off more than a hundred slaves some days earlier. The general informed Barbour that the enemy raiding force at Mundy's Point included "several platoons of uniformed negroes." Hungerford's remarks about blacks were tainted as usual by the white southerner's dread of slave revolt. Yet, all the same, he made valid points about the disadvantages under which his men labored in fighting an enemy aided by former slaves with local knowledge quite often superior to their own:

> Our negroes are flocking to the enemy from all quarters, which [the British] convert into troops, vindictive and rapacious—with a most minute knowledge of every bye path. [The blacks] leave us as spies upon our posts and our strength, and they return upon us as guides and soldiers and incendiaries. . . . From this cause alone the enemy have a great advantage over us in a country where the passes and by-ways through our innumerable necks and swamps are so little known to but very few of our officers and men, and through which they can penetrate and be conducted with so much ease by these refugee blacks.[63]

Hungerford prophesied much worse British outrages to follow:

> Unless the [Federal] Government will give this quarter more effectual aid, the ruffian system of warfare carried on by the enemy . . . will light up one universal conflagration throughout these counties.[64]

In fact, a mere nine days after Hungerford penned these words, on August 14, the troopships bearing General Ross's army cleared the Capes and entered the Chesapeake. The three regiments that had left France at the end of May—the 4th, 44th, and 85th—had been augmented in Bermuda by the 21st Regiment from the Mediterranean. On August 16, the convoy rendezvoused with Cockburn's squadron. Lieutenant Gleig of the 85th noted that the rear admiral's forces included "a battalion of seven hundred marines, a hundred negroes lately armed and disciplined, and a division of marine artillery." He marveled at the breathtaking scene of the combined British fleet:

> The sight was . . . as grand and imposing as any I ever beheld; because one could not help remembering that this powerful fleet was sailing in an enemy's bay, and was filled with troops for the invasion of that enemy's country. Thus, like a snow-ball, we had gathered as we went on, and from a mere handful of soldiers, were now become an army formidable from its numbers as well as discipline.[65]

Cockburn took new boys General Ross and Capt. Sir Peter Parker ashore to show them how easy it was to conduct warfare in the Chesapeake. He led them on a raid on a factory on St. George's Island on the Potomac. As usual, the attack was launched before daylight, with a landing five miles from the target. Advancing up a "fair road" from the landing place, Ross directed the skirmishers while Parker led a division that advanced on the factory in double-quick time. The factory was captured without opposition, and the British set it on fire.[66]

Having shown what could be achieved against the Americans, Cockburn persuaded the general that the first target should be Barney's flotilla. Capt. Harry Smith recalled that Ross's staff assembled on board Cochrane's flag-ship, H.M.S. *Tonnant*, and all the admirals came on board. He said, "After much discussion and poring over bad maps, it was resolved the force should sail up the serpentine and wooded Patuxen[t] in the frigates and small vessels."[67]

While Ross and Cockburn pursued Barney's flotilla, Cochrane ordered two diversions to distract attention from this main thrust. Capt. James Alexander Gordon in H.M.S. *Seahorse*, 38 guns, would command a small task force to sail up the Potomac to destroy the U.S. strong points on the river, confuse the Americans on the British plans, and offer an escape route for Ross's army, if necessary. Parker, in *Menelaus*, was ordered to sail up into the upper bay to likewise confuse the Yankees. Parker could also prevent Eastern Shore forces being sent to the defense of Baltimore and Washington—and perhaps draw off forces from Baltimore to the opposite shore.[68]

Ross's aide Capt. Harry Smith felt awed at the passage of the British ships up the tortuous Patuxent, which he described as being lined with "immense forest trees." He wrote later, "The appearance was that of a large fleet stalking through a wood."[69]

After entering the Patuxent, Cochrane sent a signal to get the troops ready to land. Provisions for three days were cooked, and each man was issued three pounds of pork and two and a half pounds of ship's biscuit. The cartouche

British map of the Patuxent River

Top of map is south and bottom is north; river mouth at left is east.

Courtesy Library of Congress and Donald G. Shomette

boxes were filled with fresh ammunition, the muskets and accoutrements handed out. When the larger ships and frigates began to run aground, the troops transferred to smaller boats. Late on August 18, the first British boats reached Benedict but it was too late to land. A gun brig was anchored to cover the landing next morning. The brig's broadside faced the shore, her cannons loaded and pointed at the small river town in case the Americans attacked. The British could hardly believe the Americans had not tried to resist the invasion. Particularly because, as captain of the fleet, Rear Adm. Sir Edward Codrington observed in a letter to his sister, the cliffs along the Patuxent seemed so conducive for artillery emplacements.[70]

Indeed, a more resourceful general than Winder might have anticipated that the British would land in the Patuxent as Commodore Barney had predicted to Secretary Jones. Such a commander could have had artillery and troops ready to act in concert with Barney's flotilla to resist a landing. But, President Madison had not appointed a capable commander.

Gleig noted in his diary that at dawn on August 19, "We got up, took each his haversack containing . . . [our] provisions, a spare shirt, pair of stockings, towel, &c., . . . [and with] a blanket over the other shoulder prepared for embarkation."[71] The blanket would be needed, for the troops had no tents. They would camp in the open air. Moreover, only Ross and his staff would have horses. Junior officers such as Gleig and his friends would march with their men, a fact that grieved them. In France, they had ridden horses.

After landing, the afternoon was spent dividing the troops into three brigades. The first, or light, brigade, commanded by Thornton, comprised the 85th Regiment and the light companies of the 4th, 21st, and 44th Regiments. Also added to the first brigade were the "Colonial Marines"—the former Chesapeake slaves—along with a company of Royal Marines. Col. Arthur Brooke of the 44th would lead the second brigade, made up of the 4th and 44th Regiments. Lastly, the third brigade, to be commanded by Col. William Patterson, included his own 21st Regiment and approximately one hundred sailors to pull the fieldpieces. The British artillery was skimpy at best—one 6-pounder, two 3-pounders, and a rocket battery to be served by the Royal Marines. Gleig estimated the total British force at 4,500 including the marines, sailors, sappers, and engineers. However, an official accounting of the troops at Benedict signed by Capt. Harry Smith gave a total of 4,185, and subtracting men listed as sick, the effective enlisted men with bayonets totaled 3,591.[72]

On August 20, Gleig and Lt. Garlike Philip Codd foraged the local countryside two miles beyond the British pickets. They found several houses that were deserted. Eventually, they found a woman at home and paid her "a quarter dollar" for a chicken—though other British had plundered her house already. Returning to camp to find that fellow officers had procured a pig, a goose, and a couple of chickens, they were all ready to enjoy a fine repast. It was four o'clock in the afternoon. Suddenly, "the bugle sounded the assembly and we were obliged to leave our meal and fall in. The Brigade formed and moved to the road, when General Ross passed us, and we cheered him as he passed."[73]

Ross's army was on the march—destination (though they did not yet know it), Washington, D.C. The British would do what the weak and ineffectual force under Admiral Warren in 1813 had not attempted. Attack the capital of the United States. In the words of Admiral Codrington, "The great Federal city, the capital and pride of the Virginians and all other supporters of the Jefferson and Maddison [*sic*] party, and the haters of everything English."[74]

Chapter Eight
Invasion and Defeat

On their march from Benedict, the British were aided by two renegade Americans. Capt. Harry Smith, whom Ross appointed to handle intelligence gathering, recalled how they were recruited:

> The day we landed, a most awful spectacle of a man named Calder came in to give us information. . . . The poor wretch was covered with leprosy, and I really believe was induced to turn traitor to his country in the hope of receiving medical [aid] from our surgeons. . . . He was a very shrewd, intelligent fellow, and of the utmost use to us. He was afterwards joined by a young man of the name of Brown, as healthy a looking fellow as [Calder] was the reverse, who was very useful to us as a guide and as a scout.[1]

The invaders followed the course of the Patuxent toward Nottingham. In the heat and humidity of that Maryland summer, the march proved nightmarish for the troops in their woollen uniforms, loaded down as they were with muskets, 60 rounds of ammunition, and other equipment. Moreover, they were out of shape from being nearly three months at sea.[2]

For mile after mile, the invading army marched unchallenged. Col. Arthur Brooke, leader of Ross's second brigade, wrote that the closely wooded country through which they slogged was "very favorable" to the Americans for "annoyance" of an advancing army.[3] Charles Ball, the former slave who had joined Barney's flotilla as a cook, also commented on this opportunity squandered by Winder:

> It is my opinion, that if General Winder had marched the half of the troops that he had at Bladensburg, down to the lower part of Prince George['s] county, and attacked the British in these woods and cedar thickets, not a man of them would ever have reached Bladensburg. I feel confident that . . . one

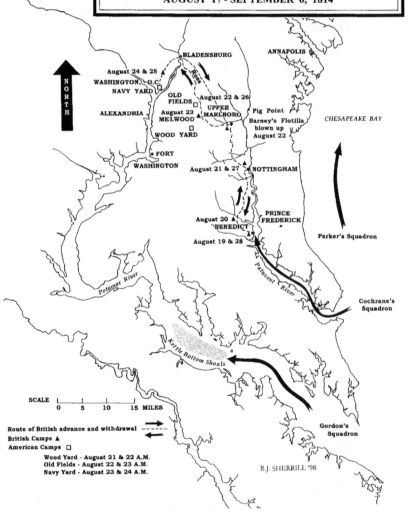

BRITISH ATTACKS AND DIVERSIONS AROUND WASHINGTON, D.C.
AUGUST 17 - SEPTEMBER 6, 1814

NORTH

BLADENSBURG

ANNAPOLIS

August 24 & 25
WASHINGTON, D.C.
NAVY YARD

OLD FIELDS

August 22 & 26
UPPER MARLBORO

Pig Point

ALEXANDRIA

August 23
MELWOOD

Barney's Flotilla blown up
August 22

CHESAPEAKE BAY

WOOD YARD

FORT WASHINGTON

August 21 & 27   NOTTINGHAM

August 20
BENEDICT

PRINCE FREDERICK

August 19 & 28

Parker's Squadron

Potomac River

Patuxent River

Cochrane's Squadron

Kettle Bottom Shoals

SCALE
0   5   10   15 MILES

Route of British advance and withdrawal
British Camps ▲
American Camps ☐

Wood Yard - August 21 & 22 A.M.
Old Fields - August 22 & 23 A.M.
Navy Yard - August 23 & 24 A.M.

Gordon's Squadron

R.J. SHERRILL '98

hundred Americans would have destroyed a thousand of the enemy, by felling trees across the road, and attacking them in ambush.[4]

What *was* Winder doing as the invaders moved closer to the capital? As he had for the last six weeks, the general dithered. On the afternoon of August 19, a dispatch from Barney had reached Washington to say the British were in the Patuxent. Secretary of State Monroe scouted the invaders, and he reported that the enemy had landed in force. Yet, although Barney gave his opinion that the British would head for the capital, Winder disagreed. He believed they would march to Annapolis. Of course, he had earlier thought of Annapolis as the *staging point* for an attack on the capital—but the British had eschewed landing there and landed in the Patuxent instead. Even now, against all logic (except for the logic that he had convinced himself of the value of Annapolis to the British as a base), Winder insisted that the Maryland capital was Ross's destination. But just as he had persuaded himself of this reasoning, he decided that perhaps they were headed for Fort Washington. Surely, he said, they intended to attack the fort, then march up the river in concert with the squadron that was at that moment tackling the treacherous shoals of the Potomac. Wherever the British were headed, Winder needed immediately to get troops down to the Patuxent to make a show of force in front of Ross's army. This is just what he did not do, or at least not in any meaningful manner, although admittedly part of the delay was caused by deficiencies in supplies for the militia.[5]

In his memoirs, Maj. Gen. James Wilkinson claimed that weeks earlier he had warned Winder about a possible British landing on the Patuxent. He said he had told the younger man that he felt that "the obstinacy and self-conceit" of Secretary Armstrong might lead to the sacrifice of the capital. He recommended that Winder consider setting up a camp of three thousand to four thousand troops at Upper Marlboro near the upper reaches of the Patuxent. To Gen. John Mason and Charles Carroll of Bellevue, he made specific proposals for fortifications in Washington in case of an attack. These included the erection of a redoubt at the junction of the Potomac and Tiber Creek and another on the heights overlooking Pennsylvania Avenue. He also suggested fortifying the Capitol and the president's mansion.[6]

On hearing of the British landings in the Patuxent, the general sent a note to Secretary Monroe. He proposed that if "my arrest [could] be suspended, and my sword restored for a short period, I would take the command of the militia, and save the city or forfeit my life."[7] He proposed a plan that would, he believed, compel the British to return to their shipping. Working parties would fell trees to obstruct the enemy's march. Artillery, infantry, and riflemen would attack the invaders from the rear. Meanwhile, "flying parties of four or five hundred infantry" would engage the enemy's front and left flank "at every exposed point or difficult defile."[8] The strategy sounds astonishingly like that proposed by flotillaman Charles Ball.

It should not surprise us that the secretary of state ignored the general's advice. First, he would not have wanted to overrule Madison's selection of Winder as commander. And second, no doubt he was wary of the slippery Wilkinson. On August 20, the general left the city to recuperate in the mountains. He said he felt "sick and disgusted" and convinced that Madison would risk "the burning up of the whole district" rather than offend Armstrong.[9]

We might question the sincerity and abilities of a general who was under fire for his own failures on the Canadian border. However, the controversial general was correct that Winder needed to take a proactive stand rather than let the invaders dictate events.

Yet, unknown to anyone in Washington, Ross had not yet made up his mind to attack the city. It seems the two commanders, Ross *and* Winder were both equally confused. Captain Smith later aired the opinion that Ross "was very cautious in responsibility . . . and lacked that dashing enterprise so essential to carry a place by a *coup de main*."[10] The general explained to his wife in a letter some days later that instructions from London enjoined him not to attempt anything at any distance from the fleet. On Monday, August 21, he continued to march parallel to the Patuxent in case the army might be able to aid Cockburn in attacking Barney's flotilla. The commodore it seemed had retreated further up the river away from the admiral's pursuing squadron of small boats.[11]

That afternoon, Gleig's whippet Mustasek caught a small hare, which he and his companions boiled for dinner. However, he said, "As usual [we] had just sat down to it, when we were obliged to fall in and march." During the day, an American detachment had fired a few shots at the British advanced guard. The invaders spent the night at the small deserted river town of Nottingham. Gleig recorded in his diary that he and his friends slept in "an old barn full of Tobacco." On Tuesday, August 22, the troops did not form up and move off until around 8:00 A.M. In Gleig's view, the delay was caused because Ross seemed uncertain whether to follow the gunboats or return to the shipping. Once the march recommenced, Gleig reported that the advance party clashed with a body of U.S. cavalry but no one was killed.[12]

Winder had gathered a force at the tobacco plantation of Benjamin Oden at the Wood Yard, about 12 miles west of Nottingham. Oden, a loyal supporter of President Madison, owned 125 slaves. He had much to lose if the British lured his slaves away. The largest contingent in Winder's army at the Wood Yard was the District of Columbia militia under Brig. Gen. Walter Smith. By Smith's later account, his militiamen numbered 1,070, including two companies of artillery with twelve 6-pounders under Maj. George Peter, and two companies of riflemen under Capt. John J. Stull. These were "riflemen" in name only because they were armed with muskets. Secretary Armstrong had been unable to provide them with rifles—one of many equipment failures. Added to the District militia were the 36th Infantry under Col. William Scott (approximately 350), the U.S. Light Dragoons under French-born Lt. Col. Jacint Lavall (estimated 125), and the Maryland cavalry under Lt. Col. Frisby Tilghman (approximately three hundred men). Winder ordered Major Peter to monitor the enemy's movements. Peters' detachment included artillery and Stull's riflemen, the cavalrymen, and the 36th Regiment. This resulted in the skirmish Gleig reported.[13]

When the Americans withdrew before the advancing British, Winder positioned part of his forces about a quarter of a mile east of Oden's house. A fork in the road, with roads leading either to the Wood Yard or north to Upper Marlboro, was screened from the Wood Yard by trees, although a portion of the British column had already been observed to enter the road to Oden's. Winder reported later that he "entertained a hope" to give the enemy "a serious check, without much risk to this detachment." But he soon learned that the British had taken the Upper Marlboro road instead, and the opportunity was lost. He, therefore, ordered his units to regroup at Long (or Battalion) Old Fields between Upper Marlboro and the District, to better resist an advance on the capital.[14]

Maj. George Peter (1779–1861)

District of Columbia militia artillery shadowed the British on their march to Bladensburg.

Collection of the Author

While this was happening, Cockburn closed in on Barney's flotilla. The admiral later reported that shortly before 11:00 A.M. his boats arrived at the upper reaches of the Patuxent, where he had been told the flotilla lay anchored. He landed the Royal Marines under Capt. John Robyns on the left bank to attack any troops defending the flotilla. Then, he proceeded with his small boats, thirsting for the kill:

> as we opened the reach above Pig Point I plainly discovered Commodore Barney's broad pendant in the headmost vessel, a large sloop, and the remainder of the flotilla extending in a long line astern of her. Our boats now advanced towards them as rapidly as possible but on nearing them we observed the sloop bearing the broad pendant to be on fire, and she very soon afterwards blew up. I now saw clearly that they were all abandoned and on fire with trains to their magazines, and out of the seventeen vessels which composed this formidable and so much vaunted flotilla, sixteen were in quick succession blown to atoms, and the seventeenth, in which the fire had not taken, we captured.[15]

Thus, Cockburn did not achieve his objective of defeating Barney in battle. The destruction of the flotilla had been realized, but at the hands of the Americans.

Destruction of Barney's flotilla *(lower right)*, and attack on Washington, D.C.—a much condensed view

Courtesy National Maritime Museum, Greenwich, London, and Donald G. Shomette

Secretary Jones had instructed Barney in a letter of August 20 to destroy the flotilla "in the event of the enemy advancing upon [it] in force." Barney left Lieutenant Frazier with a small body of seamen to do the work. Meanwhile, the commodore and the majority of his sailors proceeded to join the American army in accordance with Jones's instructions.[16]

During the day's march, Gleig reported hearing "several heavy explosions" which he learned later had been caused by the blowing up of the flotilla. Later, in the afternoon, the troops camped in a large field outside the pretty village of Upper Marlboro.[17] Ross chose as his headquarters the residence of a prominent local medical practitioner, Dr. William Beanes. A week later, after the sack of Washington, the general would order the arrest of the 65-year-old doctor after he detained some British stragglers. Beanes's arrest led to the writing of "The Star-Spangled Banner" by Georgetown lawyer Francis Scott Key. The young lawyer came out to the British fleet to obtain Beanes's release, and he and the doctor were forced to watch the bombardment of Fort McHenry.[18]

During the stay of nearly 24 hours in Upper Marlboro, Ross wrestled with himself on whether to return to Benedict. Staff officers urged him to continue to Washington. They were now only 16 miles away from the Yankee capital and still had not been seriously challenged. One of the most vehement advocates of continuing was his quartermaster, Lt. George de Lacy Evans. Evans sent word for Cockburn to come and persuade the reluctant general. The admiral arrived at Ross's headquarters early on the morning of August 23. Once more, Cockburn brought to bear all his arguments about the incompetence of the Yankee militia. He hammered home the point that the militia could not stand against the disciplined, experienced troops that Ross commanded. Finally, the general agreed to attempt an attack on the capital.[19]

That morning, Madison reviewed the American troops at Long Old Fields. Pleased with what he saw, he scribbled a note to his wife Dolley telling her that the men seemed "in high spirits & [made] a good appearance." Earlier, in a military briefing, Secretary Armstrong had assured the president that the enemy would make no "serious" attack on the capital. At most, Armstrong said, they might make a "Cossack hurrah"—a quick hit-and-run attack. Moreover, Winder informed Madison that the British had no cavalry and no artillery. The president reported these "facts" to Dolley as evidence that the British were "not very strong" and lacked the ability to carry out any extended operations. That Ross had no cavalry was perfectly true. However, although the British lacked any heavy artillery they did have some cannons. Here was an evident failure in American intelligence. Reassured by these "expert" opinions, the president comforted Dolley by saying "They are not in a condition to strike at Washington." He told her he hoped to be with her that evening.[20]

At noon, Winder received a report that the British still had not moved out of Upper Marlboro. This fitted in with one of his pet theories—that they would wait to link up with their Potomac squadron. He began to think that if the enemy remained stationary for several days, he might be able to attack them from the heights around the town. The general took stock of the forces available to him. Now that he had been joined by Barney's flotillamen and the U.S. Marines under Capt. Samuel Miller, he had approximately three thousand men at Long Old Fields. Brig. Gen. Tobias E. Stansbury had just brought 1,400 troops from Baltimore to Bladensburg on the eastern branch of the Potomac. An additional eight hundred Baltimore militiamen under Lt. Col. Joseph Sterett were shortly expected to arrive at Bladensburg. Col. William D. Beall would be bringing another eight hundred men from Annapolis. Altogether, Winder could count on a combined force of six thousand—more than enough to battle the weak British army. He would hit them hard, from all sides. Dreams of a great victory began to dance in his head. But, just as he was beginning to savor those delicious thoughts, the British columns began to move out of Upper Marlboro.[21]

Some time after 2:00 P.M., the Redcoats encountered a detachment of Americans ahead of them. Maj. George Peter was performing the same service of reconnoitering the enemy he had during the British advance from Nottingham. This time, the Americans loosed off some artillery rounds and Major Stull's "riflemen," armed with muskets, fired some volleys at the advancing Redcoats. The British returned the fire and the American detachment retreated to Long Old Fields. One rifleman was wounded in the skirmish.[22]

The British went into camp on a nearby estate known as Melwood. Winder went to confer with Stansbury in Bladensburg. In his absence, General Smith formed a battle line. He positioned Barney's artillery in advance of the main line, near a wood between the two armies. Smith felt nervous making these decisions without Winder. He sent his aide Thomas L. McKenney to find the commander. McKenney located the general eight miles away. The two officers spurred their horses and raced back to Long Old Fields. The general rode around the field looking at the battle lines. He remarked, "It is all well arranged, but the manifest object of the enemy is to attack us in the night. We have not the material for a night fight." He ordered a withdrawal to the Navy Yard in Washington. Where did Winder get the idea the British meant to attack him at night? Possibly the notion arose from his own fears, as he recalled how he was captured in the night action at Stoney Creek the previous year. If he, a regular army officer, could become confused in a night battle how much worse would it be for "untrained" militiamen?[23]

It is doubtful if the British had such a night attack in mind. Night battles were rare during this period because lack of visibility caused confusion as much among the attackers as the defenders.[24]

The District of Columbia militiamen and the other units gathered everything up and trudged back to Washington. They went into camp at the Navy Yard. It was a long night for the commanding general. Winder did not know which way the British might come. The enemy could cross the eastern branch of the Potomac (now the Anacostia River) by several bridges. There was a lower bridge, an upper bridge called Stoddert's Bridge, and one upstream at the old tobacco port of Bladensburg. If the enemy came by way of Long Old Fields,

Winder knew they would attempt to cross by means of one of the lower bridges. He decided it would be prudent to post an infantry unit at the lower crossing and to burn Stoddert's Bridge. He made arrangements with Capt. Thomas Tingey, the British-born commander of the Navy Yard, to destroy the bridge. Between 3:00 and 4:00 A.M., visible to the British pickets at Melwood, 10 miles away, a red glow colored the western sky as flames from the burning bridge leaped into the sky. Yet remarkably, at Ross's headquarters in a shed on the estate where the general and Admiral Cockburn had been sleeping on their cloaks, an early morning tussle was again taking place over whether to proceed to Washington. A despatch from Cochrane had arrived at 2:00 A.M. indicating that Ross should return to the shipping. Once more Cockburn had to browbeat the nervous general. He argued, "It is too late—we ought not to have advanced—there is now no choice to us. We must go on." The general, in the worst crisis of his career, struck his hand against his forehead. "Well, be it so," he exclaimed, "we shall proceed!"[25]

Still, Ross worried about what might happen if they failed. He later wrote to his wife that "at the moment the Attempt was made upon the City of Washington, I felt an apprehension of the Consequences of Failure. . . ."[26]

That morning, the area newspapers radiated confidence. The Georgetown *Federal Republican* assured its readers, "It is highly improbable that . . . the enemy would advance nearer to the capital." The *National Intelligencer*, as pro-administration as ever, calmly wrote, "We feel assured that the number and bravery of our men will afford complete protection for the city." However, the work of removing government documents had begun. Furthermore, many citizens had already evidenced panic. For days, they had been loading wagons and driving them out of town.[27]

At 9:30 A.M., Winder ordered Commodore Barney to take his flotillamen and man a battery of heavy guns at the end of the lower bridge. Captain Tingey positioned a barge crammed with eight barrels of powder under one of the arches, ready to blow up the bridge as soon as the enemy appeared. His former countrymen would get a surprise with this reception.[28]

Approximately 10:00 A.M., definitive word came in: the British were coming by way of Bladensburg—where even if the bridge was destroyed, the eastern branch was fordable. Winder immediately mobilized his forces to march out to join up with the Baltimore troops already at Bladensburg. By 11:00 A.M., the first troops were starting down the road. Yet, remarkably, Winder gave no thought to including Commodore Barney and his four hundred flotillamen and Captain Miller and his 120 U.S. Marines. They were left to guard the lower bridge. Not only was Winder being *forced* into a battle and unable to fight on his own terms, but he was leaving his most seasoned troops behind![29]

Here was another of Winder's fatal mistakes: Barney's flotillamen and Miller's marines should have manned a battery at the center of the line guarding the bridge at Bladensburg. If such a disposition had been made, the result of the battle might have been very different. If that had happened, perhaps the troops who did the "racing" at the Bladensburg Races might have had *red* coats.

The American troops came together at Bladensburg in a haphazard, disorganized manner. Winder failed to take control of even those troops he nominally commanded. He admitted as much three days later in an apologetic letter to Secretary of War Armstrong: "You will readily understand that it is impossible for me to speak minutely of the merit or demerit of particular troops so little known to me from their recent and hasty assemblage."[30]

Yet, as later reported by U.S. Army Surg. Hanson Catlett, the British troops heading toward Bladensburg were in poor condition. Indeed, as they approached the battlefield, the Redcoats labored along sunbaked, dusty roads in temperatures in the high nineties. Although the first five miles after leaving Melwood were through a forest, for the last five miles the men marched in the open, exposed to the unremitting sun. The tortuous conditions took their toll. Although General Ross called a halt at a stream to allow the men to refresh themselves, Gleig said that when the march resumed, within minutes stragglers littered the sides of the road. Colonel Brooke wrote that "many of [the men,] striving to keep up, fell down from actual fatigue, and breathed their last." Even Ross's trusted aide, Capt. Thomas Falls, who was mounted, fell prey to sunstroke.[31]

Although battle was about to be joined, neither side was really prepared to fight a battle.

Colonel Sterett's troops, who made up the American front line, had marched in from Baltimore the day before, exhausted from the heat. The men were also tired from being up late into the night due to false alarms. Col. Decius Wadsworth had prepared an earthwork for the Baltimore artillery. Unfortunately, though the work might be suitable for heavy cannons it little suited their lighter artillery. The parapet was too lofty for their 6-pound cannons. Knowing time was short, the men desperately used sticks to dig at the dirt to make embrasures so the cannons could be aimed at the bridge. Maj. William Pinkney, in charge of the rifle companies, knew there was no time to reduce the parapet along its whole length. Still, an effort was made to mask the cannons with brushwood. As ready as they would ever be, the riflemen sweated in their olive drab uniforms with the fuschia trim. Fifty yards behind them, in an orchard, General Stansbury's 5th Regiment in their blue uniforms with red trim also nervously awaited the arrival of the invaders.[32]

A false alarm occurred when Colonel Beall's troops marched in from Annapolis and tramped to a position in the rear. It was noon. A dust cloud rose over Lowndes' Hill to the south of the town: this time, the British *were* coming. The columns of Redcoats appeared, slogging wearily down the dirt road—the bright sunlight glinting on their muskets and bayonets. Although General Winder had arrived on the field, the time to improve the positions had evaporated.[33]

As the Americans waited for the British to attack, Major Pinkney tried to raise his men's spirits. His militiamen all knew that several years earlier, Pinkney and Monroe had served as American diplomats in London to try to head off war

Maj. William Pinkney
(1764–1822)

The former diplomat commanded the
Maryland militia riflemen at Bladensburg.
Collection of the Author

with Britain. The full-faced Baltimore attorney joked with them that he had once tried to show the British what he felt about them at the negotiating table. Now he would do it in practice.[34]

Pinkney knew his riflemen felt comforted that their fellow Baltimoreans in the 5th Regiment were stationed in the orchard only 50 yards behind. Yet, now he was alarmed to see the 5th Regiment march away from them, to the other side of the orchard, and reform some five hundred yards away. Unknown to Pinkney, Secretary Monroe, thinking he could improve the troop positions, had ordered the change.[35]

Then a calamity almost occurred. A cheer rose as President Madison's party galloped along the road. The tiny president, absurdly wearing a pair of duelling pistols buckled at his waist, was headed straight for the bridge— and the British. An American scout ran out to warn Madison. He shouted, "Mr. Madison! The enemy are now in Bladensburg!" Even as he spoke, the British were infiltrating the town. James Madison looked befuddled for a moment, and he spoke the words as if in disbelief, "The enemy are in Bladensburg!" The president and his entourage reined in and turned around, looking for Winder.[36]

The presidential party soon found the commanding general. Secretary of War Armstrong had also ridden out to the battlefield. The secretary had earlier predicted how the battle would go. He had flatly informed Madison that if the battle was between militia and regulars, the militia would be beaten. The remark appalled the chief executive. Yet even now the little president gazed at Armstrong with almost pathetic faith. It was as if Madison thought that the arrogant New Yorker might suggest some gem of wisdom to enable the Americans to snatch victory from the jaws of defeat. The president later recalled his conversation with Armstrong at Bladensburg:

> I asked [Secretary Armstrong] whether he had spoken with Genl. Winder on the subject of his arrangements and views. He said he had not. I remarked that tho' there was so little time for it, it was possible he might offer some advice or suggestion that might not be too late, to be turned to account; on which he rode up to the General as I did myself. The unruliness of my horse prevented me from joining in the short conversation that took place. When it was over I asked Genl. Armstrong whether he had

seen occasion to suggest any improvement in any part of the arrangements. He said he had not; that from his view of them they appeared to be as good as circumstances admitted.[37]

So, the author of *Hints to Young Generals* had no words of wisdom whatsoever for Brig. Gen. William H. Winder. Yet even Winder was pessimistic. As he helped place three 6-pounders under Capt. Benjamin Burch to the left of Stansbury's line, in order to rake the orchard, Winder stated, "When you retreat, take notice you must retreat by the Georgetown Road."[38]

This instruction, quite apart from its effect on morale, was yet another mistake. When the troops in the front line retreated along the Georgetown Road instead of the Washington Road, they exited at an angle *away* from the battlefield. There was no possibility that they could be reformed with the District militia on the Washington Road.

Burch had brought a total of five 6-pounders onto the field. The other two cannons were borrowed by Colonel Wadsworth and placed on the Washington Road to the rear of the Baltimore battery. The position was an exposed one, but it gave the colonel a clear line of vision to fire at the British.[39]

From the upper story of a house on Lowndes' Hill, General Ross studied the American positions through his telescope. The general observed that the Yankees were strongly posted on the opposite side of the river, their right flank resting on the road to Washington. He noted breastworks with a battery in the center of their front line. He saw that over the river stretched a long wooden bridge so narrow that only three men abreast could pass at once.[40]

Colonel Thornton, leader of his first brigade, requested permission to lead an attack over the bridge. Despite the general's earlier uncertainty about whether to attack Washington, Ross now made a quick decision that astonished Capt. Harry Smith. The general ordered that the Americans be instantly attacked. Smith protested, "General Ross, neither of the other brigades can be up in time to support this made attack, and if the enemy fight, Thornton's brigade must be repulsed." But the general's mind was made up. Thornton's brigade, the 85th Regiment, with light companies of the 4th, 21st, and 44th, would lead the attack. Then would follow the second brigade, the 4th and 44th, led by Brooke. The 4th Regiment would form line after crossing the bridge to the left to attack the American right, including the gun battery. The 44th would form line to the right, and attack the American positions on the left along the Georgetown Road. The third brigade, the 21st Regiment, would be held in reserve. In any case, they were still straggling into Bladensburg.[41]

The bugles sounded and the drummers rat-a-tatted on their drums. Thornton's brigade formed up. Led by their aggressive colonel, the 85th began to assault the bridge. The Baltimore artillery and Wadsworth's battery hammered away at the advancing British, with Wadsworth reserving his fire until the Redcoats filled the bridge. Gleig recalled the scene:

> we immediately pushed on at double quick time, towards the head of the bridge. While we were moving along the street, a continued fire was kept

up, with some execution, from those guns which stood to the left of the road; but it was not till the bridge was covered with our people that the two-gun battery upon the road itself began to play. Then, indeed, it also opened, and with tremendous effect; for at the first discharge almost an entire company was swept down.[42]

As the battle began and the initial British attack was being beaten back, the District militia formed a second line far behind the American front line. Beall's eight hundred militiamen from Annapolis had already taken a position nearby, with Lieutenant Colonel Kramer's Maryland militia in front of them. Beall had been sent by Secretary Monroe to occupy the rising ground on the present site of the Fort Lincoln Cemetery, south of the Wash-

Col. William Thornton, 85th Regiment

Thornton led the British attack at Bladensburg.

Collection of the Author

ington Road. General Smith placed his District of Columbia militiamen on a rise on the opposite side of the Washington Road, behind a small stream spanned by a small wooden bridge known as Tournecliffe's Bridge. Supporting the District militia were the raw troops of the 36th U.S. Infantry under Colonel Scott and Major Peter's six-cannon battery. These units were so far behind the men on the front line that Stansbury and Pinkney testified later that they did not even know they were on the battlefield.[43]

Still laboring to join the battle were Commodore Barney and his flotillamen plus the U.S. Marines under Miller. Barney had angrily refused to do the job that "any damned corporal" could do: mind the lower bridge. He said as much to President Madison as the diminutive executive galloped by with his entourage. The president gave him permission to join the battle—the one positive military decision the nation's constitutional commander in chief made that day. Now the commodore's sweating sailors slaved to haul the five heavy guns on naval gun carriages along the country road.[44]

Barney positioned his cannons across the Washington Road in the middle of the second line, while Miller's marines stationed themselves on his right flank. The two 18-pounders were planted directly on the road, with three 12-pounders to the right. Some of the sailors, including black man Charles Ball, would serve as artillerymen. The others joined the marines in acting as infantry. Barney's battery added fearsome firepower to the American forces. Tragically, however, they were too far back to be any help with the fight at the bridge. Serving as another indictment of Winder's incompetence that day, the American troop dispositions were absurdly out of kilter.[45]

At the bridge, the U.S. cannon and rifle fire nevertheless took a devastating toll on the British. The bombardment forced Thornton's men to take cover among the houses. The narrow wooden bridge—which the Americans had discussed chopping down but had failed to destroy—was strewn with British dead and dying. The Americans let up a loud cheer.[46]

A soldier of the 85th, a Scotsman, who had seated himself on the steps of a house and whose arm, shattered by a roundshot, dangled now by a fiber, shouted back, "Dinna halloo, my fine lads, you're no' yet out of the wood! Wait a wee, wait a wee, wie your skirling!"[47]

The Royal Marine rocket brigade had set up their rocket launcher near a warehouse. The marines loaded their three-foot long missiles on the long sticks in the angled tubes that constituted the launcher. They lit the fuses and ran for cover. The rockets arched over the river in a snaking swirl of smoke. The American militia, most of whom had never seen the rockets before, watched in awe. Some panicked.[48]

Winder, for all his disorganization, was not lacking in encouragement for his men. He called out to them that they should not be afraid—the rockets were harmless. However, he advised the president to move back. For Madison, this must have been a humbling experience. Madison told his entourage, "Let us go and leave it to the commanding general." The presidential party moved some distance back and let events unfold.[49]

The British made ready to charge the bridge once more. Knowing the 4th and 44th were now formed up to follow him, Thornton rode forward on his gray horse. His men had to run over the bodies of their own dead and wounded. This time they made it the other side. Gleig and his men began to scour the American riflemen from the willows by the river. Some of the British ran up and captured Wadsworth's two cannons. The artillerymen of the Baltimore battery, unable to fire over the earthwork now that the enemy was closer, began to limber up and withdraw their cannons.[50]

Pinkney saw that the retreat of his riflemen and the guncrew was simultaneous. There was nothing else they could do—or else risk being cut to pieces or taken prisoner. He gave orders for the riflemen to regroup in the bushes to the left of the 5th Regiment. Someone gave him a horse, which increased his ability to observe the debacle that was unfolding around him.[51]

The 5th Regiment in their blue uniforms with red trim were maintaining continuous platoon fire. They could not see the British advancing through the orchard, though the Redcoats fired with impunity on the Americans. Winder issued the order for a general retreat. A musket ball smacked into Pinkney's right arm, just above the elbow, passed through, breaking the bone. He rode painfully away with his men. Winder wrote a scribbled note to the president and his party, now some distance to the rear, to leave the battlefield.[52]

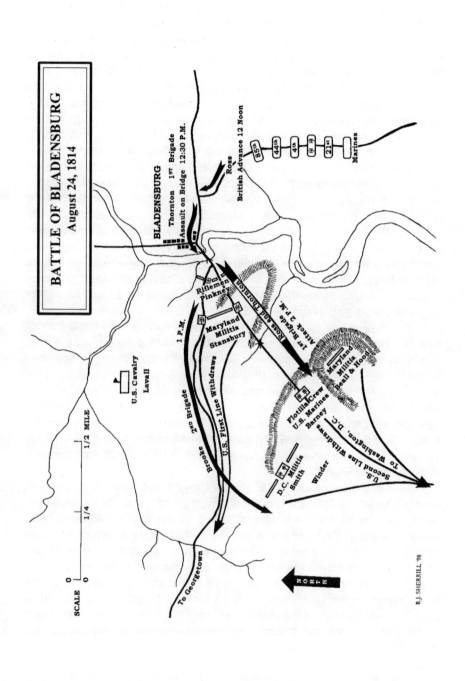

BATTLE OF BLADENSBURG
August 24, 1814

SCALE

0   1/4   1/2 MILE

BLADENSBURG

Thornton 1ST Brigade
Assault on Bridge 12:30 P.M.

Ross
British Advance 12 Noon

85th 44th 4th [ ] [ ] 21st Marines

Riflemen
Pinkney

Maryland
Militia
Stansbury

Ross and Thornton
1ST Brigade
Attack 2 P.M.

Maryland
Militia
Beall & Hood

Flotilla Crew
U.S. Marines
Barney

To Washington, D.C.

U.S.
Second Line Withdraws

D.C. Militia
Smith

Winder

U.S. Cavalry
Lavall

1 P.M.

U.S. First Line Withdraws

Brooke 2ND Brigade

To Georgetown

NORTH

R.J. SHERRILL '98

The general tried to channel the retreating militia along the Washington Road, to reform at a second line with the District militia. But as he had instructed, the militiamen mostly fled down the Georgetown Road, chased by Brooke's 44th Regiment. Meanwhile, Thornton spearheaded the advance along the Washington Road. They were approaching Tournecliffe's Bridge and coming under fire from the advance units of the second line, the Maryland militiamen under Beall and Kramer. As Thornton coaxed his tired men onward, the aggressive colonel suddenly pitched from his horse. A musket ball had slammed into his leg, splintering the bone high up in his thigh. Lt. Col. William Wood took over the command of the brigade but he too fell severely wounded.[53]

The British had encountered unexpected resistance from troops drawn up in line and from two batteries. General Ross rode up with his staff. He immediately took command of Thornton's brigade. There came a further blast of grapeshot from the Yankee cannons ahead: more scarlet-coated men fell like ninepins. The flotillamen under Commodore Barney, with their five heavy naval guns, may have arrived late for the battle, but they were losing no time. "Board 'em! Board 'em!" Barney's men shouted at the success they were having against the British regulars. They weren't under Winder's damnable orders to retreat! They even charged the enemy, waving their cutlasses in the air, and forcing the would-be victors back down the road.[54]

The second line, given strength by Barney's battery, held the British off for nearly half an hour. Then Ross led the 85th around to the left, off the road, to outflank the battery. He routed Beall's Annapolis militiamen. Barney wrote later, "To my great mortification, [the militia] made no resistance, giving a fire or two and retiring." Charles Ball, the commodore's black cook working as an artilleryman, lamented, "The militia ran like sheep chased by dogs." The Irish-born general ordered his sharpshooters to fire down on the battery from the heights that Beall's men had occupied. Meanwhile, the 4th and 44th Regiments under Brooke advanced on General Smith's District militia to attempt to turn their flank.[55]

Barney's ammunition wagon drivers drove off in panic. A lead ball hit Barney's horse, which fell dead between two of his cannons. The British continued to pour fire into Barney's battery. Sailing Master John A. Webster's horse was shot through the head and a ball drove through the crown of his hat. A musket ball shattered Captain Miller's arm. Other sailors were struck down, with two of them killed. Then the commodore received a musket-ball in his thigh. With no ammunition with which to fight, and completely outflanked, the battle was over. The commodore ordered his men to spike the guns and retreat. Three of his officers tried to help him from the field. But, faint from loss of blood, Barney sank to the ground. The Redcoats overran the battery. Some of the flotillamen, Gleig noted, "were actually bayonetted, with fuses in their hands."[56]

After the fall of Barney's battery, the District militia continued to resist the British, who were pressing strongly to turn their flanks. General Smith later

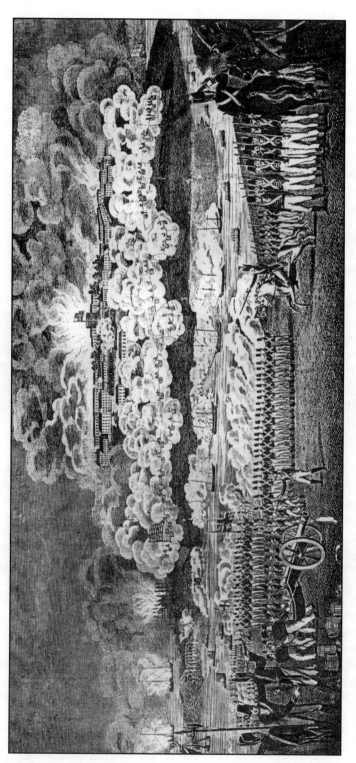

British engraving of the Battle of Bladensburg, with totally imaginary defenses fortifying the capital, Washington, D.C.

Courtesy Star-Spangled Banner Flag House

wrote that when orders came from Winder to retreat, he gave orders for his men to fall back to the city. Smith stated that he expected the commanding general would make a further stand to defend Washington.[57]

Unable to escape, Commodore Barney was captured. Ross and Cockburn were brought to him. The commodore was introduced to the admiral using the usual English pronunciation, *"Co-burn."*

Barney said, "Oh, *'COCK-burn'* is what you're called hereabouts. Well, Admiral, you've got me at last."

The admiral replied, "I regret to see you in this state, Commodore."

The general told Cockburn, "I told you it was the Flotilla men!"

The rear admiral answered, "Yes! You were right, though I could not believe you. They have given us the only fighting we have had."

Cockburn conferred briefly with the general. Then Ross told Barney he was paroled and that he would be conveyed to any place he wished. Barney chose the tavern in Bladensburg.[58]

The battle left British casualties of 249, including 56 dead, while the Americans only had approximately 50 killed and wounded. The action at the Bladensburg bridge and the assault on Barney's battery had taken a toll, particularly among the 85th Regiment. One of two officers of the regiment who was killed had been Gleig's friend, Lt. Garlike Philip Codd, struck by a musket ball that tore out his windpipe. Gleig himself was slightly wounded in the ankle. At Bladensburg, as later at North Point, the British were unable to follow up their victory and make it total because they had no cavalry. They captured 150 prisoners and 10 cannons. The militia mostly escaped, leaving wags to dub the event the "Bladensburg Races."[59]

The man who Madison had trusted to lead the American forces to victory, Brig. Gen. William H. Winder, traveled to Tenleytown and then to Montgomery Courthouse (now Rockville) with the bulk of the American troops. The District militia commander, General Smith, stated that he was shocked that Winder decided not to make a stand at the Capitol and ordered the militiamen to retreat through the city. He wrote, "It is impossible to do justice to the anguish evinced by the troops of Washington and Georgetown on receiving this order." He stated that the militiamen found it hard to accept that they were being told to leave "their families, their houses, and their homes, at the mercy of an enraged enemy. . . ."[60]

Another American officer who said he expected Winder to make a further stand to defend the capital was the commander of the U.S. Light Dragoons, Lt. Col. Jacint Lavall. The cavalryman later wrote that he had anticipated that Winder would rally the troops "and defend the capital to the last man."[61]

Despite these brave words, the French-born cavalryman could have done more at Bladensburg. Congressman Richard M. Johnson of Kentucky, who headed the congressional inquiry into the capture of Washington, observed that

It does not appear that any movement was made or attempted by the cavalry or horsemen although the enemy to the left were in open and scattered order, as they pursued or pressed upon our lines, and a most fortunate moment presented itself for a charge of cavalry and horsemen.[62]

The cavalry at Bladensburg, estimated at around 315 men, indeed could have proved a deciding factor in the battle. The British lacked adequate artillery or cavalry of their own to repel an attack by mounted horsemen.

Yet, to do them justice, it has to be admitted that the U.S. cavalrymen on the field were inexperienced, whether they were mounted volunteers (around 260 men in five separate units) or regular cavalry (a total of 55 men). Lavall said his men were exhausted from the scouting duties they had carried out for Winder prior to Bladensburg. He stated that he had been given no orders to consolidate the different corps of cavalry under his command. In fact, except for the instructions from Winder to proceed to Bladensburg, he had received no other orders of any kind, let alone orders to charge the British. The colonel pointed out, "Regular troops never act or retreat without orders." The cavalrymen therefore just sat and watched the battle. Lavall stated,

> Our being elevated, and in a conspicuous position, the balls and rockets soon showered around us. I had no other chance to form any idea, having never been at the place before. We were too late to form any judicious arrangements, not knowing how the troops and batteries were disposed at Bladensburg. . . . Yet it has been wondered at why I did not cut to pieces four or five thousand British veteran troops with fifty-five men, all recruits, and upon raw horses; the most of them had not yet been purchased two weeks; the consequences are so obvious that I did not think myself justifiable to make so certain, so inevitable a sacrifice, without a hope of doing any good; there is a distinction between madness and bravery.[63]

Lt. Col. Jacint Lavall, commander of the U.S. Light Dragoons at Bladensburg

Courtesy National Portrait Gallery, Smithsonian Institution

Lavall ordered his cavalrymen to retreat when he saw the rest of the army collapse in the face of the British advance.

By Lavall's testimony, the U.S. cavalrymen lingered a half hour at the Capitol and a further *three quarters of an hour* at the president's house because he had heard a rumor that Winder meant to rally the scattered army. When he saw no such gathering of troops, he reluctantly ordered his cavalry-men to follow the rest of the army in the retreat to the west. He left, he said, "with a heart full of sorrow, grief, and indignation," unable to comprehend that the commander would leave the city unprotected.[64]

As the victorious British rested on the battlefield before entering the city, the stunned Madison sat in the presidential mansion. His wife Dolley had fled about a half hour earlier with the full-length portrait of George Washington. She had packed documents, silverware, books, and the red velvet curtains from the drawing room. These items were loaded into a wagon and taken away for safekeeping to the Bank of Maryland outside the city. Then she had left in her private carriage with some additional pieces of silverware crammed into her reticule.[65]

The president sat dejectedly in the state dining room with his friends Jacob Barker and Robert G. L. de Peyster. A victory banquet with 40 covers lay ready on the table but all Madison took was a little wine. The president was still in shock at how the Redcoats had pushed aside the American militia and had overcome Barney's sailors and marines. Barker later recalled that the superb discipline of the Redcoats amazed the little executive:

> The president had a full view of the conflict, and noticed the havoc made [by the naval cannons]. He said the fire from Barney's guns made perfect lanes through the ranks of the enemy, but that the troops filled the voids thus created, without turning to the right or to the left to see whether their companions had lost a head, a leg, or an arm.[66]

The militarily naive president still did not realize that, under a commander other than Winder, the day could have turned out very differently. The victory banquet, shortly to be consumed by the British, could have been enjoyed by Americans. Moreover, Washington, D.C., would not have been abandoned to a night of fire and terror.

Chapter Nine
The "Frolic with the Yankees" Turns Sour

At 8:00 P.M. on August 24, British General Ross marched into the city of Washington at the head of his second brigade. The brigade comprised those troops that had not been engaged at Bladensburg—the 21st Regiment, the Colonial Marines, or former slaves, and the sailors and Royal Marines. The British would occupy the city until the following night. During the occupation, they burned the public buildings of the city, including the Capitol and the president's mansion, allegedly in retaliation for the American burning of York, the capital of British Upper Canada, in the spring of the previous year. The executive mansion would henceforth be known as the White House after it was repainted to hide the scorch marks left by the British.[1]

As the general and his staff rode onto Capitol Hill, shots rang out. Four soldiers were hit, one man killed, along with Ross's horse—his second horse to be killed that day. Exactly who fired those shots remains uncertain, although Walter Lord makes a case for some of Barney's flotillamen. Whoever fired them, it can be argued that if Ross had been killed, the city's nightmare could have been a lot worse. If Admiral Cockburn had been able to have his way, the whole city might have been torched. The moderating influence of Ross meant that the troops limited the destruction to government property and that they respected private property. Unless, that is, the people in the houses fired on them.[2]

The British broke down the door of the nearby Sewall mansion to hunt for the snipers. They found the house empty. Ironically, until recently the brick mansion had been rented by Albert Gallatin, who was now one of the five American peace commissioners in London trying to bring the war to an end. The British set fire to the house using the Congreve rockets they used with success against the militia. As the flames from the Sewall mansion leaped up to the sky, the attention of the troops was drawn to the south. The glow of a major fire

105

Sacking of Washington by the British

Courtesy of Library of Congress and Francis de C. Hamilton

reddened the sky and heavy explosions shook the ground. Captain Tingey was destroying the Navy Yard to prevent its capture by the enemy.[3]

If they could not find any snipers in the Sewall house, the invaders were not taking chances. The troops were formed in line facing the Capitol, and a volley was fired at America's seat of democracy, called by Thomas Jefferson "the first temple dedicated to the sovereignty of the people." No shots were fired back. The empty Capitol stared silently back at the invaders with shattered windows as if rebuking the British insult. Far less impressive than the Capitol we know today, the seat of the legislative branch of the United States government in 1814 lacked the distinctive dome added during Abraham Lincoln's administration. When the British attacked Washington, the Capitol comprised separate freestone buildings for the Senate and House of Representatives, linked by a one-hundred-foot wooden bridge.[4]

In order to gain entrance to the Capitol, Ross ordered the troops to break down the doors. After an interval of sightseeing in the House chamber, legend has it that Cockburn plunked himself down in the Speaker's chair. He is said to have called out to his men, "Shall this harbor of Yankee democracy be burned? All for it will say aye!" The troops supposedly yelled in reply, "Aye!"[5]

At first General Ross thought of blowing up the Capitol. However, several local people who had remained in their homes protested that an explosion might damage their houses. Besides, they said, they had done nothing to resist the British. The general relented, and decided on fire instead.[6]

The technique decided on was the one used in dizzying succession to the public buildings throughout the District: furniture and other combustibles were gathered together in the center of the room, rocket powder was sprinkled on the heap, and rockets fired into the pile to begin the conflagration.[7]

With the buildings on Capitol Hill burning merrily behind them, Ross and Cockburn rode down Pennsylvania Avenue to the president's mansion. Thinking Mrs. Madison might still be in residence, they sent a note ahead promising the First Lady "an escort to whatever place of safety she might choose." Ross later remarked to Dr. James Ewell, whose home on Capitol Hill he had requisitioned as his headquarters, "I make no war on *letters* or *ladies*"—a reference both to the First Lady and to the British burning of the Library of Congress, housed then in the Capitol, not in a separate building. The general told Ewell, in a syrupy manner, "I have heard so much praise of Mrs. Madison, that I would rather protect than burn a house which sheltered so excellent a lady."[8]

Fine as this statement appears, we might wonder why the British sent the note offering to escort the first lady *away* from the mansion if the intention was not to burn the house all along.

Lieutenant Gleig, although he did not personally witness the episode, stated that Ross and his party found "a dinner-table spread, and covers laid for forty guests. Several kinds of wine, in handsome cut-glass decanters, were cooling on the side-board." The general wrote ecstatically to his brother-in-law, "The fare . . . which was intended for *Jonathan*, was voraciously devoured by

United States Capitol, 1814

Collection of the Author

John Bull, and the health of the Prince Regent, and success to His Majesty's arms by sea and land, was drunk in the best wines."[9]

Madison's servant French John Sioussat later denied that a "victory banquet" had been prepared. However, a recent White House history supports the British claim.[10]

The British helped themselves to a number of trophies, including books and pictures from Madison's library. Cockburn took a cushion off Dolley Madison's chair, coarsely joking that it would remind him of "her seat."[11]

The job of setting the mansion on fire followed with alacrity. Cockburn's men were, after all, experts at this type of thing, having been burning property around the bay for more than a year. After the mansion had been consigned to flames, the rear admiral made a stop at the offices of the *National Intelligencer*, whose editor Joseph Gales, Jr., had been attacking him in its columns for months. He ordered his sailors to set the offices on fire. However, several ladies who lived in the block pleaded with him, saying that burning the *Intelligencer* office would endanger their homes. Acceding to their pleas not to burn the building, Cockburn left a guard at the newspaper office overnight. Next morning, he would return and see to the job of wrecking the presses, and would jest with his sailors, "Make sure all the *C*'s are destroyed, so the rascals can't abuse my name any more!" But for now it had been a very long, eventful day. The admiral and his friend, the general, retired for the night to their headquarters on Capitol Hill.[12]

The first and second brigades, the former including Gleig's 85th Regiment, entered the city well after the work of destruction had begun. He wrote of the "night of terror" for the inhabitants of Washington:

> The sky was brilliantly illumined by the different conflagrations; and a dark red light was thrown upon the road, sufficient to permit each man to view distinctly his comrade's face. Except the burning of San Sebastian, I do not recollect to have witnessed, at any period in my life, a scene more striking or more sublime.[13]

Capt. Harry Smith was less awed than the young subaltern. Smith expressed disgust that the troops were employed in "the barbarous purpose of destroying the city." He remarked that the British "burnt its Capitol and other buildings with the ruthless firebrand of the Red Savages of the woods."[14]

Back at headquarters, Ross appeared morose. He told the Ewells he deplored the tragedy he had been forced to bring to the city in retaliation for the U.S. burning of the British capital in Canada. He said he regretted the necessity for a war "between two nations so nearly allied by consanguinity and interest."[15] In writing a few days later to his wife he laid the blame for the calamity squarely on President Madison's shoulders. As usual, though, he wrote to her in a placatory manner to assure her that he would be home safe soon:

> I trust all our Differences with the Yankees will shortly be settled. That Wish is, I believe, very prevalent with them. They feel strongly the Disgrace of having their Capital taken by a handful of Men and blame very generally

The president's mansion after the British torching

Courtesy Library of Congress

a Government which went to War without the Means or the Abilities to carry it on.[16]

Toward dawn on Thursday, August 25, a summer rain squall helped dampen the fires and lessened the damage to the president's house and the Capitol. Gleig, sleeping in the open on a green space near Capitol Hill, felt the "disagreeableness of getting wet" but he still felt moved by the night of drama. "The flashes of lightning," he said, "seemed to vie in brilliancy, with the flames which burst from the roofs of burning houses, while the thunder drowned the noise of crumbling walls" and competed with the "occasional roar of cannon" and the explosions of "large depots of gunpowder."[17]

The new day began as the last ended, with more destruction. However, on several counts August 25 would not go Ross's way. A detachment of sailors entered the Navy Yard to destroy what the Americans had left unburned. Meanwhile, a British column tramped up Pennsylvania Avenue to burn the brick building west of the president's mansion that jointly housed the State, War, and Navy Departments. Suddenly, a lone horseman charged the head of the column. The brave or extremely stupid American proved to be John Lewis, errant grandnephew of Pres. George Washington. Possibly crazed with drink, Lewis galloped toward the Redcoats, wildly firing a pistol. As might be predicted, the troops fired a volley of musket fire at the wild horseman. Lewis, whether hero or fool, fell mortally wounded.[18]

At headquarters, Ross listened to the appeals of frightened but more level-headed citizens. He ordered a number of enlisted men to be flogged for looting. He spared the U.S. Marine barracks when Americans informed him it could not be burned without endangering the surrounding neighborhood. Washingtonians got the impression that the Irish-born general was a moderate man who would listen to their concerns.[19]

Around 2:00 P.M., the general sent a detachment of four officers and two hundred men down Delaware Avenue to the fort at Greenleaf's Point, the spit of land where the eastern branch meets the Potomac (now known as Fort McNair). Although the Americans had destroyed the fort itself, Ross had learned that 150 barrels of powder still lay in the magazine. The detachment had orders to destroy the barrels of gunpowder.[20]

The troops thought they could dispose of the barrels by dropping them down a well. However, there was not enough water to cover the barrels. Rumor has it—hard as it is to believe—that a soldier may have thrown a lighted brand or cigar down the well. Or perhaps a barrel struck a spark on the stone sides of the well as it tumbled down the shaft. In any case, the well blew up. The explosion killed as many as 30 men and left 44 hideously wounded. The mangled men

Admiral Cockburn

The sack of Washington was a personal triumph for him.

Courtesy National Portrait Gallery, London

were carried back to Capitol Hill, where Ross set up a hospital in a hotel on Carroll Row.[21]

If that wasn't enough, next occurred a *natural* disaster: a violent late summer storm of hurricane force struck the District. The tempest lifted the British 3-pound cannons and hurled them aside like toys. The gale also blew the drums out of camp like paper cups. Trees were uprooted and ships unmasted for miles around. The roof was torn off the patent office, which William Thornton, superintendent of patents, had persuaded the British to spare.[22]

Out of the rain emerged a delegation from Alexandria, offering to surrender to the general. A similar party that had set out from Georgetown lost their way in trying to find Ross's headquarters. Cockburn closely interrogated the Alexandrians to learn if Gordon's squadron had come in sight up the Potomac. The members of the delegation told him they had not yet seen the squadron but wanted to check the terms of surrender for when the Royal Navy ships appeared. The good citizens were prepared to surrender their town on British terms. Cockburn gave them the promise he always gave to Yankees: if no resistance would be made, private property would be respected. The Royal Navy would pay a "fair" price for provisions. Of course, government property and military stores were another story entirely: they were prizes of war.[23]

The catastrophes, manmade and natural, seemed to settle a pall of gloom over the victorious army. The disaster at Greenleaf's Point in particular seemed to make a statement on the British presence in the District, telling them to leave. It is likely that in any case Ross had already decided to evacuate the city that night. Although Winder's army had been scattered far and wide, the British commander nevertheless feared the Americans would regroup. He anticipated an American attack. Indeed, Colonel Brooke wrote in his diary that

> we could scarce think the Americans (from their immense population, and a well trained Artillery) would tamely allow a handful of British Soldiers, to advance thro' the heart of their Country, and burn, & destroy, the Capital of the United States.[24]

That night, to disguise the fact that they were leaving, Ross ordered that camp fires be left burning on Capitol Hill. The British had also previously spread the rumor that their next objective was Annapolis. As described by Capt. Harry Smith, the retreat was anything but orderly. Before they left the city, Smith had seized every type of transport possible to carry the wounded. He also planned to issue flour to the troops:

> We started at nine, and marched rapidly and in good order to Bladensburg, where we halted for about an hour to load the wounded. The barrels of flour were arranged in the streets, the heads knocked in, and every soldier told to take some. Soldiers are greedy fellows, and many filled their haversacks. During a tedious night's march through woods as dark as chaos, they found the flour far from agreeable to carry and threw it away by degrees. If it had not been for the flour thus marking the track, the whole column would have lost its road. Such a scene of intolerable and unnecessary confusion I never witnessed.[25]

Back in Washington, fears of black insurrection resurfaced after the British withdrawal. Brigadier General Stansbury of the Maryland militia reported to Congress on rumors current in the city:

> Reports from Georgetown and the city reached me, that arms of many of the enemy had fallen into the hands of the blacks, and it was apprehended that they would take advantage of the absence of the men to insult the females, and complete the work of destruction commenced by the enemy; and at the earnest solicitation of Brigadier General Smith and Major Peter, who expressed much anxiety respecting their families, and considering it all important to prevent further injury to the city, I ordered the troops of the District of Columbia to move thither for its protection.[26]

As on previous occasions, the much feared revolt did not come about.[27]

On the march back to their ships, the British were once more not harassed by the Americans. However, they were approached by runaway slaves who requested to be taken along. Lieutenant Gleig recalled:

> During this day's march [August 26], we were joined by numbers of negro slaves, who implored us to take them along with us, offering to serve either as soldiers or sailors, if we would but give them their liberty; but

as General Ross persisted in protecting private property of every description, few of them were fortunate enough to obtain their wishes.[28]

Undoubtedly Ross refused to take along these slaves because he knew they would slow up the march. He still feared an American attack. However, his refusal also shows how hollow was the British offer of freedom to slaves. The British were not offering freedom for humanitarian reasons but purely for their own ends, to use the slaves' manpower and local knowledge, as well as to sap the economic strength of the region. When it was not convenient to aid the slaves in their escape, they were turned away.

As the troops slogged their way back toward the shipping at Benedict, the British naval squadron under Capt. James Alexander Gordon was making slow, painful progress up the Potomac toward Alexandria. The squadron commanded by Gordon, a veteran who had lost a leg fighting the French three years earlier, was making a harrowing journey over the Potomac River shoals. His two frigates, *Seahorse* and *Euryalus*, constantly became stuck in the shallow water and had to be hauled off the shoals by sailors in small boats. The rest of the squadron—a rocket ship, four bomb vessels, and a despatch schooner—likewise became stuck often. Gordon observed that "each of the vessels was not less than 20 different times aground" as they tackled the river. The expedition proved a feat of extraordinary nautical expertise.[29]

On August 25, the same sudden storm that struck Washington nearly wrecked the expedition. The wind raised up the bowsprit of the *Euryalus*, slackening the stays so that the topmasts snapped off. Then the bowsprit broke. The *Seahorse* sprung her mizzenmast. The bombship *Meteor* was driven over a shoal and brought up in deep water. Luckily, Gordon effected repairs and the expedition was able to continue.[30]

On August 26, the squadron came in sight of Mount Vernon, Va., and the British saw Fort Washington ahead, high up on a hill on the Maryland side of the river. The British considered the American fort assailable, and they prepared to attack at dawn on August 27. Gordon's second in command, Capt. Charles Napier, later wrote that the bombships took positions to cover the frigates as the frigates began to throw shells at the fort. As planned, at dawn, the British began the bombardment. Then, Napier wrote,

> The garrison, to our great surprise, retreated from the fort; and a short time after, Fort Washington was blown up—which left the capital of America, and the populous town of Alexandria, open to the squadron, without the loss of a man. . . . Still, we were at a loss to account for such an extraordinary step. The position was good, and its capture would have cost us at least fifty men, and more, had it been properly defended; besides, an unfavourable wind, and many other chances, were in their favour. . . . At day-light the ships moored under the battery and completed its destruction. The guns were spiked by the enemy; we otherwise mutilated them, and destroyed the carriages.[31]

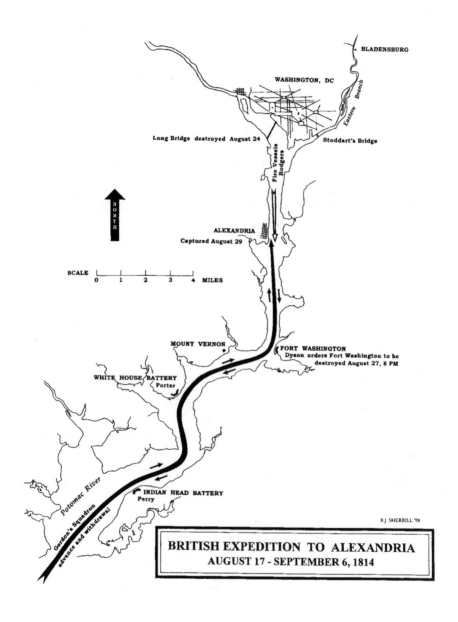

BLADENSBURG

WASHINGTON, DC

Eastern Branch

Long Bridge destroyed August 24

Stoddart's Bridge

Fire Vessels Rodgers

NORTH

ALEXANDRIA
Captured August 29

SCALE

0 1 2 3 4 MILES

MOUNT VERNON

FORT WASHINGTON
Dyson orders Fort Washington to be
destroyed August 27, 8 PM

WHITE HOUSE BATTERY
Porter

Potomac River

INDIAN HEAD BATTERY
Perry

Gordon's Squadron
advance and withdrawal

R.J. SHERRILL '98

BRITISH EXPEDITION TO ALEXANDRIA
AUGUST 17 - SEPTEMBER 6, 1814

Before the attack began, the commander of the 60-man garrison, Capt. Samuel Dyson, had decided to spike the guns and ignite the 3,346 pounds of powder in the magazine. He told his court-martial that he feared he might be attacked from the land side as well as from the river. He had orders from Winder, to blow up the fort and retire if he came under attack by land. Of course, there was no sign of a land attack, although he had heard rumors that the enemy had landed in the Patuxent. Moreover, having seen the smoke from Washington, he feared the British might be marching south from the capital to attack him.[32]

With Fort Washington destroyed, Alexandria, six miles upriver, was wide open. On the morning of Monday, August 29, the squadron anchored off the waterfront, guns trained on the town. Gordon delivered his terms. Within an hour, as he stipulated, the city's Committee of Vigilance had accepted the terms: all naval stores, public or private, to be given up; all goods intended for export to be surrendered; and all necessary provisions to be provided to the fleet and paid for at fair prices.[33]

The city fathers of Alexandria wanted no trouble from the British or from their fellow Americans. They sent a copy of their resolution to surrender to Brig. Gen. John P. Hungerford of the Virginia militia who had been hurrying to defend the town. Hungerford's subordinate Lt. Col. R. E. Parker read the resolution before it was seen by the general. Parker added his own postscript: "I send you a copy of an instrument just received and make no comment on it—my heart is broke."[34]

As Washington and Alexandria successively rolled to the conquering British, Capt. Sir Peter Parker, Lord Byron's cousin, patrolled the upper bay in the H.M.S. *Menelaus* accompanied by two smaller vessels. He enjoyed his role of diverting attention from the great events to the south while actively spying new targets for Maj. Gen. Robert Ross and the army.

On August 30, the young baronet wrote enthusiastically to Cochrane, "I may with safety give it as my opinion that Annapolis would face a very easy conquest . . ." He added smugly, "Two of my Officers walked round Fort Madison in the Night without being discovered."[35]

Parker's view that Annapolis lay virtually defenseless had basis. The civic leaders positively quaked in their boots at the specter of an imminent attack. The chairman of the Annapolis Committee of Safety, Judge Jeremiah T. Chase, wrote a panicked letter to General Winder: "We are not capable of making any Resistance to the Enemy should he attack this place and make any Demand on the Citizens. . . The Force at both Forts does not exceed Forty Regulars and many of those are unfit for Duty." The judge pleaded with Winder to order the commander of the regulars, Lt. H. A. Fay, not to fire a shot at the British and thus provoke them.[36]

But Winder had a bigger worry than Annapolis. Baltimore would likely be the next major British target, and the general was working with nettlesome Baltimore commander Gen. Samuel Smith to try to organize the city's defenses.

The audacious Captain Parker had also probed the channel into Baltimore harbor, as Rear Adm. George Cockburn had done the year before. Again, a tone of superiority and confidence suffused his letter as he wrote to Cochrane, "On the 27th in the Morning I proceeded into the Patapsco in the *Jane* tender close to the Forts of Baltimore and completely sounded the Passage and reconnoitred the port where there is a large frigate with topmast rigging [Oliver Hazard Perry's *Java*, being fitted out in Fell's Point], two sloops of war, and several gun vessels . . ."[37]

Parker's task, given to him by Cochrane, it will be recalled, was to create a *diversion* from the main British thrust and prevent Eastern Shore forces being sent to the defense of Baltimore—and perhaps to draw off forces from Baltimore to the opposite shore.

However, after his morning jaunt into the Patapsco, a development on the Bay shore opposite the city astonished him: "Running down the Eastern shore of Maryland on the 27th . . . I was surprized to observe the Enemy's Regular Troops and Militia in Motion along the whole coast . . ."[38]

These troop movements might have served as a warning to the baronet. However, the young commander's cockiness knew no bounds. Having found that the Americans had "taken up a strong position close to a large depot of stores," he adopted Cockburn's tactic of deciding to punish them for their temerity. He had, after all, learned from a master.

In phraseology comparable to Cockburn's, Parker said that the American battery "induced me instantly to push on shore with the small arm men and Marines." The result was the usual one seen around the bay for over a year. The baronet expressed his "great satisfaction" of reporting "the total Defeat of the Enemy's force who were dispersed in every Direction and driven into the Woods."[39]

One of Parker's crew, Midshipman Frederick Chamier, later wrote a revealing account of life on board the *Menelaus*, as well as a detailed account of the events of the early hours of Wednesday, August 31, 1814, when Parker met his death.[40]

Chamier had served for the last six years on the *Menelaus*, with its appropriately warlike name, from Menelaus, King of Sparta, husband of Helen of Troy. On joining the frigate in Plymouth in 1808, in time to transport Lord William Bentinck, new commander in Sicily, to the Mediterranean, he had been immediately impressed with the spotless nature of his new vessel, under Parker's strict discipline:

> Every thing here differed from the frigate I had just left; the yards of the ship were painted white instead of black; the men wore white hats, so did the officers; the gaskets for the sails were covered with bleached canvas; the mast-heads were white . . . green painted bulwarks, decks as white as snow, officers in their proper uniforms. . . . If on deck, we were obliged to be scrupulously correct; for Peter used to say, if ever he had occasion to find fault with a sailor for being deficient in respect to a midshipman— "By

the god of war (his favorite oath) I will make you touch your hat to a midshipman's coat, if it's hung on a broomstick to dry."[41]

As might be expected, the handsome young captain felt envious of the fame other British naval commanders had gained fighting the French, and he yearned to gain similar laurels. Chamier said Parker constantly muttered, "I'll do it yet, if they will only give me one chance."[42]

The type of warfare he was forced to engage in with the Americans must have been a frustration and a bother—hardly the glorious activity in which he had envisioned he would be employed: intercepting Yankee schooners, burning Yankee houses, and chasing off the Yankee militia.

Capt. Sir Peter Parker

Lossing's *Field Book of the War of 1812*

But the "incompetent" militia had something different in store for him in the wee hours of August 31. Parker learned on August 30 from a runaway slave of a chance to attack a body of militia in their camp. He understood "that one man out of every five [men] had been levied as a requisition on the eastern shore, for the purpose of being sent over for the protection of Baltimore. . . ."[43] If he could destroy the militia camp, perhaps this would give him the laurels for which he so yearned.

Whether Parker actually boasted that "he must have one more frolic with the Yankees before he left them," as Americans subsequently claimed, is debatable. On that day, he would have no way of knowing how much longer he would be required to serve in the Chesapeake. However, as with many of these tales that have entered legend, it makes for a grand story.[44]

All the same, preparing for the battle to come, Parker appears to have experienced a mixture of trepidation and exuberance, as shown by a note that he wrote on Tuesday, August 30, to his wife:

My Darling Marianne:

I am just going on desperate service and entirely depend on valor and example for its successful issue. If anything befalls me I have made a sort of will. My country will be good to you and our adored children. God Almighty bless and protect you all. Adieu, most beloved Marianne, adieu!

Peter Parker

P.S. I am in high health and spirits.[45]

Chamier, if he is to be believed, described an incident that appears to show that Parker had a premonition that the night's battle would not go as planned:

That morning, Sir Peter Parker, in leaning over the taffrail, to make some remarks upon the rigging at the mizen-top-mast-head, lost his gold-laced cocked-hat overboard. He said very thoughtfully, and in a very unusual manner, "my head will follow this evening." We had an American captain of a schooner we had captured, on board; and he was kind enough to enact prophet on the same subject, and to the same effect. From that moment, Sir Peter was more thoughtful and reserved: he prepared his will with the purser; he destroyed his letters; he made several allusions concerning his wife and family; in short, spoke like a man who had some apprehension of impending fate.[46]

Parker landed north of present-day Tolchester with approximately 250 sailors and marines with 20 men armed with pikes. Lt. Col. Philip Reed, commander of the local 21st Regiment of Maryland Militia, later charged that Parker purposely armed his men with pikes to cut the militiamen's tents.[47]

Reed said that about 11:30 P.M., he learned that enemy barges were coming ashore near Waltham's Farm. He stated that he at first believed the British meant "to land and burn houses," but that while marching toward Waltham's he "discovered that the blow was aimed at our camp."[48]

Reed, aged 54, a United States senator for Maryland from 1806 to 1813 (and thus a colleague in the Senate of Baltimore's Sam Smith), was no wet-behind-the-ears officer. A veteran of the American Revolution, as a lieutenant in 1779 he took part in the bayonet charge under Gen. "Mad" Anthony Wayne at Stoney Point, New York, on the Hudson on the night of July 15. A measure of the man's character was that, as a congressman after the War of 1812, his Revolutionary War record was debated in the Committee on Military Affairs when considering Gen. Andrew Jackson's execution of two British subjects during the Seminole War. As a lieutenant under Wayne prior to the bayonet charge, Reed is said to have carried out Gen. George Washington's order of executing deserters by cutting down an American he had found skulking, and sending the man's head to the commander in chief. Reed acknowledged to his fellow committee members that he had done this.[49]

There is confusion on where Reed's camp was located when the British landed. Most later accounts, and the historical sign at Caulk's Field, locate Reed's camp at Fairlee (then known as Belle Air), probably going by the address on his September 3, 1814 letter to Brig. Gen. Benjamin Chambers, "Camp at Belle Air." However, on the night of August 30, the militia were camped considerably nearer the beach, probably near the present-day Georgetown crossroads. If they had been at Fairlee, two and a half miles from the scene of the Battle at Caulk's Field, this would have necessitated a forced march toward the British. In fact, Reed's despatch reveals that on learning of the imminent British attack, he ordered the breakup of the camp and instructed the troops to face about and march to a position "three hundred paces" to the rear of the camp:

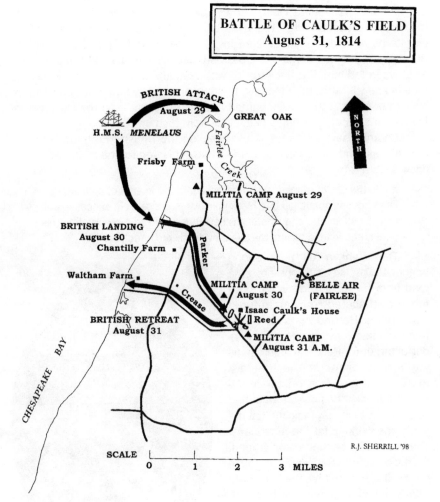

BATTLE OF CAULK'S FIELD
August 31, 1814

BRITISH ATTACK
August 29

GREAT OAK

NORTH

H.M.S. *MENELAUS*

Fairlee Creek

Frisby Farm

MILITIA CAMP August 29

BRITISH LANDING
August 30

Chantilly Farm

Parker

Waltham Farm

MILITIA CAMP
August 30

Crease

BELLE AIR
(FAIRLEE)

Isaac Caulk's House
Reed

BRITISH RETREAT
August 31

MILITIA CAMP
August 31 A.M.

CHESAPEAKE BAY

SCALE

0   1   2   3   MILES

R.J. SHERRILL '98

Orders were immediately given to the quarter-master to remove the camp and baggage, and the troops to countermarch, pass the road by the right of our camp, and form on the rising ground about three hundred paces in its rear—the right towards Caulk's house, and the left resting on the road—the artillery in the centre, supported by the infantry on the right and left.[50]

Reed arranged his troops in a fringe of woods, with the whole line facing the open area of Caulk's Field, with five cannons positioned in the center, to the north of present Route 21, and his left flank resting on the road, east of the granite battlefield marker erected in 1902. Meanwhile, the British blithely marched toward the Georgetown crossroads, led by their "intelligent black man," as they termed him. But the surprise was over, and according to Chamier, the raiders knew it. After their landing, their advance party had engaged in an exchange of shots with some mounted American pickets—and the exchange of fire was answered by a single field-piece from the camp.[51]

Chamier says prudence would have led the British to retreat. However, Parker's ego and the disdain the British had cultivated for the militia would not allow such a retreat. Chamier added,

> It was the height of madness to advance into the interior of a country we knew nothing about, led by a black man, whose sincerity in our cause was very questionable, and who might have been paid to run away from his owner, and to lead us into the snare evidently prepared for us.[52]

That night, a full moon shone brightly. Parker led his troops along the road from the beach, mounted on a horse confiscated from a captured cavalryman. He and his sailors and marines must have presented a wonderful target for Reed's militiamen lying in wait for them. They made a march of some five miles—much longer than the "half mile" Parker had been told—which may indicate that the slave *was* working for the Americans. Then, they approached rising ground. On the rise stood Caulk's Field House (and still stands today), the large date "1743" inlaid in shellacked brick, after the fashion of the area, in the brick of the east gable.[53]

Reed had positioned himself in the woods with an advance party of riflemen commanded by Capt. Simon Wickes covering the road. As soon as the enemy column appeared, he ordered

Lt. Col. Philip Reed

Collection of the Author

the riflemen to fire a volley "at seventy paces distance." As he saw the company being pressed by the enemy's superior numbers, he told the riflemen to form on the right of the main line. Reed took his place in command by the artillery in the center of the line of militia.[54]

The firing became general along the whole U.S. line. The British charged across a 50-acre open field, but suffered casualties from the sustained American fire. Parker's invasion force included a Congreve rocket unit. However, because the man carrying the staffs for the rockets fell early in the engagement, the Royal Marines never brought their rockets into action. Moreover, under Reed's command, the Yankee militia did not run as Parker had come to expect. Parker ordered the Royal Marines to attack Reed's left flank (Capt. Ezekiel F. Chambers' company), and the sailors under Lt. Henry Crease were ordered to assail Reed's right flank.[55]

Chamier described the British attack:

> we advanced at double-quick time, in the hopes of closing with our foes and finishing the fight; but they cautiously retreated as we advanced towards the woods in the rear; at last they made a halt, and we distinctly heard one of the officers telling his men to stand firm against the attack "of the British lions, as they called themselves." . . . Up to this moment, Parker had cheered on the marines with his usual determined courage; his Turkish saber sparkled in the moonlight as he waved it over his head, and his continual cry of "Forward! Forward!" resounded amidst the firing; but now his voice failed, and he fell in my arms.[56]

Reed attributed Parker's mortal wounding to "a buck-shot." In 1902, Justice Robert Calder, whose father reportedly fought in the battle, maintained that the fatal shot was fired by Henry Urie, a militiaman from Rock Hall, who was "strategically located . . . on the over-hanging limb on a huge willow tree . . . his blunder-buss loaded to the muzzle with all the hardware, bolts, nuts, nails, etc., in his barnyard."[57]

Reed says the British fire had almost ceased when he learned some militiamen had almost used up all their cartridges (though each had brought about 20 rounds into the field), and that the artillery had already completely exhausted their ammunition. He therefore ordered a retreat.[58]

It is likely that the sudden wounding of Parker and their other casualties blunted the British effort to pursue the withdrawing militiamen. Officially, the British lost 14 killed and 27 wounded compared with no Americans killed and only three wounded.[59]

Indeed, as characterized by Chamier, there was little thought among the British other than to carry the wounded commander from the field of battle and get back to the ships. Chamier wrote:

> In vain we asked where he was wounded; for he was unable to speak, and had fainted. On lifting him on the marines' shoulders (six of whom carried him off the field), [Lt.] Pocock, who had assisted, and who had placed his

hands under the thighs of the captain, remarked that the dew was very heavy, for the captain was wet through; but on holding his hands to the moonlight, he discovered them dyed in blood. It was instantly proposed to strip Sir Peter on the spot—and had this been done, he might perhaps have been saved; but we were in no situation to delay operations—a hasty retreat was determined, and we instantly began to retrace our steps. The wound was occasioned by a buck-shot, which had cut the femoral artery, and poor Sir Peter was bleeding to death.[60]

By the time the British reached the beach, the young captain had died. Among the detritus of battle the morning after the battle, a young American soldier found an elegant leather shoe "richly gilt around the vamp and quarters" and stained with blood. Inside, he saw the mark of the London shoe manufacturer, "No. 20169, Parker, Capt., Sir Peter, Bt." It was the first clue the Americans had that they had killed the British commander. Returning the shoe to the British during the truce the next day, a militia officer commented, "We guess that your captain was not a man to run away without his shoes."[61]

Caulk's Field, though a small battle in terms of numbers engaged, can be viewed as a turning point for the tussle for the Chesapeake, if only in terms of what it did for American morale. No longer would everything go the way of the British. The bravery of the Kent County militiamen, so well led by the veteran Reed, proved an inspiration to the militiamen of Baltimore two weeks later. Reed could with justification tell Brigadier General Chambers, "When it is recollected that very few of our officers or men had ever heard the whistling of a ball, . . . I feel justified in the assertion, that the gallantry of the officers and men on this occasion could not be excelled by any troops."[62]

In Washington, D.C., events were also taking a turn for the better. There was a new feeling of confidence despite the trauma the capital had been through. The Madisons had returned and were living in the Octagon House, loaned to them by French Ambassador Louis Serurier. Secretary of War John Armstrong had been forced to resign. President Madison named James Monroe as acting secretary of war. Monroe immediately decided to take action against the British squadron in the Potomac. He ordered three key commanders in the U.S. Navy, Coms. John Rodgers, Oliver Hazard Perry, and David Porter, to set up batteries to pound the British ships as they attempted to pass back down the Potomac River from Alexandria.[63]

At 5:00 A.M. on September 2, the British squadron began to move away from the wharves of Alexandria. The British ships were packed with their spoils from the capitulation of that city: 13,786 barrels of flour, 757 hogsheads of tobacco, as well as tons of cotton, beef, tar, and sugar. Captain Gordon also had with him 21 prize vessels. The British had found rich pickings in Alexandria. Now, the three veteran U.S. Navy commodores would try to make them pay for their greed.[64]

Next morning, Rodgers left Washington with a flotilla of cutters. He planned to use three fire vessels against the rear of the British squadron. He caught up

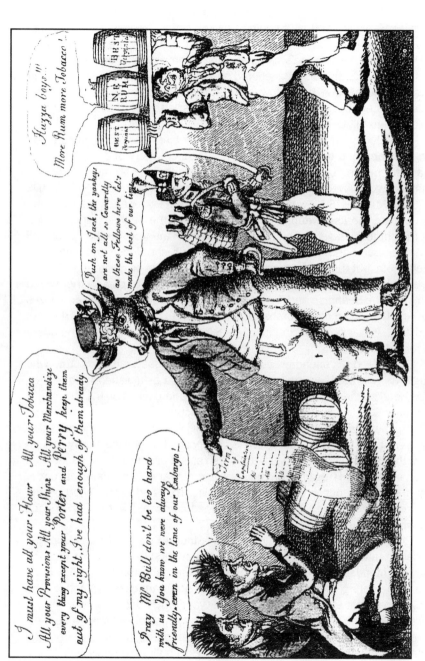

Johnny Bull and the Alexandrians

Contemporary cartoon by William Charles

with the British and found that the bombship *Devastation* had grounded several miles below Alexandria. It seemed a likely target. Rodgers sent three fire vessels to try to burn her, while covering them with his five cutters. But then the wind died. The *Devastation*'s skipper, Capt. Thomas Alexander, lowered his boats. The other British ships, anchored off Fort Washington, also lowered their boats. The Royal Navy boats towed the fire ships astern and then chased Rodgers' cutters back up to Alexandria. The first attempt to attack Gordon's squadron had failed.[65]

On a bluff on the Virginia shore called the White House, Commodore Porter had established by September 3 a formidable battery of 10 guns with a furnace for heating the shot and entrenchments for supporting infantry. The commodore displayed a huge white banner which proclaimed "FREE TRADE AND SAILORS RIGHTS." It was the same banner that Porter and his sailors had flown aboard the *Essex* during her epic voyage in the South Pacific. Gordon sent the bombships *Aetna* and *Erebus* to interrupt the work on the battery. All day September 4 and the morning of September 5, the British and Americans traded shots, but the match proved a standoff. At noon on September 5, Gordon brought up his whole squadron, weighting his ships to port so they would fire higher. The *Seahorse* and *Euryalus* led, with the smaller vessels and prizes following. The British naval bombardment brought to bear a total of 63 guns as against 13 Porter now had in place. Hopelessly outgunned, the commodore was forced to withdraw.[66]

Gordon led his squadron down river past the beaten battery. Yet, if he thought he had escaped, he was wrong. Perry had established a battery on Indian Head on the Maryland side. As the British approached on the morning of September 6, they expected another heated action. Napier wrote that "From fourteen to eighteen guns were mounted in this new position, and a considerable interruption was expected." However, Perry only had one gun heavy enough to give the British any difficulties. The British sailed past this meek opposition. This time, they were free to go on their way to meet up with the main fleet under Admiral Cochrane out in the bay. The mauling they had experienced on the Potomac had cost them 7 killed and 35 dead compared with 11 Americans dead and 19 wounded.[67]

Gordon's squadron was immediately added to the fleet that Cochrane planned to take up to Baltimore. Although the admiral had written to England to say he intended to sail up to Rhode Island for the winter and attack Baltimore in the spring, plans had changed. A full-scale attack was planned. The attack also meant a change of plans for lawyer Francis Scott Key. Key was on his way to find the British fleet to try to obtain release of Dr. William Beanes, who had been arrested in the middle of the night during the retreat from the capital. The elderly physician was held captive on board the *Royal Oak*.[68]

Several days earlier, Key dashed off a letter to his mother. He told her,

I am going in the morning to Baltimore to proceed in a flag-vessel to Genl. Ross. Old Dr. Beanes of [Upper] Marlbro is taken prisoner by the Enemy, who

Com. David Porter's battery at White House, Virginia, on the Potomac
Courtesy of Joseph W. A. Whitehorne

threaten to carry him off. Some of his friends have urged me to apply for a flag & go & try to procure his release.[69]

Detained on board a British ship during the attack on Baltimore, Key would be a witness to the British bombardment of Fort McHenry. In a joint naval and land attack, the British planned to do to Baltimore what they had done to Washington and Alexandria. Although the news of Parker's death had dampened the spirits of the British, the intelligence of the vulnerability of Baltimore that Parker had obtained during his reconnaissance of the Patapsco gave room for optimism. What the British apparently did not know was that militia units from around Maryland and neighboring states were flocking to the defense of Baltimore. These militiamen even included at least one Eastern Shore unit which Parker's diversion had been intended to prevent from coming to the defense of the city.[70]

Chapter Ten
The Defense of Baltimore

The public buildings of Washington, D.C., stood in charred ruins. Would Baltimore be next? News of the American defeat at Bladensburg jolted the cocky city on the Patapsco. On the night of August 24–25, 1814, the glow of the fires in the nation's capital, 50 miles to the south, had been visible all night long. Rumors swept Baltimore that the British were marching up the Washington road to lay waste the city. The stifling pessimism that gripped the city is evident in a letter of August 25 from David Winchester to his brother Brig. Gen. James Winchester:

> You may be sure this is the most awful moment of my life. Not because, if the place is defended, I shall put my life at hazard in common with my fellow citizens, but because I am positively sure we shall not succeed.[1]

Another observer noted that Baltimore, under threat from the British, bore a deserted, fatalistic aspect:

> The City as yet wears a most gloomy appearance. All furniture has been moved and but a few stores are open, and the few genteel females that have remained have been in a state of preparation to fly at a moment's warning.[2]

There was talk of capitulation, as had happened at Alexandria. Yet, surrender remained unthinkable to Maj. Gen. Samuel Smith. Gritty and determined, Smith would not give up without a fight.[3]

Indeed, because of the general's fine-tuned planning, Baltimore was better prepared to defend itself than the District had been under the dubious command of Brig. Gen. William H. Winder. However, after the debacle at Bladensburg, Winder came to Baltimore, tail between his legs but nevertheless cocksure that he would command the defense of Baltimore. In truth, the

126

loser of Bladensburg could legitimately claim the command. He had been appointed by President Madison to be chief of the 10th Military District, which included the city of Baltimore. Additionally, as a regular army general, he outranked Smith, who held the rank of a major general of militia. Anticipating Winder's challenge to Smith's authority, a cadre of prominent military officers lobbied the city's Committee of Vigilance and Safety on August 25. The men who insisted that Smith should retain the top command were Brig. Gen. John Stricker, Fort McHenry commander Maj. George Armistead, Com. Oliver Hazard Perry, hero of the Battle of Lake Erie, and Lt. Robert T. Spense, new chief of the Baltimore naval station. In response to this powerful lobby, the committee resolved that in "this important crisis" Smith should take "command of the forces that may be called out for the defense of our city."[4]

Three leading citizens were called on to tell Smith of the committee's unanimous opinion. Significantly, and as if once more to emphasize that Smith was the correct man for the job of saving Baltimore from the enemy, one of these citizens was wealthy property owner Gen. John Eager Howard. Despite their bitter political differences, Smith and Howard, hero of the Battle of Cowpens in 1781, resolved to work together in the face of the crisis facing the city.[5]

To make certain of his authority, Smith also wrote to Governor Winder to request confirmation of his command. The governor obligingly wrote a letter on August 26 that went further than he had in his instructions of March 13, 1813, when he named Smith as commander of the militia in defense of the city. To the detriment of his nephew Brig. Gen. William H. Winder who had gone down to ignominious defeat in the dust of Bladensburg, Winder implied that Smith's assignment was also a federal appointment. The governor declared, "By the requisition of the President of the United States of the 4th of July last, one Major General is required of this state. In conformity to which, you [i.e., Gen. Samuel Smith] have been selected."[6]

When General Winder arrived in the city the following day, Smith triumphantly showed him an endorsed copy of his uncle's letter. The younger man flew into a rage. In the following days, the brigadier general wrote whining letters to Madison and Secretary Armstrong, but to no avail.[7] The controversy was resolved on September 11, the eve of the British attack on Baltimore, by which time Armstrong had departed from the capital in disgrace. Acting Secretary of War James Monroe wrote to the still steaming general emphasizing that "Gen'l Smith's command must extend to Annapolis, & to other points along the bay, to which the enemy may direct their movements." The acting secretary added, "There can be but one commander . . . [and] the troops must be under his control."[8] Monroe sounded like a headmaster chiding a petulant schoolboy.

Meanwhile, the work of strengthening the city's defenses continued at a pace. The Committee of Vigilance and Safety proclaimed that "The inhabitants of the city and precincts are called on to . . . [furnish] all wheelbarrows, pickaxes, spares and shovels that they can procure."[9] Slaves and free black volunteers alike were among those who helped construct the defenses. The committee also invited patriotic individuals from surrounding states to help in improving the defenses as well as in taking up arms for the protection of the city. Although many of the volunteers undoubtedly were motivated by patriotism, men from neighboring states no doubt also flocked to the city's aid because they feared what would happen to the commerce of the region if the enemy sacked Baltimore. Pennsylvania and Virginia militia companies began arriving on August 29. Smith ordered the militiamen to be drilled from reveille to dusk. He was determined that the militia would be made to stand their ground against the disciplined Redcoats and not run as had the militia at Bladensburg. There was to be no repetition of the "Bladensburg Races" at Baltimore.[10]

After the debacle of August 24, there remained the problem of reassembling the militia units that had scattered in the wake of the U.S. defeat. Notices appeared in the *Patriot and Evening Advertiser* requesting that Pinkney's riflemen and the American artillerists reassemble in order to fight again. A call also went out for "Elderly men, who are able to carry a firelock, and willing to render a last service to their Country."[11]

A number of senior citizens volunteered, among them David Poe, grandfather of Edgar Allan Poe. Ulster-born Poe had been a quartermaster during the Revolution, when he served with Lafayette, earning himself the affectionate local nickname "General" Poe. At age 71, the spinning-wheel maker offered his services as a private in the Maryland 5th Regiment company of "Baltimore Patriots" under Capt. Robert Lawson. Another elderly volunteer was Uriah Prosser, a shoemaker and Revolutionary War veteran who served alongside his son, Pvt. Samuel Prosser, a grocer. Father and son were privates in Capt. Benjamin Edes' company of the Maryland 27th Regiment.[12]

Although the defenses on the western side of the city were minimal, those on the eastern side, the direction from which an attack would likely come, now stretched from Bel Air Road in the north, south to Harris Creek in the harbor, a full mile in length. The earthworks were designed by Robert Cary Long and William Stuart. The key strong point was the redoubt in the center of the defensive line, which quickly became known as "Rodgers' Bastion" for its commander, Havre de Grace favorite son Com. John Rodgers. The commodore fortified the redoubt, located on Hampstead Hill (present-day Patterson Park) with 16 guns that included a mix of naval and field artillery. Among the cannons were 12-pounders that Rodgers had borrowed from the U.S. sloop of war *Erie*. Rodgers' battery adjoined redoubts armed with 4- and 6-pound field pieces manned by seven companies of the 1st Regiment of Maryland Artillery. Capt. George Stiles's Marine Artillery, manned by seaman and officers of blockaded Baltimore privateers and letters of marque, were positioned on the Philadelphia Road. Stiles's sailors stood at five 18-pound field guns, waiting for Ross and his Redcoats to come up the road from North Point. From Philadelphia Road south to the harbor, four batteries that made up the rest of the defensive line, ending west of Harris Creek, were similarly crewed by experienced naval gunners. The entrenchments between the batteries were manned by U.S. Marines and Maryland and Pennsylvania militia.[13]

If General Smith exhibited a single-minded determination to save Baltimore from the enemy, Rodgers too had a personal need to ensure that the British did not burn the city. The commodore undoubtedly still smarted from the insults the British had visited on Havre de Grace, when Admiral Cockburn burned two-thirds of the town and damaged the Rodgers family home. The commodore was a tough, determined sailor. Even so, his wife Minerva worried about him, as shown by the letter she wrote to him on hearing of the fate of the capital:

> I have just heard that Washington is in ashes. . . . Oh my husband! Dearest of men! All other evils seem light when compared to the danger which threatens your precious safety. When I think of the perils to which your courage will expose you, I am half-distracted, yet I would not have you different from what you are. . . .[14]

On September 3, George Douglass , a local merchant serving as a private in the Baltimore Fencibles, wrote to his friend Henry Wheaton, editor of the *National Advocate* in New York, and described the hectic work of preparing the city's defenses. He marveled at how everyone had united in the common cause, determined that Baltimore would not suffer the same fate as Washington:

> Everyday, almost every hour, bodies of troops are marching in to our assistance. At this moment we cannot have less than 10,000 men under arms. The whole of the hills and rising grounds to the eastward of the port are covered with horse-foot and artillery exercises and training from morning until night.[15]

The attack on Baltimore for which Baltimoreans prepared was about to happen. Yet, despite all the activity in the city, unbelievably, the British almost left the bay *without* attacking the city.

Ross's aide, Capt. Harry Smith, later insisted that when he left for London with the general's report of the capture of Washington, Ross assured him that he did not intend to attack Baltimore. He said he departed for London secure in the knowledge that such an attack would not be attempted. On reaching the British capital, Smith briefed the Prince Regent and Lord Bathurst on the capture of Washington, the joyous news of which caused church bells to ring and fireworks to be set off in celebration. Then the newly promoted major and his Spanish wife Juana traveled to Bath to visit Ross's wife, Elizabeth.[16]

Soon after Smith sailed for London, Ross came under pressure from his aggressive quartermaster Lt. George de Lacy Evans and Admiral Cockburn. The same two men had forced the general to attack Washington. Now they compelled him to see that he could not leave the Chesapeake without attempting an attack on Baltimore. After all, they told him, the capture of Washington had been relatively easy. Why not crown that triumph by destroying that "nest of pirates" as they termed Baltimore? Moreover, as noted by British army historian

Militia on Hampstead Hill, Baltimore

The militia await the British attack, September 1814.

Contemporary painting by Thomas Ruckle, courtesy Maryland Historical Society and Joseph W. A. Whitehorne

Sir John Fortescue, the admirals were undoubtedly lured by the possibility of plunder if Baltimore capitulated or was captured. However, one wonders after a blockade of 18 months, how full the warehouses of Baltimore could have been with goods to plunder.[17]

On Tuesday, September 6, Lieutenant Gleig wrote in his diary: "An order went through the Fleet by telegraph for every ship to give in a return of the number of seamen she could land with small arms besides Marines." The British were bolstering their army with sailors due to the losses sustained at Washington. On Friday, September 9, after anchoring in the Potomac to rendezvous with Gordon's victorious (if battered) Alexandria task force, the fleet turned north. Young Gleig noted joyously, "We now put about again all in a body and took the direction of Baltimore which is confidently stated to be the next point of attack."[18]

Unwilling passengers in the British race up the bay were Upper Marlboro physician Dr. William Beanes and the two men who had come to try to negotiate his release, Francis Scott Key and U.S. Agent for Prisoners John S. Skinner. The American negotiators had joined the fleet on September 7 after several days of hunting for it in a truce vessel. They discovered that the elderly prisoner was being held incommunicado in the forecastle of Cochrane's flagship, H.M.S. *Tonnant.* The Upper Marlboro doctor was treated with contempt by the whole crew. Rear Admiral Cockburn allegedly sneered that Beanes should be sent to Halifax in chains.[19]

The normally humane Ross viewed Beanes with particular scorn. He apparently felt that the elderly physician had broken a "gentleman's agreement" by entertaining himself and other British officers in his home during their march to Washington, then arresting those stragglers during the retreat four days later. The general felt personally affronted that the doctor had acted in such a hostile manner after his earlier accommodating, if not to say obsequious, manner. Ross was a man of his word. Because he felt bound by his personal code of honor, he had struggled over the decision to disobey his instructions not to try to attack Washington. It appears that in Ross's view, Beanes had exhibited a Jekyll-and-Hyde personality. In a matter of days, he had transformed himself from a supposed immigrant

Francis Scott Key
Courtesy Star-Spangled Banner Flag House

Scotsman of honor, Federalist in sympathy with the British, to a Yankee of "low cunning"—to borrow Lieutenant Gleig's characterization of the former colonials.[20]

Although an unwritten rule decreed that prominent prisoners were to be treated with civility by either side, the beleaguered physician suffered in the hands of his captors. Key and Skinner knew that for the aged doctor's well-being it was essential that they secure his release.

The negotiators had brought with them letters from the wounded British prisoners at Bladensburg testifying as to how well they were being treated. Hopefully, the letters would hold some weight with Ross. The two Americans were invited by Admiral Cochrane to join the Royal Navy and British army officers for dinner on board *Tonnant*. During the meal, as the wine flowed, captain of the fleet Admiral Codrington launched into a tirade about Com. David Porter. Skinner, who had served as purser of Barney's flotilla and thus had been on the "receiving end" of Cockburn's naval attacks, let go with a salvo of his own. In this hostile atmosphere, the prospects for obtaining Beanes' release did not look good.[21]

General Ross salvaged the situation by inviting Skinner—though, according to Skinner's account written years later, pointedly *not* Key—to Admiral Cochrane's cabin. Skinner produced the letters from the wounded British prisoners. Ross perused them carefully. Several tense minutes passed as the general digested the contents of the correspondence. Then, the Irish-born general indicated that he was reassured by the prisoners' account of their treatment by the Americans. He informed Skinner, "Dr. Beanes . . . shall be released to return with you."[22] However, he perhaps did not indicate that release would be immediate—the British could not afford to allow Key and Skinner to spread word of the planned attack on Baltimore.

Ross wrote a letter to Gen. John Mason, the U.S. commissioner for prisoners, in which he further explained his attitude toward Beanes and the reason for his change of mind about detaining him:

> Dr. Beans [*sic*] having acted hostilely towards certain soldiers under my command, by making them prisoners when proceeding to join the army, & having attempted to justify his conduct when I spoke to him on the subject, I conceived myself authorized & called upon to cause his being detained as a prisoner. . . . The friendly treatment, however, experienced by the wounded officers and men of the British army left at Bladensburg enables me to meet your wishes regarding that gentleman; I shall accordingly give directions for his being released, not from any opinion of his not being justifiably detained, nor from any favorable sentiments of his merit, as far as the cause of his detention is to be considered, but purely in proof of the obligation which I feel for the attention with which the wounded have been treated. . . .[23]

The Americans, forced to accompany the invaders in their rush up the bay, must have had very mixed emotions as the British sailed under full press of sail toward their new target. Lieutenant Gleig noted in his diary that as the fleet swept up the western shore of Maryland, Americans "fired alarm guns all along the coast and showed every symptom of terror."[24]

In his *Narrative of the Campaigns,* Gleig describes the effect on Annapolis:

In passing Annapolis . . . we stood in so close as to discern the inhabitants flying from their houses; carts and wagons loaded with furniture hurrying along the roads, and horsemen galloping along the shore, as if watching [for] the fearful moment when the boats should be hoisted out, and the troops quit the vessels.[25]

Around noon on September 11, the fleet arrived at the mouth of the Patapsco and anchored off North Point, some 14 miles from Baltimore. In the city, a quiet sabbath was broken at 1:30 P.M. by the firing of three rounds from the cannon on Courthouse Green. At that moment, the churches of the city were packed. One preacher told his congregation, "May the God of battles accompany you." Rev. John Gruber at the Light Street Methodist Church even pronounced, "May the Lord bless King George, convert him, and take him to heaven, as we want no more of him."[26]

In contrast to his pessimistic letter of August 25, David Winchester jotted off a letter to his brother General Winchester telling him of the confidence that now abounded in the city:

The enemy have at length appeared before our river in great force—the fleet consists of upwards of Fifty sail. . . . We can muster upwards of 15,000 men. Great confidence prevails in our ability to repel them, and if our troops will but stand, there can be no doubt of the force being what every American could wish.[27]

With the enemy off the mouth of the Patapsco, Commodore Rodgers' sailors set about sinking the hulks in the channel between the Lazaretto Point and Fort McHenry as he and General Smith had previously agreed.[28] Lt. Solomon Rutter of the Chesapeake flotilla prepared for battle a line of barges positioned as floating batteries behind the hulks. In all, there were 11 barges, bristling with long 8- and 12-pound cannons as well as carronades. Approximately 340 sailors manned the barges.[29]

So much had happened since the battles in St. Leonard's Creek in the summer. At St. Leonard's Creek, as at Bladensburg, Rutter, Barney, and their brave sailors had held off the best that the British could throw at them.

Closely watching the activity of the British fleet for Commodore Rodgers was Sailing Master George De La Roche who was in charge of sinking the hulks in the channel off Fort McHenry. Roche had seen previous action against the British in the Chesapeake. He had commanded gunboat *No. 74* when the British were beaten off at Craney Island in their attempt to attack Norfolk in June 1813.[30]

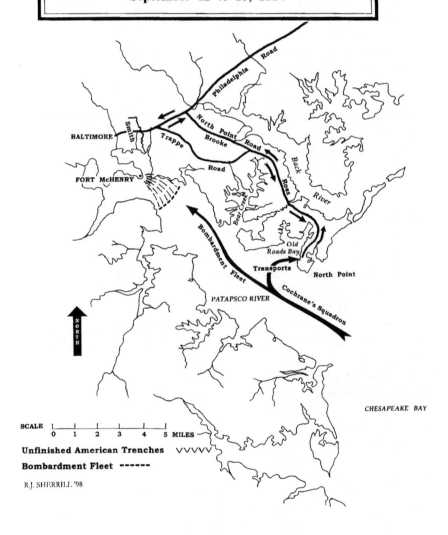

BRITISH OPERATIONS AROUND BALTIMORE
September 12 to 15, 1814

Philadelphia Road

North Point Road

BALTIMORE

Smith

Trappe

Brooke Road

Back River

Ross

FORT McHENRY

Bear Creek

Old Roads Bay

Bombardment Fleet

Transports

North Point

PATAPSCO RIVER

Cochrane's Squadron

NORTH

CHESAPEAKE BAY

SCALE

0 1 2 3 4 5 MILES

Unfinished American Trenches ∨∨∨∨∨

Bombardment Fleet ------

R.J. SHERRILL '98

In Fort McHenry, popularly known as the "Star Fort," commander Maj. George Armistead stood ready for the expected British onslaught. His garrison of 60 regulars of the U.S. Corps of Artillery had been strengthened with flotillamen. Shortly, he would be joined by 80 volunteer artillerymen commanded by Capt. Joseph H. Nicholson, a local judge who was the brother-in-law of Francis Scott Key. Additional reinforcements to arrive soon would be detachments of the 36th and 38th U.S. Infantry together with an incomplete company of the 12th Infantry, for a total of six hundred regular (if recently recruited) troops. Adding two companies of U.S. Sea Fencibles under Capts. Matthew Bunbury and William H. Addison, Fort McHenry and nearby batteries could shortly boast a complement of approximately one thousand defenders.[31]

Fort McHenry was supported by several smaller batteries established in 1813 after the British first threatened the city. To the east, on Lazaretto Point, Lt. Solomon Frazier of Barney's flotilla commanded a three-gun earthen battery garrisoned by 45 flotillamen. West of the fort lay two other, mud-walled forts. Sailing Master John A. Webster of the flotilla commanded an additional 52 flotillamen at Fort Babcock, mounting six 18-pounders. Further along the shoreline of the Ferry Branch, an even stronger earthen battery, Fort Covington, was garrisoned by 80 seamen under Lt. Henry S. Newcomb, of the *Guerriere,* who had served under Commodore Rodgers in the attempts to destroy Gordon's squadron on the Potomac.[32]

Events were shaping up toward a decisive moment in history at Baltimore because the British had no conception of the powerful concentration of drilled militia and experienced naval forces that awaited them. Because their decision to attack Baltimore had been made on the spur of the moment, their intelligence of the military developments in the city was hazy at best.

Once more Ross had listened to and accepted Cockburn's arguments about the incompetence of the American militia. In June 1813, in the attack on Norfolk, the admiral had underestimated the capabilities of U.S. commander Brig. Gen. Robert B. Taylor and his miscalculation had led to disaster. Similarly, Cockburn underestimated (or rather had no inkling of) the resourcefulness and stubbornness of General Smith. He could not know that Smith was cooperating with a cabal of equally capable fellow commanders: Armistead, Rodgers, Porter, and Perry. The overwhelming force Smith had accumulated at Baltimore would be more than a match for the disdainfully overconfident and unprepared British attackers.

As the British made ready to tackle the shoals of the Patapsco to bring their bomb ships and rocket ship close to shore to bombard Fort McHenry, Major Armistead should have been feeling confident. Instead, he was worried sick. On a personal level, his wife Louisa, whom he had sent away to safety at Gettysburg, was expecting a baby. Yet, he had a much more serious worry: only he knew that the magazine at Fort McHenry was not bombproof.[33]

Within three hours of the firing of the alarm gun, Brig. Gen. John Stricker mobilized his 3rd Brigade. The British, as anticipated, were preparing to land their troops at North Point. As had been planned for months, Stricker and his militiamen would march down the Patapsco Neck peninsula that day and camp for the night near the Methodist meetinghouse. As Stricker's force marched down the neck, southeast from the city, General Smith sent Brig. Gen. William H. Winder to guard the western approaches. The losing general at Bladensburg was not given any duty he might foul up. The delegation of this task was just rubbing salt in the brigadier general's wounds. The real fighting would be entrusted to Stricker.[34]

Stricker had an aggregate of 3,185 effective men in five regiments, the 5th, 6th, 27th, 39th, and 51st Regiments of Maryland militia. He planned to hold the 6th Regiment under Lt. Col. William McDonald in reserve and go into battle with the British using the other four regiments. By their own account, the British would land at North Point with 4,419 men—not counting sailors, which probably brought their total force to upward of five thousand. Stricker marched his men to the Methodist meetinghouse near the head of Bear Creek, about seven miles from the city. Beyond the meetinghouse lay one of the possible grounds where he and Smith had discussed he could plan to meet the enemy. Just adjacent to the intersection of Trappe Road and the main North Point Road was a grove of trees known as Godley Wood behind a rail fence. Beyond the fence lay a wide expanse of farmland belonging to the Bouldin Farm. The British would have to approach him over the open field. This made the location an excellent place to meet Ross's army, especially because the peninsula narrowed at this point. As the militiamen looked toward North Point, an arm of Bear Creek glinted on their right, while Back River lay on their left, with marshland of glutinous black mud down toward the river.[35]

Cpl. John McHenry of the 5th Regiment, nephew of the former secretary of war who gave his name to the Star Fort, wrote an account of marching down the peninsula. He remembered, "We lay that night without tents on the bare ground" by the Methodist meetinghouse just beyond Bread and Cheese Creek. On board the troopship *Golden Fleece,* Lieutenant Gleig, unable to sleep, could not remember seeing a more heavenly night. He later recalled, "The heat of the day was past, a full clear sun shone brightly, in a sky where not a cloud could be discerned."[36]

It was a tense night for the American and British troops alike.

Brig. Gen. John Stricker

Portrait by Rembrandt Peale, 1816, courtesy of the Star-Spangled Banner Flag House

Gleig wrote in his diary, "We expect to disembark tonight, so every man sleeps with his clothes on." Gleig reported that at 3:00 A.M. he was roused out of bed. "All that I take with me this time is a blanket and a haversack with three days provisions on my back."[37]

As at Benedict, to cover the landing, a gun brig lay offshore with cannons pointed at the shore. However, yet again, to their amazement, the Americans did not challenge the landing. The landings carried on until after dawn. After General Ross reached shore, he decided to advance with the light troops, leaving Colonel Brooke to disembark the rest of the army. The colonel had orders to advance as soon as the 21st Regiment and four 6-pounders came ashore. When the sun came up, it turned into a brutally hot day. Brooke noted in his diary: "The men were falling in Twentys, from the heat of the sun." He gave orders for them to get as quickly as possible into the shade afforded by the trees.[38]

Meanwhile, Ross and Cockburn enjoyed breakfast at the Gorsuch house about five miles from the landing place. Here, on being asked by Mr. Gorsuch if they would be back for dinner, Ross reportedly boasted, "I'll sup in Baltimore tonight—or in hell." He also questioned three captured dragoons. The prisoners told him that 20,000 Americans manned the defenses of Baltimore. The Irishman asked if they were mainly militia and they allowed that this was so. Legend maintains that Ross remarked, "I don't care if it rains militia."[39]

Because the captured dragoons had only told Ross about the defenders in the entrenchments some 11 miles ahead, the general apparently did not realize Stricker's "City Brigade" was less than four miles away. The misleading information undoubtedly helped contribute to the event that followed—the fatal wounding of Robert Ross. No doubt the general and his friend Admiral Cockburn anticipated a "stroll" to Baltimore much like their easy march to Bladensburg. Three weeks earlier, during that march, Winder's forces had rarely showed themselves let alone presented them with any serious opposition.

Stricker later wrote that he felt "insulted" that "the enemy in small force was enjoying himself at Gorsuch's farm." Earlier in the morning, Stricker had ordered his riflemen to the skirts of a thick, low pine wood beyond the blacksmith's shop, miles ahead of his main line. However, the men had panicked and retreated when they thought the British were landing on Back River on the east side of Patapsco Neck to cut them off. With the report of the British activity at the Gorsuch Farm, he decided to send the riflemen and some other units back down the neck. Included were 150 men of the 5th Regiment under Maj. Richard Heath and 70 riflemen, among them Capt. Edward Aisquith's rifle company, which had been on the front line at Bladensburg.[40]

Soon after noon, Ross was riding through a wooded section of North Point Road with the light troops. The casualties the British incurred three weeks earlier made for a more hazardous situation than during the advance from Benedict. Key officers in the 85th Regiment who led the advance then had been seriously wounded and left at Bladensburg. Moreover, the British still lacked the cavalry support that could give them better intelligence of the situation up ahead.

Firing broke out between the American and British skirmishers. According to Gleig, Ross rode ahead to investigate the firing and in doing so was struck down:

> As soon as the firing began, he had ridden to the front, that he might ascertain from whence it originated, and, mingling with the skirmishers, was shot in the side by a rifleman. The wound was mortal: he fell into the arms of his aid-de-camp. . . . He was removed towards the fleet, but expired before his bearers could reach the boats.[41]

American surgeon Dr. James H. McCulloh, Jr., who helped tend to the wounded of both sides after the Battle of North Point, later wrote that he was told by a British surgeon that "Genl. Ross was shot through the lungs." In a letter to the general's elder brother, Rev. Thomas Ross, Cockburn said, "a Musket Ball . . . passed thro' his right Arm and entered his right Breast."

The admiral told the general's brother, "He lived about two Hours after receiving the Wound, during which time he only Expressed Anxiety on account of his Family and seemed to suffer little or no bodily Pain."[42]

Baltimore legend maintains that the fatal shot was fired by one of two riflemen in Aisquith's rifle company. Pvts. Henry G. McComas and Daniel Wells, aged 18 and 19 years, respectively, were killed by British fire at the same time Ross was shot. The teenagers were both apprentices in the city's leather trade.[43]

The general's sudden incapacity stunned the British. Gleig described the chilling effect on the troops as the British column with which he was marching neared the site of the shooting:

> [Ross's aide, Capt. Duncan MacDougall] came at full speed towards us, with horror and dismay on his countenance, and calling loudly for a surgeon. . . . [The aide] had scarcely passed, when the general's horse, without its rider, and with the saddle and housings stained in blood, came plunging onwards. . . . In a few moments we reached the ground where the skirmishing had taken place, and beheld poor Ross laid by the side of the road, under a canopy of blankets, and apparently in the agonies of death. . . . All eyes were turned upon him as we passed, and a sort of involuntary groan ran from rank to rank, from the front to the rear of the column.[44]

Gleig then makes the statement,

> By the fall of our gallant leader the command now devolved upon Colonel Brook [sic], of the 44th Regiment, an officer of decided personal courage, but, perhaps, better calculated to lead a battalion, than to guide an army.[45]

This damning statement, made by a man who at the time was a second lieutenant aged 18 years, has led some writers to the conclusion that Brooke was incompetent. Indeed, Franklin R. Mullaly, historian at Fort McHenry, wrote baldly that "[Brooke] was not qualified to lead an operation of this type."[46] Such a

"Death of Gen. Ross at Baltimore."

Engraving of an original painting by Alonzo Chappel

conclusion is not supported by the facts. Baltimoreans may not wish to acknowledge the point, but Brooke did win the Battle of North Point that followed Ross's mortal wounding. Admittedly, the militia stood their ground and fought a better battle that did the militia at Bladensburg under Winder, but ultimately they were forced from the field.

American and British accounts of the battle differ greatly. Brooke recorded in his diary that he took command after Lt. George de Lacy Evans galloped up to him to tell him "General Ross was wounded, and he feared mortally." Brooke said he hurried forward and suddenly found himself faced with Stricker's force arranged in battle order. He wrote, "[I] had but little time for thought, knowing nothing of the intentions of the General, and without a single person to consult with, I determined on an instant attack." The Americans, he said, were "strongly posted in a wood, and behind a strong paling . . . with six or eight guns, and a flat of about five hundred yards between us."[47]

By his own account, Brooke ordered his skirmishers to fire to cover the front of the American line. He directed the first, or light, brigade to wheel off the road to the right, and after extending as far as they could, to form line. Meanwhile, he ordered the 4th Regiment, under the command of Maj. Alured Faunce, to advance across the swampy ground to the right, by Back River, to turn the militia's left flank. As the 4th would begin to turn the flank, the first brigade, including Gleig's 85th Regiment, would form line and attack the center.[48]

In a letter to his mother, Lieutenant Gleig described the opening of the battle:

Col. Arthur Brooke (1772–1843), in a portrait done later in life

Courtesy Ulster American Folk Park, Omagh, County Tyrone, Northern Ireland

> We . . . drew up in order of battle under cover of a rising ground, the light brigade forming a thick line of skirmishers in front, and the rest of the troops in line behind us. We now lay down under the shade of some trees, with a nice little breeze blowing while the 4th and 44th moved round to the left of the American line. In this state of ease we remained for nearly half an hour when the word was given and we sprang over a railing in front of us and advanced. The Americans instantly opened a tremendous fire of grape upon us, but reserved their musketry till we should get closer. I carried upon my back a haversack with three days provisions in it which

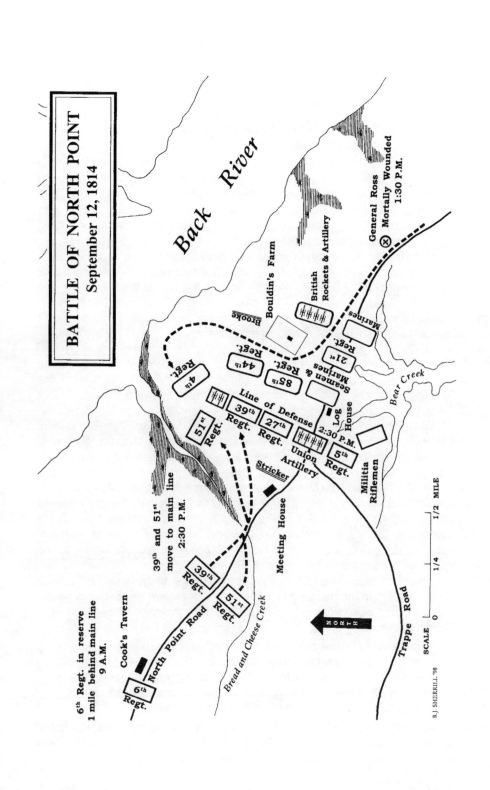

BATTLE OF NORTH POINT
September 12, 1814

Back River

General Ross Mortally Wounded 1:30 P.M.

British Rockets & Artillery

Bouldin's Farm

Brooke

Marines

21st Regt.

4th Regt.

44th Regt.

85th Regt.

Seamen & Marines

Bear Creek

Line of Defense

39th Regt.

27th Regt.

Log House 2:30 P.M.

51st Regt.

5th Regt.

Union Artillery

Militia Riflemen

Stricker

39th and 51st move to main line 2:30 P.M.

Meeting House

39th Regt.

51st Regt.

Bread and Cheese Creek

6th Regt. in reserve 1 mile behind main line 9 A.M.

Cook's Tavern

North Point Road

6th Regt.

Trappe Road

NORTH

SCALE   0   1/4   1/2 MILE

R.J. SHERRILL '98

filled it completely, and to it I owe the preservation of my life. The motion of walking shifted the haversack round and it rested on my left groin, when a grape shot struck it with such violence, that it pounded the biscuit to powder, but did not hurt me in the least. Had the haversack not been there it would certainly have killed me. As it was it nearly brought me to the ground but all I suffered was a slight bruise.[49]

Capt. John Montgomery, the states attorney of Maryland, commanded the six cannons of the Union Artillery stationed in the middle of the line of militia on the main road. His cannonfire of canister and roundshot ploughed into the ranks of the advancing British. Meanwhile, Brooke ordered his field artillery and the Royal Marine rocket battery to open up on the Americans to distract attention from the flanking movement he had ordered in order to turn Stricker's left flank. Congreve rockets snaked over the field, igniting a haystack by the Bouldin house. Approximately seven hundred sailors in a special naval brigade under Capt. Edward Crofton made up the center of the British line with the 1st Brigade of Royal Marines under Capt. John Robyns deployed on the left toward Bear Creek. The 21st Regiment and the 2nd Brigade of marines were ordered to remain in column behind them. Meanwhile, the 44th Regiment under Lt. Col. Thomas Mullins moved to the right of the naval brigade.[50]

Stricker later wrote that his orders from General Smith were "that the 5th and 27th should receive the enemy, and if necessary, fall back through the 51st and 39th, and form on the right of the 6th or reserve regiment." Before the battle commenced, he had placed the more experienced regiments, the 5th and 27th, on either side of Long Log Lane, the 5th to the right of the lane, with their right flank on a branch of Bear Creek, and the 27th to the left side of the road, extending in line toward Back River. The 51st and 39th were initially deployed in a second line around a half mile in the rear behind Bread and Cheese Creek beyond the Methodist meetinghouse. At approximately 2:30 P.M., seeing the advancing British 4th Foot picking their way over the gluey marshy ground by Back River, Stricker ordered the 39th and 51st into line on his left to counter the flanking movement. He placed the 39th immediately to the left of the 27th, detaching two cannons from Montgomery's artillery battery to the left of the 39th to better secure his left flank.[51]

Stricker wanted the 51st, under Lt. Col. Henry Amey, to deploy in a perpendicular line to the main line, in order to better receive the British advance. This order began to cause confusion among the untrained militia of the 51st. Stricker wrote:

> Colonel Amey . . . was ordered to form his regiment at right angles with my line, resting his right near the left of the 39th. This order being badly executed, but was soon rectified by the efforts of my aid[e-de-camp Maj. George Pitt Stevenson] and brigade majors, who corrected the error of Colonel Amey, and posted the 51st in its ordered position.[52]

The efforts of Stevenson proved to no avail in bringing steadiness to the raw militiamen of the 51st Regiment. Stricker's report betrays frustration and anger at the behavior of the 51st as the enemy continued to advance:

The 51st, unmindful of my object to use its fire in protection of my left flank in case an attempt should be made to turn it, totally forgetful of the honour of the brigade, and regardless of its own reputation, delivered one random fire and retreated precipitately, and in such confusion, as to render every effort of mine to rally them ineffective.[53]

As Colonel Amey's militiamen fled, a few of the men of the 39th also succumbed to the temptation to run. Nevertheless, after the retreat of these men, Stricker managed to rally his remaining men for an hour more to withstand the advancing British, musket volley for musket volley. Then, he said, "Finding my line, now 1,400 strong, was insufficient to withstand the superior numbers of the enemy . . . I was constrained to order a movement back" to the reserve 6th Regiment at Cook's Tavern. Finding the British did not follow, he then directed his men to fall back to Worthington's Mill, to which his men withdrew "in good order to receive the enemy on his nearer approach to the city."[54]

Cpl. John McHenry of the 5th Regiment mentions the collapse of the 39th and 51st but also seems to indicate that the retreat was less orderly than Stricker might have us believe. His recollection also calls into question whether the reserve 6th Regiment stood its ground:

The contest . . . was maintained for some time very vigourously by the 5th & 27th Reg'ts & a company of artillery commanded by [Capt. John] Montgomery. . . . The 39th & 51st Reg'ts fired one round at they knew not what & immediately fled. . . . the 6th Reg't . . . retreated long before the enemy approached them. . . . In the 27th Reg't adjutant [Lt. James] Lowry Donaldson was killed. As our reg't, the 5th, carried off the praise from the other reg'ts engaged so did the company to which I have the honor to belong cover itself with glory. When compared with the [other] reg'ts we were the last that left the ground. Our loss was nearly $1/3$ of the company engaged, [Pvt. William] McClennan the best soldier in the company, [Pvt. John C.] Byrd, . . . & a young man named [Pvt. Jacob] Haubert were killed; there were ten wounded, & three taken prisoners. I had the honor to carry the colours of the Reg't, which I brought off Safe, & was not hurt myself. Had not our company retreated at the time it did we should have been cut off in two minutes. . . .[55]

Cockburn's aide, Lt. James Scott, writing years later, thought the battle "a second edition of the Bladensburg Races." Lieutenant Gleig wrote to his mother, "I never in my life saw a more complete route. Horsemen, Infantry, Guns and all mixed together running like a flock of sheep, and our fellows knocking them over in dozens. . . .[56]

Scott reported, "Again we felt the loss of cavalry, and the effect of our previous fatiguing march." He noted because the British "were unable to pursue [the Americans], . . . the scattered forces effected their escape with a comparatively trifling loss of prisoners."[57]

Stricker's militiamen may have retreated but, despite British claims to the contrary, they were not completely routed and scattered as were the militia

Musket ball from the North Point battlefield

The musket ball showing teeth marks, evidence of its use in the field hospital at the meetinghouse for men to "bite the bullet" during surgery.

Courtesy Kathy Erlandson Liston and the Samuel D. Harris National Museum of Dentistry

after Bladensburg. They were still a fighting unit. Although bruised in the fight, they remained largely intact to face the British again as they neared the city. Moreover, they had taken a toll on the British forces. The British casualty figures show that the battle was a costly one to the invaders. By their own official reports, they lost 46 killed and 295 wounded. By contrast, the Americans had approximately half those amounts in killed and wounded. A report published three months after the battle in the *Niles' Weekly Register* claimed only 24 Americans killed and 139 wounded, and 50 Americans made prisoner (some of the wounded were prisoners who were exchanged two days after the battle). One of the American dead was elderly Uriah Prosser, the shoemaker and Revolutionary War veteran, who had volunteered as a private to defend his city.[58]

Because his Redcoats were exhausted from the battle and the hot weather, Brooke camped for the night on the battlefield. The Methodist meetinghouse was converted into a hospital for both sides. At midnight, heavy rain began to drench the British troops, who were camping in the open without tents. The men did what they could to protect the firelocks of their muskets, wrapping leather cases around the firelocks or keeping them dry under their elbows. The greatest fear was that the incessant rain would swell their musket stocks and prevent the muskets from firing. This was also a problem eight months later at Waterloo, where a torrential downpour soaked the battlefield on the morning of the battle.[59]

By dawn on September 13, when the companies formed to march the rest of the way to Baltimore, the rain was still falling in a deluge. For the Redcoats, their general dead, it must have been a dispiriting trudge along muddy, rutted roads. Progress was not aided by the fact that the Americans had chopped down trees at intervals to impede their progress. Gleig reported that they had to stop constantly for their "pioneers" to remove the felled trees. Even though the troops were only going seven miles, the march was so slow that the main body of the British did not reach the vicinity of the American entrenchments until evening.[60]

When the troops began their march, the Royal Navy positioned their bombardment vessels in order to begin the assault on Fort McHenry. The Royal Navy had performed the brilliant feat of kedging their bomb vessels, rocket ship, and other small war vessels over the shoals of the Patapsco. Admiral Cochrane had transferred his broad pennant to the frigate *Surprize* in order to move close enough to command the bombardment. Key, Skinner, and Beanes had been transferred to the truce vessel in which Key and Skinner had sailed to obtain Dr. Beanes' release. They would be forced to watch the bombardment, their truce vessel under the guns of British warships off Old Roads Bay.[61]

In a letter to his wife, captain of the fleet Rear Adm. Sir Edward Codrington expressed delight that at last the rascals of Baltimore would be attacked by both land and sea:

> The work of destruction is now about to begin, and there will probably be many broken heads tonight. . . . The bomb vessels, brigs, and frigates are

all pushing up the river with an eagerness which must annoy the enemy, I presume, as much as it delights me. Three frigates are aground abreast of us, hauling themselves over the banks into deep water by main strength, each trying to surpass the other. . . . I do not like to contemplate scenes of blood and destruction; but my heart is deeply interested in the coercion of these Baltimore heroes, who are perhaps the most inveterate against us of all the Yankees.[62]

At 6:00 A.M. on September 13, five bomb ships and other vessels of war maneuvered into line abreast of Fort McHenry two and three-quarter miles out from the fort. A half hour later, the bomb ship *Volcano* fired two mortar shells toward the fort to check the range. The shells fell short, and *Volcano* moved closer. The bombardment squadron formed a semicircle two miles out from the fort. The deadly long guns of the French warship *L'Eole,* mounted in the fort in the spring of 1813, prevented the British coming closer. As the bombardment began, Sailing Master Beverly Diggs and a team of flotillamen hastily sunk more merchant vessels in the channel between the fort and the Lazaretto Point. The work was done, with little thought of who owned the vessels or what might be in them; court cases would ensue for years afterward. The bomb vessels *Aetna, Devastation, Meteor, Terror,* and *Volcano* commenced their bombardment of Fort McHenry. The bombs were immediately answered by brisk fire from the fort's batteries.[63]

Major Armistead later estimated that in the next 25 hours the British would hurl at the fort 1,500 to 1,800 of the spherical 10- and 13-inch exploding shells. A few fell short or long, while some burst directly over the fort, threatening to shower destruction on the defenders. About four hundred actually landed within the ramparts damaging buildings and wounding and killing men. In addition to the bomb ships, each of which fired about five bombs an hour, the British schooner *Cockchafer* opened up on the fort along with the rocket ship *Erebus.* The American artillerymen scored a success at 8:40 A.M. when one of their cannonballs ripped through the mainsail of *Cockchafer.* Admiral Cochrane then withdrew the *Cockchafer* and *Erebus* leaving the work to the bomb vessels which, when moved back out of the range of Armistead's guns, could still rain terror on the fort.[64]

The Reverend James Stevens, a Methodist preacher, wrote to his sister in Pennsylvania to tell her of the panic caused by the British onslaught:

I do not feel able to paint out the distress and confusion half as it was with us—to see the wagons, carts and drays, all in haste moving the people, and the poorer sort with what they could carry and their children on their backs flying for their lives while I could plainly see the British Sail which was engaged in a severe fire on our fort for 24 Hours. I could see them fire and the Bombs lite and burst on the Shore at which explosions the whole town and several miles out would shake. . . .[65]

The fiery assault on Fort McHenry continued long into the morning and afternoon. By evening, with the naval bombardment still shaking the ground,

"Bombardment of Fort McHenry, Sept. 13–14, 1814."

Painting, ca. 1830, by Alfred Jacob Miller,
courtesy of the Maryland Historical Society

Colonel Brooke and his advance British troops came to within two miles of the city trenches. The sight was not encouraging: the colonel saw a strong line of entrenchments and in front of them, a stretch of open farmland almost all cleared of cover. The American preparations hardly bespoke the "inept" militia that Cockburn had spoken about so often. Nevertheless, Brooke later wrote in his diary:

> I . . . reconnoitred him, and found his left was not so secure, and that by making a night attack, I might gain his flank, and get into his rear, so came to a resolution of attacking him in two Columns, whilst the third was to make a feint on his right.[66]

General Smith observed Brooke's reconnoitering column moving toward the left of his defenses "as if with the intention of making a circuitous march and coming down on the York or Harford roads." He immediately ordered Stricker with his 3rd Brigade and Winder with the Virginia Brigade into action. He ordered them "to adapt their movements to those of the enemy, so as to baffle his supposed intention." The major general said the two generals "executed this order with great skill and judgement" forcing Brooke back to a position in front of the entrenchments. The colonel's advance troops came within a mile of the Hampstead Hill trenches, driving in the American pickets. Smith realized that the British commander showed every sign of planning to attack him that night.[67]

Indeed, Brooke had formed his plan to attack at three in the morning when the militia would likely be lulled into complacency.[68] This was a good plan. It is true that the contemporary military thinker Claus von Clausewitz cautioned against night attacks.[69] Yet, Brooke's men *were* after all professionals with battle experience. They might be expected to succeed whereas the American amateur soldiers might be expected to panic.

That panic which could easily have occurred among at least some of the militiamen is graphically shown in the diary of Capt. Matthias Bartgis of the 16th Regiment of militia from Frederick in western Maryland:

> There was an unfortunate incident happened, during our march this night [to Fort McHenry] . . . as our company had just passed the Eastern bridge in Baltimore street, a great confusion was discovered in front of us. The night was very dark. . . . The 3rd regiment, in front of us, became confused in consequence of a team of horses approaching them, in full drive, . . . when some of the officers and men, becoming alarmed, not knowing what was meant by it, while the women, who took alarm from the confusion in the street came running out of their houses crying the British! the British! Oh, the British! And officers and men whom fear had operating on, supposing it to be an attack from the British took to their heels. . . . All the companies to the right and some on the left of us broke, but our company, not knowing and not caring, what was the matter, stood the shock with firmness and not a man moved from the ranks. . . . In . . . this disgraceful affair . . . some of the deserters fled and reported that the enemy had attacked the whole line on Horseback. . . . As it was, some were never seen in Camp afterwards.[70]

But the feared attack by the Redcoats would not happen. The bombardment of Fort McHenry was not going as the cocky Royal Navy admirals had anticipated. Against the odds, Armistead and his garrison of defenders in the Star Fort still held out. At 8:00 P.M., a messenger arrived at Brooke's camp with a letter for Admiral Cockburn from Cochrane, in which the commander in chief indicated his inability to assist the army. The channel leading to the harbor was too well blocked. The Royal Navy could not force a passage past the fort in order to bombard the entrenchments as Cochrane had planned. The Americans at Baltimore were much better prepared to resist his forces than he could have dreamed possible. Now he was afraid that if the army attacked Baltimore and suffered serious losses that might cause problems for other projects he had in mind, notably the capture of New Orleans.

Cochrane ended his letter to Cockburn with the words:

> it is for Colonel Brooke to consider . . . whether he has force sufficient to defeat so large a number as it is said the enemy have collected, within say twenty thousand strong, and to take the town, without this can be done, it will be only throwing the men's lives away. . . .[71]

In his diary, Brooke recorded the dilemma he faced: "If I took the place, I should have been the greatest man in England. If I lost, my military character was gone for ever."[72]

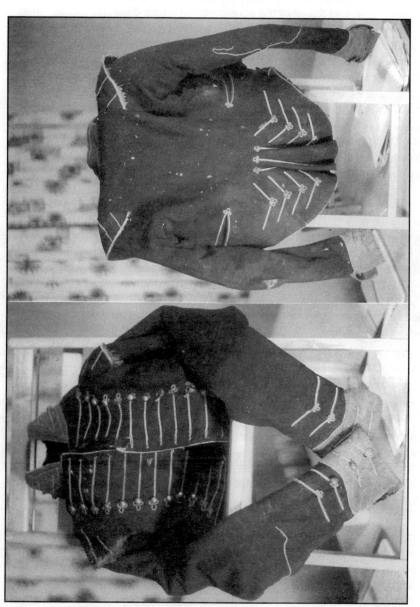

Uniform of Sgt. Jacob Huyett

Captain Barr's cavalry company, 1st District, Washington County—a western Marylander who came to the aid of Baltimore

Courtesy Ross Kimmel and the Washington County Historical Society

150   *Chapter Ten*

In his usual aggressive way, Cockburn urged that an attack be attempted. He told Brooke that his seamen had volunteered to storm the American lines. But the colonel was less sure of the success of an attack if the navy could not help by simultaneously bombarding the entrenchments. The assault would be hazardous at best in the dark and with the slippery conditions after the hours of rain. Brooke disliked the idea that he might be responsible for the deaths of hundreds if not thousands of men or that he might be held accountable for damaging other schemes the commander in chief was planning. He called a meeting of his staff. The army men wrangled for hours about whether to chance the attack. Eventually, at midnight, a beleaguered Brooke wrote to Cochrane that the "Council of War" had advised that he should retire. He said, "I have therefore ordered a retreat to take place tomorrow morning and hope to be at my destination the day after tomorrow—that is, the place we disembarked from."[73]

Although many among the British grumbled that an attack was not attempted, logic says that the right choice was made. Brooke almost undoubtedly avoided a slaughter on the order of that seen in New Orleans on January 8, 1815. In that battle, the British suffered 2,057 casualties when they tried to assault the trenches manned by Maj. Gen. Andrew Jackson's army. By contrast, in that battle, the Americans only suffered 13 dead.[74]

Lieutenant Gleig wrote to his mother that all appeared ready for the planned night attack when he learned that instead of assaulting the trenches they would withdraw:

> when the order was given to fall in, and we were all in high hopes of obtaining *death or immortal honor,* to our great mortification we found the troops formed on the main road for a retreat. This was commenced at 4 o'clock A.M. in the best order, and finished without the loss of a single man or even a musket.[75]

Employing the same tactic they used on their retreat from Washington, the Redcoats built fires and stole away into the night.

Cochrane, not knowing Brooke had already decided to withdraw, ordered a last-ditch attempt to try to end the stalemate. He ordered Capt. Charles Napier of H.M.S. *Euryalus* to attempt a landing near the fort. Cochrane instructed Napier to

> row up close to the [western] shores . . . about one or one and a half miles. . . . and remain perfectly quiet until one o'clock, at which hour the Bombs will open upon the fort and sky rockets will be thrown up when you will begin a regular fire. . . . This is intended to take off the attention of the enemy opposite to where our army is and an attack [that] is to be made upon their lines directly at two o'clock. . . .[76]

Napier's attempt to save British credibility was foiled by the vigilance of Sailing Master John A. Webster, one of Commodore Barney's flotillamen. Webster commanded Fort Babcock, one of the small earthen-walled batteries to the

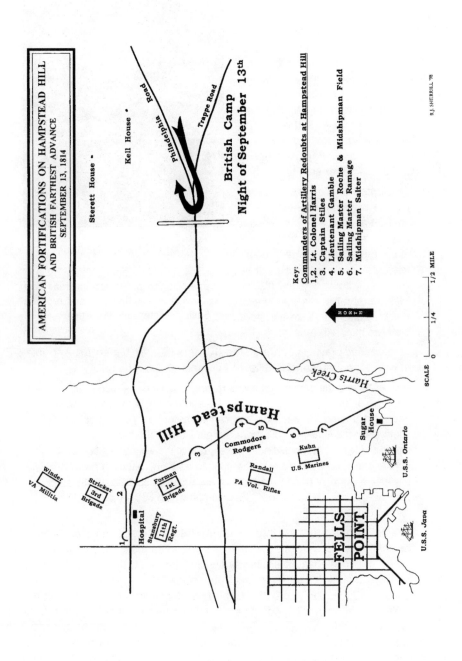

AMERICAN FORTIFICATIONS ON HAMPSTEAD HILL
AND BRITISH FARTHEST ADVANCE
SEPTEMBER 13, 1814

Sterett House

Kell House

Philadelphia Road

Trappe Road

British Camp
Night of September 13th

Key:
Commanders of Artillery Redoubts at Hampstead Hill
1,2. Lt. Colonel Harris
3. Captain Stiles
4. Lieutenant Gamble
5. Sailing Master Roche & Midshipman Field
6. Sailing Master Ramage
7. Midshipman Salter

NORTH

SCALE 0 1/4 1/2 MILE

R.J. SHERRILL '98

Harris Creek

Hampstead Hill

Winder
VA Militia

Stricker
3rd
Brigade

Forman
1st
Brigade

Commodore
Rodgers

Randall
PA Vol. Rifles

Kuhn
U.S. Marines

Sugar
House

U.S.S. Ontario

Hospital

Stansbury
11th
Regt.

FELLS
POINT

U.S.S. Java

west of Fort McHenry. He had previously helped man Barney's battery at Bladensburg, which gave the British so much trouble in the closing stages of that battle. It was therefore only fitting that he set the seal on denying the enemy the capture of Baltimore.[77]

On that cold, rainy night, when other men might have let their minds wander, Webster detected a line of British barges attempting to enter the ferry branch. Webster said later,

> I could hear a splashing in the water. The attention of the others was aroused and we were convinced it was the noise of the muffled oars of the British barges. Very soon afterwards we could discern small gleaming lights in different places. I felt sure that it was the barges, which at that time were not more than two hundred yards off.[78]

Capt. Charles Napier
(1786–1860)

Napier led the barge attack near Fort McHenry that was detected and repelled by Sailing Master John Webster.

Collection of the Author

Webster had previously ordered the six cannons in his battery to be double-shotted with 18-pound cannonballs and grapeshot. Now, he said,

> I . . . examined the priming, as it was raining fast. All being right I trained the guns and opened on them, which caused the boats to cease rowing and a rapid firing followed from the barges, as well as from ourselves. I could distinctly hear the balls from our guns strike the barges. My men stated to me that they could hear the shrieks of the wounded. Soon after I commenced firing, Fort Covington opened on them, although they had not gotten up to it. During the firing of the enemy, I could distinctly see their barges by the explosion of their cannon which was a great guide to me to fire by.[79]

The flotillaman could see that the enemy had 22 barges and a long schooner. The schooner was mounted with an 18-pound cannon, which could have severely damaged Webster's small mud-walled fort—but, as he put it, "They fired too high, their shots taking effect in the bank."[80]

The other American gun batteries and Fort McHenry itself opened on the invaders and beat back the landing party. Despite being in severe pain from a twice-broken shoulder, Webster bravely stayed in command of his battery. The initial injury came about when he found one of his sailors, "an obstinate Englishmen," as he termed him, attempting to lay a train of powder to the magazine. Webster said, "I laid him out for dead with a handspike," but in doing so he injured himself severely.[81]

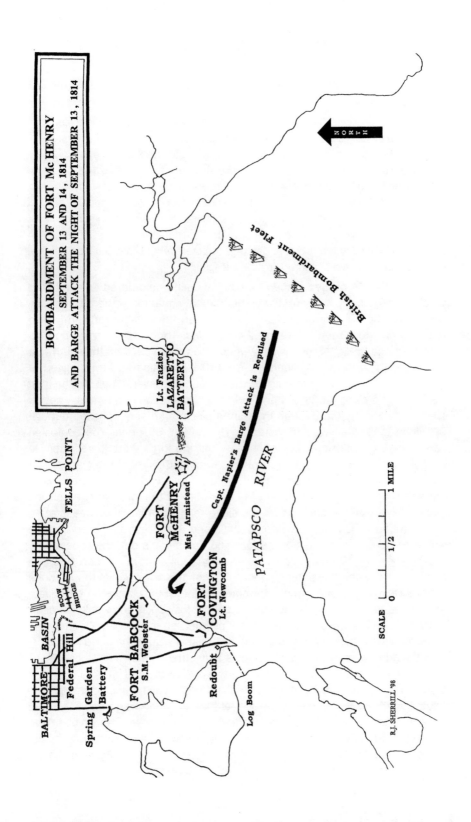

BOMBARDMENT OF FORT McHENRY
SEPTEMBER 13 AND 14, 1814
AND BARGE ATTACK THE NIGHT OF SEPTEMBER 13, 1814

NORTH

British Bombardment Fleet

Lt. Frazier
LAZARETTO
BATTERY

FELLS POINT

FORT
McHENRY
Maj. Armistead

Capt. Napier's Barge Attack is Repulsed

PATAPSCO RIVER

BALTIMORE

BASIN

Federal Hill

Spring Garden Battery

SCOW
BRIDGE

FORT BABCOCK
S.M. Webster

FORT
COVINGTON
Lt. Newcomb

Redoubt

Log Boom

SCALE

0   1/2   1 MILE

R.J. SHERRILL '98

In his report to Secretary Monroe, Major Armistead described the repulse of Napier's landing attempt:

> it was discovered that [the British] . . . had thrown a considerable force above to our right; they had approached very near to Fort Covington, when they began to throw rockets; intended, I assume to give them an opportunity of examining the shores—as I have since understood, they had detached 1,250 picked men, with scaling ladders, for the purpose of storming the fort. We once more had the opportunity of opening our batteries, and kept up a continued blaze for nearly two hours. . . . One of [their] sunken barges has since been found with two dead men in it—others have been seen floating in the river. . . . Had they ventured to the same situation in the day time, not a man would have escaped.[82]

At 7:00 A.M. on September 14, Admiral Cochrane ordered an end to the bombardment of the fort, and the bombardment squadron withdrew. Remarkably, given the number of shells the British had fired at the fort, Armistead reported only four men killed and 24 wounded. The worst damage had occurred around 2:00 P.M. on Tuesday when a bomb exploded on the southwest bastion, dismounting a 24-pounder. The explosion killed Lt. Levi Claggett of Captain Nicholson's volunteer artillery and wounded several men. As the men were trying to clear the debris and help their wounded compatriots, another shell came zooming in through the rain. A piece of shrapnel passed through Sgt. John Clemm killing him instantly. The British, observing the confusion caused by the explosions, came in closer but the fort's guns forced them to retreat once again. Then, a bomb crashed through the roof of the magazine. A quick-thinking defender doused the fuse and Armistead ordered the powder barrels taken out and scattered at the rear walls of the fort. Worry about the magazine as well as tension over the siege rendered him ill for weeks afterward. Around 3:00 P.M., three bomb ships and the rocket ship *Erebus* came within one and a half miles of the fort, and Armistead's batteries opened up with all they had. The bomb ship *Devastation* took a hit in her port bow and started to leak, and her sister ship *Volcano* took five straight hits though none serious. Despite this punishment, the commanders of the bombardment squadron wanted to go in close to shore and blast the fort. Cochrane would not allow it. He needed his ships and men for his planned attack on New Orleans, the same reason he cautioned Colonel Brooke about attacking the entrenchments. Now the admiral recalled his bomb ships altogether. The siege was over.[83]

As the squadron retreated down river, Major Armistead ordered the small storm flag that had flown during the bombardment to be hauled down. His men hauled up the huge flag 42 feet by 30 feet that Mary Pickersgill had sewn. The fort's band struck up with "Yankee Doodle." Eight miles down river, on board the truce vessel in Old Roads Bay, Francis Scott Key was intensely moved by the end of the bombardment and the sight of the huge flag waving above the battlements. On the back of an envelope, he jotted down the words of a poem. He

By the Dawn's Early Light

Painting by E. Percy Moran,
courtesy Star-Spangled Banner Flag House

called the poem, "The Defense of Fort McHenry," but his composition would be soon known to the world by a more famous title: "The Star-Spangled Banner."[84]

As the bombardment fleet kedged its way back down the Patapsco, Colonel Brooke's bedraggled troops trudged back to their ships. During their withdrawal, the troops crossed over the North Point battleground where they had fought Stricker's force. The dead lay where they had fallen. Lieutenant Gleig noted that the bodies appeared not to have been stripped, unlike the dead at Bladensburg they had seen on the morning of August 26.[85]

Some American riflemen hung in the trees where they had been shot. The British, upset at the way American sharpshooters concealed themselves in trees, felt they had got their just desserts. The *honorable* and only way to fight, they reasoned, was to fight in the open as they had been taught.[86]

General Smith has been criticized for not launching a full-scale attack on the retreating British. The only blow struck against the retreating Redcoats was a late harassing cavalry charge which netted a handful of prisoners. Smith was lobbied by officers who wanted to attack the invaders. The general replied that there was an ancient saying, "Make a bridge for a retreating enemy," in which he thought there was much wisdom. If the enemy were disposed to retreat, he said, he would not impose any obstacle. Smith remarked that to pit the citizens of the United States against the "hirelings of Britain" was like "staking dollars against cents."[87] In the end, Smith did the smartest thing possible and waved Brooke and his bedraggled Redcoats good-bye.

"The Flag Was Full of Stars."

Maj. George Armistead and his triumphant garrison raise the Star-Spangled Banner above Fort McHenry on the morning of September 14, 1814.

Painting by Dale Gallon, courtesy of The Patriots of Fort McHenry

Epilogue

The British departed, bloodied by their experience at Baltimore and hardly the victorious army that had captured Washington only three weeks earlier. They had suffered losses both in casualties and prestige.

In his official report on the operations at Baltimore, Admiral Cochrane tried to pretend that he had not planned a real attack on Baltimore. He and Ross, he wrote later, had decided to make "a demonstration on the city of Baltimore, which might be converted into a real attack, should circumstances appear to justify it. . . ." In other words, the admiral had only planned a grand fireworks display to impress the Baltimoreans. Capt. Robert Rowley of the troopship *Melpomene* scoffed, "The general term of the Affair is a Reconnaissance."[1] There were more than 50 dead British, including General Ross, and four times as many wounded to prove these British obfuscations to be a big lie. Moreover, in addition to the blood they spilled at Baltimore, the British had expended thousands of tons in firepower.

The failure of the attack did little to modify the superior attitudes of most of the British. They ascribed the death of Ross and the turning back of the attack to "bad luck" and as no tribute to American military skill. Yet, at least one British serviceman viewed the situation differently. Young Lt. Gordon Gollie MacDonald of the Royal Navy with a dozen sailors had the grim task of transporting the body of General Ross down to the beach on the afternoon of September 12. He said the general's servant was "leading a magnificent black horse, the animal actually appearing as if conscious of his loss." The lieutenant wrote that he was not sorry to leave the Patapsco. He added, "These Americans are not to be trifled with—"[2]

In Baltimore, citizens celebrated a great victory. Francis Scott Key, freed to return home after his time aboard the truce ship, showed brother-in-law Judge

158

Joseph H. Nicholson the poem he had written about the defense of Fort McHenry. Shortly, his verses would be set to music, to the tune of an English-drinking song, "To Anacreon in Heaven." Within weeks, the fame of the song spread throughout the land. Key's composition, written in the aftermath of the harrowing enemy onslaught, would be the future United States national anthem, "The Star-Spangled Banner."[3]

Pres. James Madison in his address to the U.S. Congress on September 20 was able to exult that the enemy attack on Baltimore "was received with a spirit which produced a rapid retreat. . . ." He noted that a powerful British attack on Plattsburgh, New York, by Canadian Governor Sir George Prevost was also repulsed at the same time.[4]

Despite the apparent triumph of Ross and Cockburn at Washington, world opinion quickly turned against the British for their incendiary actions in the American capital. President Madison forecast this twist of fate in his address to Congress:

> In the events of the present campaign the enemy. . . . will find . . . transient success, . . . [but] no compensation for the loss of character with the world by his violations of private property and by his destruction of public edifices protected as monuments of the arts by the laws of civilized warfare.[5]

Moreover, the American defensive triumph at Baltimore and the defeat of Prevost at Plattsburgh had a direct effect on the peace negotiations in Ghent, Belgium. British negotiator Henry Goulburn realized the grimness of the situation. Because the attack on Baltimore "did not terminate in the capture of the town," he wrote, "[it] will be considered by the Americans as a victory, and not as an escape." If the British had burned Baltimore, he thought peace might have been achieved within a month. "As things appear to be going on in America," he forecast, "the result of our negotiations may be very different."[6]

British Prime Minister Lord Liverpool lamented that the "success" at Baltimore had been "dearly bought" by the death of Maj. Gen. Robert Ross. He expressed regret that "such large reinforcements" had been sent to Prevost, whom he said had managed the northern campaign "as ill as possible." If the troops had been given to Ross instead, he thought the general "might have taken possession of every considerable town in America south of Philadelphia."[7] This rosy scenario ignored that Ross had two horses shot from under him at Washington and lost his life in the firefight preceding the Battle of North Point. If Prevost was an ineffective commander, possibly Ross, though undoubtedly a brilliant and brave officer, was foolhardy.

Liverpool asked the Duke of Wellington for his opinion of the state of affairs of the North American campaign. The Iron Duke frankly pointed to the British failures. They had not, he said, won naval superiority on the Great Lakes or captured any territory. His advice was to conclude peace with the Americans.[8]

The troops that had retreated from Baltimore lingered on board the ships in the Chesapeake for three weeks. On September 19, Lieutenant Gleig noted

"John Bull and the Baltimoreans."

A contemporary cartoon by William Charles poking fun at the British retreat from Baltimore.

Collection of the Author

in his diary that a court-martial was held on board the *Royal Oak* to decide the fate of two seamen accused of desertion. The following day, the sailors were hanged from the yardarm of the *Royal Oak*.[9]

Desertion was a chronic problem for the British while they were in the Chesapeake but possibly more so for the fleet than for the army due to the harsh discipline in the Royal Navy. For the Americans, desertions likewise posed a major problem. Considerable numbers of militiamen deserted both before and after the Battle of Baltimore. In a letter of September 20, Brig. Gen. Thomas M. Forman, commander of the 1st Maryland Brigade made up of Cecil and Harford County troops of an estimated 2,900 men, possibly the rawest and least steady of the brigades defending Baltimore, mentioned the post-Battle of Baltimore desertions to his wife. He lamented, "A great many of my Brigade have deserted, . . . and nearly all, are extreem[ly] anxious to return to their homes."[10]

On October 4, the British made a landing on the Potomac to attack a force of militia said to be at Northumberland Courthouse. A battalion of Royal Marines landed at Nomini Bay while the 21st Regiment and 44th Regiment under Brooke landed at Coan Bay. They could not locate the rumored militia but came under fire from Col. Thomas D. Downing's 27th Regiment of Virginia Militia before returning to their ships, with the loss of one man and two wounded. In mid-October, the invasion force quit the Chesapeake entirely and sailed for Jamaica.[11] It was not, however, an end to the British presence in the bay. The Royal Navy continued to blockade the Chesapeake until the war's end. British depredations continued, particularly in the southern bay. All the same, never again would they menace any large town or city in the region.

This more tentative approach by the enemy was recognized by Brig. Gen. John H. Cocke in reporting on a British raid on Tappahannock, Virginia, on December 4, 1814:

> The plundering of the Enemy has been confined . . . [to] a few plantations. Indeed, his whole course has been marked with the most circumspect caution and evident alarm. He has never trusted himself on land a single night.[12]

Cocke said that he understood the British intent "was to harass the Militia." The following day, a British incursion was repulsed in the Battle of North Farnham Church. Royal Marines landed near the mouth of the Rappahannock River and advanced within 12 miles of Warsaw. Capt. Vincent Shackleford's artillery company of the 41st Regiment of Virginia militia from Richmond County opposed the invaders near the church. Although Shackleford himself was severely wounded and captured, the militiamen drove the British back to their ships.[13]

On Christmas Eve, 1814, Great Britain made peace with the United States at Ghent, approximately three months after the ignominious withdrawal from Baltimore.[14]

The British maintained a presence on Tangier Island until word of the signing of the treaty reached the Chesapeake in mid-February. On February 7, 1815, two British barges were captured when they became grounded and hemmed in by ice on Maryland's Eastern Shore off the mouth of Parson's Creek near Cambridge in the so-called "Battle of the Ice Mound." Companies of the 48th Regiment of Maryland militia under Lt. Col. John Jones rounded up Lt. Matthew Phipps, a midshipman, 12 sailors, and three Royal Marines. They also secured a 12-pound carronade, a swivel gun, and the small arms of the British landing parties from the two barges. This was the last incident of any significance of the war in the Chesapeake Bay.[15]

The news of the peace reached New York on February 11, brought personally by Henry Carroll, secretary to American negotiator Henry Clay. Carroll sailed into New York harbor aboard the British sloop of war *Favourite* flying a flag of truce. At 4:00 P.M. on February 14 Carroll arrived by coach in Washington, D.C. He delivered the glad tidings to President Madison at the interim presidential mansion at the Octagon House at 18th Street and New York Avenue. The capital went wild with joy. Church bells rang, cannons fired, and rockets were fired into the skies.[16]

In Baltimore, the *Niles' Weekly Register* announced the news with the words, "Long live the republic! All hail! Last asylum of oppressed humanity!" The same paper had cause to exult again in April when the privateer *Chasseur*, victor of a February 27 engagement with the British schooner *St. Lawrence*, swept into Baltimore harbor. Capt. Thomas Boyle ordered the schooner's cannons to be fired to salute the fort that six months earlier had withstood the might of the Royal Navy. The newspaper reported that the famed privateer was universally acclaimed the "Pride of Baltimore."[17] Baltimore could justly claim to be a city that had beaten the British on land and sea.

Symbolic of Baltimore's triumph

The Battle Monument which was begun in 1815, commemorating the 41 Americans who died at North Point and Fort McHenry, was as famous in its day as was the new patriotic song called "The Star-Spangled Banner."

Courtesy Star-Spangled Banner Flag House

Appendix One
Rear Adm. George Cockburn, Terrorizer of the Chesapeake

American newspapers during the war and for decades afterwards castigated Cockburn as a "negro stealer," a firebrand, a pirate, and a brigand. Yet he was also, if grudgingly, acknowledged as a formidable enemy. In the winter of 1813–1814, rumors circulated that Cockburn would be named overall British commander for the coming campaign. If that were indeed to happen, it was thought, Cockburn would endeavor "to do all the harm he could." There was even a story that when he first arrived in the bay the admiral had cunningly disguised himself as a common fisherman and talked his way on board the *Constellation*. Using such subterfuge, the story went, Cockburn succeeded in obtaining "all and every information he wished to acquire" about the U.S. Navy frigate.[1]

As a commander and as a man, Cockburn elicited widely divergent opinions even among men on his own side. While one junior Royal Navy man thought that the admiral was as decisive as Nelson, army man Lt. Col. Charles Napier thought him reckless.[2] When Cockburn transported the deposed emperor Napoleon to exile on St. Helena in 1815, one of the emperor's aides found the admiral to be "capricious, irascible, vain, and overbearing."[3]

Midshipman Frederick Chamier described Cockburn as "a very austere man." He related a story in which Cockburn threatened to burn a house in southern Maryland despite the tearful protests of three young ladies. Having determined that the house belonged to a colonel of militia, Cockburn declared, "In ten minutes' time, I shall set fire to this house" and suggested they use the time to remove their "most valuable effects." Then the admiral—"his countenance unchanged and unchangeable"—coolly placed his watch on the table. When 10 minutes had expired, the sailors were ordered to bring fireballs (ropeyarns covered in pitch) to set fire to the house. Then Cockburn "walked out with his usual haughty stride, followed by the two eldest girls, who . . . vainly implored him to countermand the order." Chamier concluded, "By the light of [the burning] house we embarked. . . ."[4]

Morriss provides insight into Cockburn's disdain for the American militia. He states, "The guerrilla warfare practiced by the local inhabitants . . . seemed dishonourable to Cockburn."[5] This aids us in understanding why, for example, Havre de Grace was treated so severely after its militia had showed an American flag and fired a gun. In a private memorandum on his career, Cockburn noted,

> [The Americans] took every opportunity of firing with their rifles from behind trees or haystacks, or from the windows of their houses upon our boats, whenever rowing along the shore within their reach, or upon our people when employed watering. . . . in short, whenever they thought they could get a mischievous shot at any of our people without being seen or exposed to personal risk in return.[6]

As a result of these provocations, Morriss says, Cockburn "felt justified in adopting and publicising a policy of strict retribution."[7] Cockburn felt that his policy reduced such sniping incidents. Indeed, the admiral bragged that the people of the Chesapeake "suffered perhaps less real loss and inconvenience than was ever experienced by people inhabiting a country made the theater of hostile operations."[8]

After the British withdrawal from Baltimore, Cockburn was not included in the plans to attack New Orleans. Although the four British army regiments that had arrived in the Chesapeake with Ross were part of the invasion force for New Orleans, supplemented with other regiments, Cockburn and the Colonial Marines were excluded from the expedition. As a result, in early 1815, he and the Colonial Marines were operating out of a base on Cumberland Island, Georgia, conducting raids on the Carolina and Georgia coasts. Although the British suffered the reverse at New Orleans, until word of the peace treaty reached him, it was Cockburn's expectation that he would be ordered to cooperate with Indians in western Florida, southern Alabama, and Louisiana to further prosecute the war against the Americans. Cognizant of his reputation among Americans, and even proud of it, he wrote, "I think the savage Cockburn, as I am termed among my Yankee neighbours, when joined by the Indians will create no small consternation in the country. . . ."[9]

Appendix Two
British Atrocities or Yankee Propaganda?

There can be no doubt of the excesses committed in June 1813 at Hampton, Virginia, by the "Canadian Chasseurs" or French former prisoners of war in the employ of the British. Those outrages were well documented by both the Americans and British (see chapter 5). However, what of the other outrages of which the British were accused of committing?

At Chaptico in southern Maryland, which was raided by Cockburn on July 30, 1814, did the British *really* stable their horses in the church? Did they smash tiles and windows and use the communion table as a dinner table, before smashing it? Did they use sunken graves as barbecue pits? Did they break open graves looking for treasure? Did they, as charged, open the Key vault, and tear the winding sheet off the corpse of the wife of Judge Philip Key? Did several British officers actually make some of the young women of the neighborhood strip naked in front of them and make them stand in front of them for an hour and a half? Did they, before departing, fill in the town wells? All of these "atrocities" were charged in a letter to the anti-British *National Intelligencer* on August 4, five days after the raid.[1]

Historian Donald Shomette says that these accusations seem ghoulish even for the British. He also notes that Cockburn had few if any horses that would need to be stabled.[2] On the other hand, the alleged activities at Chaptico appear to match those at Havre de Grace on May 3, 1813, where St. John's Episcopal Church was vandalized, and at Tappahannock, Virginia, on December 4, 1814, where a family vault "was broken into and the coffins searched."[3]

Among the acts of "willful destruction" of which the British stand accused are allegations that they intentionally killed and maimed animals. At Specutie Island at the end of April 1813, Cockburn's men are said to have willfully slaughtered cattle and sheep grazing there. Moreover, at Havre de Grace, it is said,

166

"They cut hogs through the back, and some partly through, and then left them to run." However, in his contemporary account, Wilmer reports no such wanton destruction of animals on Specutie Island or such cruelty to animals at Havre de Grace. He says that on Specutie Island the British paid for the cattle they took. Moreover, he makes a point of commenting on the good behavior of the British on the island compared with their acts elsewhere.[4]

Operating as they were in a foreign bay, the British were desperately in need of provisions. Would they really have slaughtered what they could carry off to eat?

When I discussed these incidents with researcher and archeologist Kathy Lee Erlandson, she thought that perhaps where such outrages actually occurred it was a case of "blood-lust." In other words, the raiders were caught up in a rollercoaster of destruction. Such wanton destruction could have been carried out either with the approval of their officers or (if without approval) by men who were out of control. In either case, the acts fitted into the general British plan to create havoc in the bay.

Cockburn's recent biographer Roger Morriss admits that "some seamen, marines and soldiers who landed did behave with abandon." However, he maintains, "there is evidence that Cockburn did attempt to check excesses, with a determination to punish offenders."[5]

That officers often did not exercise full control over their men is indicated by an episode of pillaging that took place late in the war. The incident at the Jesuit chapel at St. Inigoes manor house, St. Mary's County, Maryland, well illustrates the type of havoc and misery that the British wreaked in the Chesapeake.

On October 30, 1814, a British naval raiding party from the sloop of war *Saracen* commanded by Capt. Alexander Dixie looted and vandalized the Jesuit chapel in the manor house. Next day, Brother Joseph P. Mobberly wrote to Father John Grassi of Georgetown College to tell of the calamity that had befallen the chapel. Mobberly said he had tried to remonstrate with the officer in charge of the raiding party that ransacked and vandalized it (most probably *not* Dixie though Mobberly refers to him as "Capt."):

> I ran to the Chapel, saw 4 or 5 ruffians at work, ran back & begged the Capt. to interfere. He ran with me & ordered them out. But Oh! painful to relate. The sacred vestments thrown & dragged here & there, the Vessels consecrated to the service of God prophaned, the holy altar stripped naked, the tabernacle carried off and the most adorable Sacrament of the altar borne away in the hands of the wicked. Great God what were my feelings. I entreated [the officer] over & over again to protect the Church & have all things restored. He promised he would. He instantly ran with me to the barge— He stormed & swore if they did not restore the sacred vessels, the Sacrament & vestments, he would have all their plunder thrown on shore & deprive them of it. Seeing the Chalice I pointed it out to him and observed it was sacred. He ordered it to be restored—I received it from the hands of a villain & turning to the Capt. observed: "What an indignity to

the church!" . . . After a short pause [the officer] replied: "Sir, the truth is, I did not come on shore to plunder—I came for stock; but I cannot command these men. They are nothing but real ruffians." . . . [I] begged him to restore the [sacred] vessels, etc. He promised he would, seated himself in the barge & ordered his men to move off without taking any more notice of us. . . . This is certainly the most outrageous attack that has been witnessed on our shores in the present war. The prophanation is distressing, our losses great. . . . The Cruets & plates were broken & scattered on the floor. . . . Never was there a mechanic more perfect in his trade than these villains. The whole was compleated in about 10 or 15 minutes. . . . Had nothing been said they would certainly have taken every article of any value that was in the House. They had no pity. They are men of no sensibility, they respect neither God nor man. Like ravenous blood hounds, they rushed forward with hellish fury, only intent on seizing their prey. . . .[6]

In a letter of November 14, Mobberly gave a long list of everything that had been stolen, making a total value of $1,033.70. On November 18, nearly three weeks after the incident, a British naval lieutenant came ashore under a flag of truce and restored a number of the stolen articles.

Included among the returned property was the "ciborium lined with gold," which Mobberly says he received "into my trembling hands." Indeed, he said "[I] fell on my knees . . . [before I] carried [it] . . . to the Chapel." The officer promised to hunt for the remaining articles. He gave Mobberly a British government bill for £22 and a piece of gold worth $9. He said a court-martial was being held to punish the men who ransacked the chapel. Mobberly was also given a letter from Captain Dixie. Dixie expressed regret about the incident, saying, "Such proceedings being unauthorized by me, I have taken the earliest opportunity of causing restitution to be made of the property so taken."[7]

Years later, Mobberly would write that a claim of $2,000 worth of damages done to forestry land on St. George's Island had been ignored by the British Parliament. He recalled, "[The British] set the Island on fire twice: 1st, to burn down all the houses, in order to deprive our militia of shelter; 2nd, to find two deserters who had hidden themselves in the high grass of the marshes." The Jesuit brother wrote with bitterness, "Eight years have since elapsed, and perhaps eight hundred more may pass away before justice will be done; thus showing that every nation as such, is just and honorable as the time and circumstances may suit its interest."[8]

Appendix Three

Napier's Plan to Use Ex-Slaves to win the War for the British

British army officer Lt. Col. (later General Sir) Charles Napier recorded in his memoirs that he proposed the following plan to the British command in 1813 to use former slaves to help win the war:

Seeing a black population of slaves ruled by a thin population of whites, the blacks thinking the English demi-gods [for liberating them] and their Yankee masters devils, I said to the authorities[,] "Give me two hundred thousand stand of arms, and land me in Virginia with only the officers and non-commissioned officers of three black regiments, that is to say about one hundred persons accustomed to drill black men. Let the ships with store of arms lay off while I strike into the woods with my drill men, my own regiment [the 102nd], and proclamations exciting the blacks to rise for freedom: forbidding them however to commit excesses under pain of being given up or hanged. The multitude of blacks who nightly come to our ships, and whom we drive back to death or renewed slavery, shews that we can in a week assemble a million—certainly one hundred thousand before any force could reach us, indeed before the American government can be aware of our descent, as we shall lie hidden in the forests until the influx of blacks discovers us. All the blacks can use arms, and in twelve hours can be organized in regiments and brigades. . . . When this vast mass shall be collected and armed, we shall roll down the coast, and our large fleet can pass us into the Delaware country, out of which we shall instantly chase the whole population. Then, with half our fleet in the Delaware River, with provisions in the Delaware country, and a handful of corn or rice is all a black slave will want for that occasion, we shall people the deserted space, set all the women and children to cultivate the ground,

169

and with our enormous mass of males, will have entrenched a position across the isthmus [i.e., between the Delaware River and the Chesapeake Bay] in twenty-four hours, for the fleet will supply us with tools, powder, cannon, engineers and marines." Such was my proposal, nothing could have approached us, and in a month a drilled army of two hundred thousand men, well appointed, would have been formed with one hundred thousand in reserve, to supply losses. At the head of that army I would have sallied from our lines and taken Washington, while Sir George Prevost from Canada followed the American army, which must perforce have retired on the first alarm either to the Indian country or to the south: the British force from Canada could then have joined my black force at Washington. . . . Had this plan been accepted, two things must have happened: we should have dictated peace, and abolished slavery in America![1]

Appendix Four

G. R. Gleig, British Chronicler of War in the Chesapeake

Even with his faults, which are many, George Robert Gleig remains the contemporary British chronicler *par excellence* of the British campaign for the Chesapeake in 1814. In his diary, his letters to his parents, and in two books, he has left an invaluable record of the events of August and September 1814.

Despite the fact that Gleig's views are probably better known from his much quoted books than from any other source, modern readers should understand that at the time of the events of the summer to fall 1814, Gleig was an 18-year-old subaltern, or second lieutenant, in the British 85th Regiment. His family letters and diary better reveal the immaturity of the man than do his books, where he strives to sound like a military strategist.

Indeed, the editor of the American edition of Gleig's best-known book, *Narrative of the Campaigns*, takes exception to a number of the author's statements. In an appendix to the American edition of the work, the editor seeks to correct a number of the writer's "principal mistakes."[1] For example, he points out confusion in Gleig's narrative in regard to the Battle of Bladensburg. Indeed, Gleig makes several explicit characterizations that the engagement at the bridge at Bladensburg was hard fought by the Americans. Gleig writes that "a continued fire was kept up," that the two-gun battery opened up on the British, "with tremendous effect" (such that "almost an entire company was swept down"), and that despite the advance of the British, the militiamen "stood firm" and even "advanced to recover the ground which was lost." Yet Gleig then goes on to discount that resistance entirely in his eagerness to note the bravery of Barney and his sailors. He remarks that "with the exception of a party of sailors from the gun-boats, under the command of Commodore Barney, no troops could behave worse than they did."[2] The critic validly notes that "if 'no troops could behave worse,' how was it . . . that the loss of the British on the

171

field, in killed and wounded, amounted, out of so small an army engaged, to not less than FIVE HUNDRED MEN!"[3]

In London, new editions were supposedly revised and corrected, although not of course to remove any of the writer's aspersions about his American foe. Indeed, the work changed little except to introduce further typographical mistakes (e.g., "Bain" instead of "Bean" for Dr. Beanes's name). Gleig's errors of judgement and fact are left intact. It is irritating to read that Gleig says the British landed at "St. Benedict's" on the Patuxent—rather than Benedict—and that Sir Peter Parker was killed "at a distance of a few miles from the banks of the Potomac, and about nine leagues below Alexandria"—not in Kent County, Maryland.[4]

Debate has lingered whether Gleig is also the author of *A Subaltern in America*.[5] This work appears to give a number of different incidents to those recounted in *Narrative of the Campaigns*. Although Walter Lord believed Gleig was the author of *Subaltern,* based on its similarities with the lieutenant's diary, a writer in the *Journal of the War of 1812* recently made a case that it was another British officer entirely. However, that same researcher later discovered that the Blackwood's files at the National Library of Edinburgh indicate that Gleig was indeed the author of this work. *Subaltern* originally appeared in Great Britain in serialized form in Blackwood's *Edinburgh Magazine* and when offering the work to the magazine, Gleig requested that his name never be revealed as the author.[6]

Historians should probably use the material in *Subaltern* with care. For example, we might note that the account of the wounding of General Ross at North Point in *Subaltern* diverges from the account that Gleig provides in his letters and diary and in the *Narrative of the Campaigns*. In *Subaltern,* the narrator *witnesses* the shooting, instead of coming on the scene afterward as in those other descriptions of the event.[7] This might indicate that *Subaltern* shows a tendency toward a more colorized if not to say fictionalized treatment. Possibly Gleig has supplemented his own experiences with those of fellow officers.

Gleig is at his best in describing private moments rather than meditating on grand military strategy. Possibly one of his most absurd pronouncements is when when he asserts in *Narrative of the Campaigns* that "had [Gen. Ross] lived, we should have fought two battles in one day."[8] And this in the heat of a late Maryland summer! But would Ross have attacked? Or would he have made the same decision that Colonel Brooke made—that to withdraw would be the better part of valor? As humane as Ross is said to have been, I doubt if he would have thrown his troops' lives away when he learned the Royal Navy could not force a way past Fort McHenry to bombard the American entrenchments on Hampstead Hill. He too would have recognized the determination of the defenders to expend their last ounce of courage to prevent the capture of their city.

Appendix Five

American "Dirty Tricks" during the War in the Chesapeake?

As mentioned in chapter 5, following a directive from Congress in spring 1813, Americans actively tried to blow up Royal Navy vessels with the use of "torpedoes." Although such attacks were not successful in the Bay, an attack on H.M.S. *Ramilies* off New London did succeed. The latter attack was characterized by one British Royal Navy captain who served in the Chesapeake as "[a] *most* dastardly method of carrying on the war." The same captain stated, "The endeavouring to destroy our men-of-war by torpedoes . . . [was] among the causes which led to our system of warfare."[1]

Another tactic that distressed the British was use of scrap metal as ammunition by the Americans. Lt. Col. Charles Napier complained:

> [The Americans] fight unfairly, firing jagged pieces of iron and every sort of devilment, nails, broken pokers, old locks of guns, gun-barrels, everything that will do mischief. On board a 20-gun ship that we took, I found this sort of ammunition regularly prepared. This is wrong. Man delights to be killed according to the law of nations. . . . A 24 lb. shot in the stomach is fine, we die heroically: but a brass candlestick for stuffing, with a garnish of rusty twopenny nails makes us die ungenteelly, and with the cholic.[2]

British officers in the Chesapeake constantly warned their men that any food and drink the men found might be poisoned. The British commanders complained of "poisoned" beverages and well water to their American counterparts in Virginia, southern Maryland, and during the Battle of Baltimore. Was the idea that the Yankees were deliberately trying to poison them just British paranoia?

American commanders hotly denied there was any plan to poison the British troops. In one such incident, poisoned whiskey is said to have been left enticingly on the porch of a house at Nomini, Virginia, in July 1814. After the British complained that an attempt had been made to deliberately poison them, Brig. Gen. John P. Hungerford of the Virginia militia told the governor of Virginia that he would immediately convene a court of enquiry, "deeming it essential to the character of our Arms as well as our persons to wash off completely so vile an imputation."[3]

Because the British complained about attempts at poisoning repeatedly, in different locales, one begins to wonder if there might have been some secret American plan to injure the British war effort on land, much as the "Yankee torpedoes" were meant to injure the British naval effort at sea. At least two alleged poisoning incidents took place after the British landing at North Point in September 1814. As reported by Lt. Christopher Claxton to Capt. Sir Thomas Hardy, in one of these incidents, Claxton said that an American deliberately tried to give poisoned liquor to a British sailor:

> Henry Dent a seaman attached to the small arm party of this ship [H.M.S. *Ramilies*] deposed that while looking for some hay for a bed he met a man in a drab colour coat with a pint bottle and asked him what it contained—told him it was spirits would he take some. Dent took the bottle and drank about a gill when some Marines making their appearance the stranger snatched the bottle from his mouth and ran hastily away into the wood close by. Dent came to me (he says in about half an hour after) in great pain and looking very ill. He stated the above circumstance and told me he thought himself poisoned by an American, he vomited a great deal, complained of pains in his head and belly, his Eyes appeared much inflamed, he talked rationally, and I am certain was perfectly sober.

> We were then on the point of marching. I took him to the surgeon of the 44th Regt. who examined him and said he thought him to have been slightly poisoned, that the vomiting had possibly saved his life, he ordered some warm water for him which I had not time to give him, as we began our march and I left him in the care of Alexander Robinson, who states, that almost immediately after our leaving them he was seized with the cramp all over & swelled a great deal, that in about half an hour he succeeded in getting him into a house where a woman gave him some warm tea which he could not keep down, that he was in great agony for upward of an hour when a surgeon of the Army arrived who gave him two doses of salts which he also brought up, but after which he began gradually to recover, that this surgeon told him if he had drank a little more it would have done [its] business.

> He states further that the man who gave him the spirits was nearly six feet high and that he called himself one of the Commander in Chiefs servants. What Commander in Chief he does not know.

> I feel perfectly certain myself that the man had been poisoned but the opinion of the surgeon of the 44th who examined him would be more conclusive and satisfactory.[4]

Notes

Abbreviations

Adm, Admiralty Papers; *CVSP, Calendar of Virginia State Papers*; JWP, James Winchester Papers, Tennessee Historical Society Collection, Tennessee State Library and Archives; LC, Library of Congress; *MHM, Maryland Historical Magazine*; MHS, Maryland Historical Society; NA, National Archives, Washington, D.C.; NLS, National Library of Scotland; NMM, National Maritime Museum, Greenwich, England; PRO, Public Record Office, Kew, England; WO, War Office.

Chapter One

1. Two modern biographies of Cockburn have been published. An admiring portrait of the admiral is provided by James Pack, *The Man Who Burned the White House: Admiral Sir George Cockburn 1772–1853* (Annapolis, Md.: Naval Institute Press, 1987). Despite the documented cases of indiscriminate looting and burning under Cockburn, Pack (161) praises Cockburn for his "outstanding humanity." A more recent but similarly noncritical view of the admiral is given in Roger Morriss, *Cockburn and the British Navy in Transition: Admiral Sir George Cockburn 1772–1853* (Columbia, S.C.: University of South Carolina Press, 1997). See Appendix 1, "Rear Adm. George Cockburn, Terrorizer of the Chesapeake" for further discussion of the controversial admiral.

2. J. Mackay Hitsman, *The Incredible War of 1812: A Military History* (Toronto: University of Toronto Press, 1965), 107.

3. Quoted in Edwin Warfield Beitzell, *The Jesuit Missions of St. Mary's County, Maryland* (Abell, Md.: published by the author, 1959), 107.

4. See Donald G. Shomette, *Flotilla: Battle for the Patuxent* (Solomons, Md.: The Calvert Marine Museum Press, 1981), 20–186.

5. See Ian Beckett, "The Amateur Military Tradition" in David Chandler and Ian Beckett, eds., *The Oxford Illustrated History of the British Army* (New York: Oxford University Press, 1994), 402–16. See also John R. Elting, *Amateurs to Arms! A Military History of the War of 1812* (New York: Da Capo Press, 1995), 6–10, for a discussion of the condition of the militia at the beginning of the war, as well as the ongoing problems of lack of supplies and poor leadership as the war progressed.

175

6. See Lords Commissioners of the Admiralty to Warren, December 26, 1812, Warren to Secretary of the Admiralty John W. Croker, January 5, 1813, and Croker to Warren, January 9, 1813, in William S. Dudley, ed., *The Naval War of 1812: A Documentary History*, 2 vols. (Washington, D.C.: Naval Historical Center, Department of the Navy, 1985–92), 2:11, 14–15.

7. William James, *The Naval History of Great Britain from the Declaration of War by France in 1793 to the Accession of George IV*, 6 vols. (London: Macmillan and Co., Ltd., 1902), 6:82.

8. Warren to Cockburn, February 13, 1813, Cockburn Papers, LC.

9. On November 7, 1775, Royal Governor Lord Dunmore issued a proclamation offering freedom to any slaves who promised to bear arms against their former masters. Dunmore employed the former slaves in an "Ethiopian Regiment" that fought against the Patriots. See "Lord Dunmore's Ethiopian Regiment" in Benjamin Quarles, *The Negro in the American Revolution* (New York: W. W. Norton & Co., 1973), 19–32.

10. Benson J. Lossing, *Pictorial Field Book of the War of 1812* (New York: Harper & Brothers, 1869), 667–68, and John M. Hallahan, *The Battle of Craney Island: A Matter of Credit* (Portsmouth, Va.: St. Michael's Press, 1986), 48–52.

11. On President Jefferson's gunboat navy see Dudley, 1:12–15, and Howard I. Chappelle, *The History of the American Sailing Navy* (New York: W. W. Norton & Co., 1949), 179–241.

12. Norfolk's river forts and gunboat defenses are discussed in Hallahan, 14–15, 38–47.

13. Cockburn to Warren, March 13, 1813, in Dudley, 2:320–24.

14. Taylor to Barbour, March 11, 1813, *Calendar of Virginia State Papers and Other Manuscripts from January 1, 1808 to December 31, 1835; Preserved in the Capitol, at Richmond* (hereinafter, *CVSP*), 10 vols. (Richmond, Va.: State of Virginia, 1892; reprint, New York: Kraus Reprint Co., 1968), 10:200.

15. Stewart to Jones, March 17, 1813, in Dudley, 2:315–16.

16. For information on the recalcitrance of militia at the Battle of Queenston, see Arnold Blumberg, "The United States Invades Canada. Queenston Heights: The Battle That Saved British North America," *Journal of the War of 1812*, 3 (Spring) 1998: 5–7, and Elting, 38–50.

17. Pack, 147.

18. John C. Stagg, *Mr. Madison's War: Politics, Diplomacy, and Warfare in the Early American Republic, 1783–1830* (Princeton, N.J.: Princeton University Press, 1983), 298, and Stewart to Jones, March 22, 1813, in Dudley, 2:316–17.

19. Monroe to Barbour, March 21, 1813, *CVSP*, 10:212.

20. Stewart to Jones, March 22, 1813, in Dudley, 2:316–17.

21. Polkinghorne to Warren, April 3, 1813, in Dudley, 2:339–40. Also see Pack, 150.

22. Dudley, 2:340.

23. Pack, 150.

24. Ibid., 151.

Chapter Two

1. J. Thomas Scharf, *History of Baltimore City and County from the Earliest Period to the Present Day: Including Biographical Sketches of Their Representative Men* (Philadelphia, Pa.: Louis H. Everts, 1881; reprinted in 2 vols., Baltimore, Md.: Regional Publishing Co., 1971), 1:78.

2. *Niles' Weekly Register*, August 15, 1812. See also "Privateering in the War of 1812" in Dudley, 1:166–70, and John Philips Cranwell and William Bowers Crane, *Men of Marque: A History of Private Armed Vessels out of Baltimore During the War of 1812* (New York: W. W. Norton & Co., 1940).

3. Editor's note in Dudley, 1:248. Dudley (248–60) publishes an extract from Barney's journal of his July to October 1812.

4. Barney's colorful career is chronicled in Mary Barney, ed., *A Biographical Memoir of the Late Joshua Barney from Autobiographical Notes and Journals in Possession of His Family and*

Other Authentic Sources (Boston, Mass.: Gray and Bowen, 1832), and Hulbert Footner, *Sailor of Fortune: The Life and Adventures of Commodore Barney, U.S.N.* (New York: Harper & Brothers, 1940; reprinted Annapolis, Md.: Naval Institute Press, 1998).

5. For more on the War of 1812 and Thomas Boyle, see Fred W. Hopkins, Jr., *Tom Boyle, Master Privateer* (Cambridge, Md.: Tidewater Publishers, 1976).

6. Cranwell and Crane, *Men of Marque*, 90.

7. Ibid., 90, 393, and *Niles' Weekly Register*, November 14, 1812.

8. Cranwell and Crane, *Men of Marque*, 180–83, and Dudley, 1:318–20.

9. Scharf, *History of Baltimore City and County*, 1:78.

10. See Bruce Wheeler, "Urban Politics in Nature's Republic: The Development of Political Parties in the Seaport Cities in the Federalist Era," Ph.D. diss., University of Virginia, Charlottesville, Va., 1967), 144–209.

11. Scharf, *History of Baltimore City and County*, 1:84, 2:782–84. Also see Frank A. Cassell, "The Great Baltimore Riot of 1812," *MHM* 70 (Fall 1975): 241–59, and Paul A. Gilje, "'Le Menu Peuple' in America: Identifying the Mob in the Baltimore Riots of 1812," *MHM* 81 (Spring 1986): 50–66.

12. J. Thomas Scharf, *Chronicles of Baltimore* (Baltimore, Md.: Turnbull Brothers, 1874), 309–10.

13. For a biography of General Lee, see Charles Royster, *Light-Horse Harry Lee and the Legacy of the American Revolution* (New York: Alfred A. Knopf, 1981).

14. Cassell, "The Great Baltimore Riot of 1812," 249–51.

15. Ibid., 249. See John Stricker, Jr., "Memoir of General John Stricker," Ms. 1490, Maryland Historical Society (hereinafter MHS).

16. Cassell, "The Great Baltimore Riot of 1812," 251.

17. Scharf, *Chronicles of Baltimore*, 320.

18. Cassell, "The Great Baltimore Riot of 1812," 251–52.

19. Barney to Stricker, August 25, 1812, published in the *Maryland Gazette*, August 27, 1812.

20. Cassell, "The Great Baltimore Riot of 1812," 252–53.

21. Federalist account in Scharf, *Chronicles of Baltimore*, 326–28.

22. Narrative of John E. Hall, *Maryland Gazette*, September 3, 1812. Also Cassell, "The Great Baltimore Riot of 1812," 256–57.

23. Royster, 232–52.

24. Cassell, "The Great Baltimore Riot of 1812," 258–59.

25. Ibid.

26. Joseph A. Whitehorne, *The Battle for Baltimore 1814* (Baltimore, Md.: The Nautical & Aviation Publishing Co., 1997), 16. Whitehorne notes that stories of the violence in Baltimore "may have influenced British perceptions as to the degree of division in the region." Ibid.

27. See Donald E. Graves, *The Battle of Lundy's Lane: On the Niagara in 1814* (Baltimore, Md.: The Nautical & Aviation Publishing Company, 1993).

28. Gaines to Armstrong, August 16 (?), 1814, and Ripley to Armstrong, August 17, 1814, in T. H. Palmer, ed., *The Historical Register of the United States, Part II for 1814* (Washington, D.C.: T. H. Palmer, 1816), 4:73–78, 82–84.

29. Capt. Charles Gordon to Secretary of the Navy Jones, February 16, 1813, in Dudley, 2:331.

30. Frank A. Cassell, *Merchant Congressman in the Young Republic: Samuel Smith of Maryland, 1752–1839* (Madison, Wisc.: University of Wisconsin Press, 1971), 181–83.

Chapter Three

1. Cockburn to Warren, April 19, 1813, in Dudley, 2:340–41. See also William L. Calderhead, "A Strange Career in a Young Navy: Captain Charles Gordon," *MHM* 72 (Fall 1977): 373–86.

2. Gordon to Jones, April 27, 1813, in Dudley, 2:351.

3. Smith to Armstrong, March 13 and April 16, 1813, Smith Order Book, and Governor Winder to Smith, March 13, 1813, Samuel Smith Papers, LC.

4. Cassell, *Merchant Congressman in the Young Republic*, 181. For discussion of Smith's Revolutionary War service in the Continental army and militia, see ibid., 12–31. As de facto commander of Fort Mifflin in the Delaware River in the fall of 1777, Colonel Smith took part in a difficult and bloody siege situation that for more than four weeks helped delay the British fleet from reaching Philadelphia. His experience in that siege prepared him well for a possible siege of Baltimore.

5. Scharf, *History of Baltimore City and County*, 1:85, and Scott S. Sheads, *The Rockets' Red Glare: The Maritime Defense of Baltimore in 1814* (Centreville, Md.: Tidewater Publishers, 1986), 14.

6. Cockburn to Warren, April 19, 1813, in Dudley, 2:340–41.

7. Gordon to Jones, March 13, 1813, in Dudley, 2:331–32. During their time in the Patapsco, British dropped buoys to mark the shoals. Gordon removed some of the buoys and placed them elsewhere to confuse the enemy. Ibid., 348.

8. Hopkins, *Tom Boyle: Master Privateer*, 31. Also see William L. Calderhead, "Naval Innovation in Crisis: War in the Chesapeake, 1813," *American Neptune* 36 (July 1976): 206–21.

9. Smith's comments about the deficiencies of the fort are in Smith to Armstrong, March 13, 1813, Samuel Smith Papers, LC. For more on Wadsworth's improvements see Sheads, "Defending Baltimore in the War of 1812: Two Sidelights," *MHM* 84 (Fall 1989): 252–58.

10. Smith to Armstrong, April 21, 1813, Samuel Smith Papers, LC. For the terms of Beall's appointment, see Secretary of War Henry Dearborn to Beall, "Letters Sent, Office of the Adjutant General," RG 107, NA. Also see Cassell, *Merchant Congressman in the Young Republic*, 185–86.

11. Governor Winder to Smith, May 13, 1813, Samuel Smith Papers, LC.

12. Sheads, *The Rockets' Red Glare*, 16–17.

13. Quoted in Lord, 274.

14. Ibid., 274–75.

15. Cassell, *Merchant Congressman in the Young Republic*, 184–85.

16. Whitehorne, 45; Sheads, *The Rockets' Red Glare*, 35–37.

Chapter Four

1. William M. Marine, *The British Invasion of Maryland 1812–1813* (Baltimore, Md.: Society of the War of 1812 in Maryland, 1913), 29. See also James J. Wilmer, *Narrative Respecting the Conduct of the British from Their First Landing on Specutia Island Till Their Progress to Havre de Grace. . . By a citizen of Havre de Grace* (Baltimore: Printed by P. Mauro, 1813), and Christopher T. George, "Harford County in the War of 1812," *Harford Historical Bulletin* 76 (Spring 1998): 1–61.

2. Cockburn to Warren, April 29, 1813, Cockburn Papers, LC. Also see Pack, 151; Marine, 32.

3. Ibid.

4. Robert J. Barrett, R.N., "Naval Recollections of the Late American War. I.," *United Service Journal* 149 (April 1841): 455–67.

5. Frederick Chamier, R.N., *The Life of a Sailor by a Captain in the Navy*, 2 vols. (New York: J. & J. Harper, 1833), 1:201.

6. Ibid., 200.

7. Cockburn to Warren, April 29, 1813, Cockburn Papers, LC.

8. Pack, 151.

9. Chamier, 1:201.

10. George Johnston, *History of Cecil County, Maryland* (Elkton, Md.: 1881, reprinted Baltimore, Md.: Regional Publishing Co., 1967), 413–15; and bounty land application of John C. Hull, in F. Edward Wright, *Maryland Militia War of 1812. Vol. 3. Cecil & Harford Counties* (Silver Spring, Md.: Family Line Press, 1980), 54.

11. *Harford County Directory, 1953* (Baltimore, Md.: State Directories Publishing Co., 1954), 143, and *Maryland: A Guide to the Old Line State* (New York: Oxford University Press, 1948), 323.

12. Cockburn to Warren, May 3, 1813, in Dudley, 2:341–44.

13. Ibid.

14. Account of Rev. Jared Sparks, *North American Review*, July 1817, quoted in Marine, 35–42. At the time of the British attack, Sparks (1789–1866) was a tutor in the Pringle household. I am assuming the "commanding officer" meant by Sparks was Lt. Col. William Smith, commander of the 42nd Regiment, but he might have been referring to Capt. Thomas Courtney, under whose command several companies of men had been consolidated at Havre de Grace on April 18. See Wright, *Maryland Militia War of 1812. Vol. 3. Cecil & Harford Counties*, 26.

15. Cockburn to Warren, May 3, 1813, in Dudley, 2:341–44.

16. Marine, 32–33. For more on the Congreve rocket, see Donald E. Graves, *Sir William Congreve and the Rocket's Red Glare* (Alexandria Bay, N.Y.: Museum Restoration Service, 1989).

17. Letter of John O'Neill, May 10, 1813, in *Niles' Weekly Register*, quoted in Marine, 33.

18. Cockburn to Warren, May 3, 1813, in Dudley, 2:341–44.

19. Account of Sparks in Marine, 39.

20. Lossing, 672.

21. Latrobe to Fulton, May 4, 1813, in John C. Van Horne, ed., *The Correspondence and Miscellaneous Papers of Benjamin Henry Latrobe*, 3 vols. (New Haven, Ct.: Yale University Press, 1988), 3:452–55. As Van Horne notes (454), "Later accounts of the event modify Latrobe's hastily constructed narrative." Of course, horses could have been viewed by the British as a military target. See appendix 2, "British Atrocities or Yankee Propaganda?"

22. Quoted in Swepson Earle, *Chesapeake Bay Country* (Baltimore: Thomsen-Ellis, 1923), 245–48.

23. T. H. Palmer, ed., *The Historical Register of the United States. Part II. From the Declaration of War in 1812, to January 1, 1814* (Washington, D.C.: T. H. Palmer, 1814), 2:86.

24. Brig. Gen. Henry Miller to Warren, May 8, 1813, quoted in Marine, 34. When Miller wrote this letter, it seems that O'Neill and the others may already have been released. For more on O'Neill's defense and detention, see George, "Harford County in the War of 1812," 32–34, and Wilmer, 11–13.

25. Cockburn to Warren, May 3, 1813, in Dudley, 2:341–44.

26. James L. Kochan, "The Development of Heavy Ordnance in the United States Army, 1802–1815," paper delivered at the 31st Annual Military History Conference of the Council on America's Military Past, Buffalo, New York, May 7–10, 1997. See also Earl Chapin May, *Principio to Wheeling, 1715–1945: A Pageant of Iron and Steel* (New York: Harper and Brothers, 1945), 1–58, 69–74.

27. Pack, 151.

28. Lt. Gen. Sir William Napier, *Life and Opinions of General Sir James Napier, G.C.B.*, 4 vols. (London: John Murray, 1857), 1:218.

29. Jones to Manuel Eyre, May 12, 1813, in Dudley, 2:117–20.

30. Cockburn to Warren, May 6, 1813, in Dudley, 2:344–46.

31. Edward C. Papenfuse, Gregory A. Stiverson, Susan A. Collins, and Lois Green Carr, eds., *Maryland: A New Guide to the Old Line State* (Baltimore, Md.: The Johns Hopkins University Press, 1976), 364–65. Today, the Kitty Knight House is a well-known inn and restaurant.

32. Cockburn to Warren, May 6, 1813, in Dudley, 2:344–46, and Whitehorne, 49–51.

33. Probably the detachment that Cockburn had sent up to Lapidum was not powerful enough to attack Port Deposit. See Albert P. Silver, "Lapidum and its Surroundings. A Sketch Before the Harford County Historical Society, April 28th, 1888," typescript, Archives of the Historical Society of Harford County.

34. Wilmer, 21.

35. Philip Reed, "The Late War," undated manuscript memorandum, War of 1812 Papers, Archives of the Historical Society of Harford County.

36. Jones to Eyre, May 12, 1813, in Dudley, 2:117–20.

37. See Frank A. Cassell, "Slaves of the Chesapeake Bay Area and the War of 1812," *Journal of Negro History* 57 (April 1972): 144–55. Also Christopher T. George, "Mirage of Freedom: African Americans in the War of 1812," *MHM* 91 (Winter 1996): 426–50.

38. Charles Ball, *Slavery in the United States: A Narrative of the Life and Adventures of Charles Ball, a Black Man* (Lewistown, Pa.: John S. Tayloe, 1836; reprinted New York: Negro Universities Press, 1969), 469.

39. *National Intelligencer*, April 30 and May 1, 1813.

40. *Niles' Weekly Register*, August 21, 1813.

41. Croker to Warren, May 17, 1813, in Dudley, 2:356–57.

42. Richard Peters, ed., *The Public Statutes at Large of the United States of America, from the Organization of Government in 1789, to March 3, 1845 . . . ,* 8 vols. (Boston: Little, Brown, Boston, 1846–67), 2:816.

43. In the years before the war, Fulton, masquerading under the name of "Mr. Francis" had tried to get the Royal Navy interested in torpedoes. See "Infernal Machines" by Michael Phillips, Maritime History web page, http://www.cronab.demon.co.uk/mines.htm.

44. Warren, General Orders, July 19, 1813, in Dudley, 1:164.

45. Jones to Gordon, May 7, 1813, in Dudley, 2:355. Architect Benjamin Henry Latrobe helped Mix by supplying and modifying Fulton's torpedoes for the sailor to deploy. Latrobe's correspondence proves that Captain Stewart of the *Constellation* was also involved in the endeavor. See Fulton to Latrobe, April 22, 1813, Latrobe to Fulton, April 23, 1813, Latrobe to Mix, May 7, 1813, and Latrobe to Fulton, June 6, 1813, in Van Horne, 3:440–44, 3:445–47, 3:456, 3:467–69, respectively.

46. Editor's note in Dudley, 2:356. It would not be until the Civil War that the torpedo would be considered a practical weapon of war. See Phillips, "Infernal Machines."

Chapter Five

1. See editor's note in Dudley, 2:309, Hallahan, 56–57, and J. Mackay Hitsman and Alice Sorby, "Independent Foreigners or Canadian Chasseurs," *Military Affairs* 25 (Spring 1961): 11–17. Both Hallahan and Lossing incorrectly term these troops *Chasseurs Britanniques*.

2. Beckwith to Warren, July 5, 1813, published in Dudley, 2:364–65. Also Hitsman and Sorby, 12–14.

3. Col. Sir William F. Butler, *Sir Charles Napier* (New York: Macmillan and Co., 1890), 55. Napier (1782–1853), an Anglo-Irishman, made his reputation in India, as conqueror of Scinde. For a modern assessment of him, see Byron Farwell, *Eminent Victorian Soldiers: Seekers of Glory* (New York: W. W. Norton & Co., 1988), 62–101.

4. Warren and Beckwith to Cockburn, with replies by Cockburn, undated, Great Britain Navy box, Manuscripts and Archives Division, New York Public Library.

5. Pack, 157–58.

6. Taylor to Armstrong, June 18, 1813, quoted in Hallahan, 52–53, 58–59.

7. Pack, 158.

8. Hallahan, 59.

9. Hallahan, 59–61. Sanders to Cockburn, June 20, 1813, and Cassin to Jones, June 23, 1813, in Dudley, 2:357–59.

10. Hallahan, 61.
11. Lossing, 679–80, and Hallahan, 63–64.
12. Hallahan, 65–66.
13. Ibid., 62–63.
14. Ibid., 64–65.
15. Napier, *Life and Opinions*, 1:217.
16. Hallahan, 64.
17. Ibid., 64, 67.
18. Robertson, quoted in Napier, *Life and Opinions*, 1:213.
19. Ibid., and Hallahan, 67–69.
20. Napier, *Life and Opinions*, 1:224.
21. Robertson, quoted in Napier, *Life and Opinions*, 1:213–14.
22. Hallahan, 70–71.
23. Ibid., 71–72.
24. Ibid., 72.
25. Robertson, quoted in Napier, *Life and Opinions*, 1:213. Also see Hallahan, 72.
26. Beatty to Taylor, June 25, 1813, in Palmer, 2:259–60. Also see Robertson, quoted in Napier, *Life and Opinions*, 1:213–14, and Hallahan, 72–73.
27. Napier, *Life and Opinions*, 1:217.
28. Beatty to Taylor, June 25, 1813, in Palmer, 2:259–60. Warren to Croker, June 24, 1813, in Dudley, 2:360–61. Warren to Croker, June 25, 1813, enclosing Beckwith's return of killed, wounded, and missing. Admiralty Papers (hereafter Adm) 1/503, Public Record Office (PRO).
29. Pack, 158.
30. Hallahan, 70.
31. T. H. Palmer in Palmer, 2:87.
32. Crutchfield to Barbour, June 21, 1813, *CVSP*, 10:231–32.
33. Crutchfield to Barbour, June 28, 1813, in Palmer, 2:260–63. Also see Crutchfield to Barbour, June 25, 1813, *CVSP*, 10:232–33.
34. Beckwith to Warren, June 28, 1813, in Dudley, 2:362–63.
35. Crutchfield to Barbour, June 25, 1813, *CVSP*, 10:232–33.
36. Ibid.
37. Napier, *Life and Opinions*, 1:218.
38. Beckwith to Warren, June 28, 1813, in Dudley, 2:362–63. Crutchfield to Barbour, June 28, 1813, in Palmer, 2:260–63.
39. Crutchfield to Barbour, June 28, 1813, in Palmer, 2:260–63.
40. Napier, *Life and Opinions*, 1:224.
41. Robertson, quoted in Napier, *Life and Opinions*, 1:214.
42. Napier, *Life and Opinions*, 1:221.
43. Farwell, 93–94.
44. Ibid., 1:224.
45. Ibid., 1:222.
46. Taylor to Warren, June 29, 1813, in Palmer, 2:264.
47. Myers to Taylor, July 2, 1813, in Palmer, 2:264.
48. Dudley, 2:373.

Chapter Six

1. Donald G. Shomette, *Flotilla: Battle for the Patuxent*, 19–20.
2. Barney to Jones, July 4, 1813, in Dudley, 2:373–76.

3. Ibid., 373.

4. For Jones' correspondence of February to April 1813 in regard to the Potomac flotilla, see Dudley, 2:332–36.

5. Barney to Jones, July 4, 1813, in Dudley, 2:373–76.

6. Jones to Madison, April 17, 1813, quoted in editor's note in Dudley, 2:373.

7. Barney to Jones, July 4, 1813, in Dudley, 2:373–76.

8. Jones to Barney, August 20, 1813, in Dudley, 2:376–77.

9. Shomette, *Flotilla*, 23.

10. Ibid.

11. Ibid., 24.

12. Pack, 159, and Cockburn to Warren, July 12, 1813, in Dudley, 2:184–86.

13. Com. James Rattray to Warren, July 14, 1813, and Mdn. Henry M. MClintock [*sic*] to Jones, July 19, 1813, in Dudley, 2:366–68.

14. Warren to Croker, July 29, 1813, in Dudley, 2:368–69, and Warren to Lord Melville, June 1, 1813, National Maritime Museum (hereafter NMM), LBK/2.

15. Irving Brant, *James Madison, Commander in Chief, 1812–1836* (New York: The Bobbs-Merrill Company, Inc., 1961), 206–7. The 36th and 38th Regiments were among those authorized by Congress on January 29, 1813, when it sanctioned the raising of 20 additional regiments to be enlisted for one year instead of the usual five years.

16. Ibid. Maj. Gen. James Wilkinson wrote that the two secretaries were trying to outdo each other "in demonstrations of zeal." In his view, Monroe's plan "was marred by the jealousy or invidious spirit of the war minister. . . ." Gen. James Wilkinson, *Memoirs of My Own Times*, 3 vols. (Philadelphia, Pa.: Abraham Small, 1816), 1:734.

17. Warren to Croker, July 29, 1813, in Dudley, 2:368–69.

18. Wilkinson, 1:733.

19. Lord, 21. Pitch describes Secretary Armstrong as "officious, stubborn, and cocksure." Anthony Pitch, *The Burning of Washington: The British Invasion of 1814* (Annapolis: Naval Institute Press, 1998), 18.

20. Wilkinson, 1:732.

21. Ibid., 1:741. For a biography of Wilkinson (1757–1825), see James R. Jacobs, *Tarnished Warrior: Major-General James Wilkinson* (New York: Macmillan & Co., 1938). On Crysler's Farm and the lead-up to it, see Pierre Berton, *Flames Across the Border: The Canadian-American Tragedy, 1813–1814* (Boston: Little, Brown & Co., 1981), 228–43. It was the opinion of Brig. Gen. Winfield Scott and others that Wilkinson was drunk. However, Berton thinks that the repeated draughts of opium the Marylander had taken to alleviate his dysentery may have given him the appearance of being drunk.

22. John Armstrong, Sr., (1717–1795) was born in County Fermanagh, Ireland, and came to Carlisle, Pennsylvania, as a surveyor. See Trevor N. Dupuy, Curt Johnson, and David L. Bongard, *The Harper Encyclopedia of Military Biography* (Edison, N.J.: Castle Books, 1995), 45–46.

23. Kohn notes, "The Newburgh conspiracy was the closest an American army has ever come to revolt or coup d'etat. . . ." Richard H. Kohn, *Eagle and Sword: The Federalists and the Creation of the Military Establishment in America, 1783–1802* (New York: The Free Press, 1975), 17. The most seditious passage in the first Newburgh Address points out that if Congress failed to do justice, "the army has its alternative." Skeen maintains that the passage "was [only] included for shock value. . . ." C. Edward Skeen, *John Armstrong, Jr., 1758–1843: A Biography* (Syracuse, N.Y.: Syracuse University Press, 1981), 12.

24. Skeen, 19–112.

25. Armstrong to Alida Armstrong, August 8, 1812, quoted in Skeen, 123. Also see John Armstrong, *Hints to Young Generals By an Old Soldier* (Kingston, N.Y.: J. Buel, 1812).

26. Skeen, 124.

27. Ibid., 133–34.

28. Statement of Maj. Gen. John P. Van Ness, November 16, 1814, in "Report on the Capture of the City of Washington," *American State Papers*, Military Affairs, Class V, I. (Washington, D.C.: Gales and Seaton, 1832), 580–83.

29. Wadsworth to Armstrong, May 28, 1813, quoted in Skeen, 188.

30. Wilkinson, 1:735–36.

31. Statement of Van Ness, "Rport on the Capture of the City of Washington," 580–83.

32. Mark Lloyd, *History of the United States Army* (London: Chevprime Ltd., 1988), 31–33, and T. Harry Williams, *The History of American Wars from 1745 to 1918* (Baton Rouge, La.: Louisiana State University Press, 1985), 84–90.

33. *A Declaration of Rights*. Broadside published by the Virginia Convention, May 16–June 29, 1776, James Madison Papers, LC.

34. James Madison, *The Papers of James Madison, Vol. 7, 3 May 1783–20 February 1784*, ed. by William T. Hutchinson and William M. E. Rachal (Chicago, Ill.: University of Chicago Press, 1971), 177. See also Lawrence D. Cress, "The Standing Army, the Militia, and the New Republic: Changing Attitudes toward the Military in American Society," Ph.D. diss., University of Virginia, 1976, 222–27; Kohn, *Eagle and Sword*, 42–48.

35. Margaret Bayard Smith to Mrs. Jane Kirkpatrick, July 20, 1813, in Smith, *The First Forty Years of Washington Society*, 89–91.

36. Ibid.

37. William S. Dudley, review of Donald G. Shomette, *Tidewater Time Capsule: History Beneath the Patuxent*, MHM 90 (Fall 1995): 357–59. Marine (53) says, "A large number of the inhabitants, unable to bear the burdens of war, abandoned their homes to the pillagers and moved to the new settlements then opening in the far west."

38. Warren to Croker, July 29, 1813, in Dudley, 2:368–69.

39. Marine, 53–54; Sheads, *The Rockets' Red Glare*, 22–23.

40. Ibid.

41. Whitehorne, 79.

42. Marine, 54. Also see letters of August 12 and 29, 1813, from Secretary Jones to Capt. Charles Morris in Dudley, 2:383–84.

43. Warren to Croker, August 23, 1813, in Dudley, 2:382–83.

44. Ibid.; Marine, 54.

45. Ibid.

46. Warren to Croker, August 23, 1813, in Dudley, 2:382–83, and Whitehorne, 78.

47. Robertson, quoted in Napier, *Life and Opinions*, 1:215–16, and Marine, 54–55.

48. Ibid.

49. *Niles' Weekly Register*, August 14, 1813.

50. Warren to Cockburn, August 7, 1813, Cockburn Papers, LC.

51. See Norman H. Plummer, "Another Look at the Battle of St. Michaels," *The Weather Gauge* 31 (Spring 1995): 10–17. Also Donald G. Shomette, *Tidewater Time Capsule: History Beneath the Patuxent* (Centreville, Md.: Tidewater Publishers, 1995), 60. Even after building of vessels for the flotilla began in St. Michaels, no additional attack on the town was made by the enemy.

52. Polkinghorne to Cmdr. Henry Loraine Baker, August 10, 1813, in Dudley, 2:381; Napier, *Life and Opinions*, 1:220.

53. Marine, 55–56.

54. Ibid. Local legend has it that the residents of St. Michaels extinguished all lights near the ground and hung lanterns in upper story windows and treetops to make the British cannoneers overshoot the town. However, Papenfuse (164) points out, "Contemporary accounts

make no mention of the ruse." Plummer (13–14) said that the attack was apparently made at daybreak, and that in daylight no lanterns would have fooled the British. He stated, "Not until 1913 in anticipation of the centennial did the lantern story gain prominence." Ibid., 14.

55. Polkinghorne to Baker, August 10, 1813, in Dudley, 2:381. Another myth that Plummer discusses is a well-circulated story that Cockburn lost his "favorite nephew" in the attack. No reference to this incident can be found in the admiral's correspondence. Plummer, 16.

56. Editor's note in Dudley, 2:381, and Pack, 162.

57. Napier, *Life and Opinions*, 1:369, 4:393.

58. Ibid., 1:369–70.

Chapter Seven

1. Pack, 166. Sir Alexander Forester Inglis Cochrane (1758–1832) was the younger son of Thomas Cochrane, eighth earl of Dundonald. His elder brother, Maj. the Hon. Charles Cochrane (1749–1781) had performed the service of ferrying letters from Sir Henry Clinton to Lord Cornwallis at Yorktown by running through the French fleet in an open boat. Because of his courageous conduct, he was made an aide to Cornwallis. Two days before the British surrender at Yorktown, on October 17, 1781, he was killed while standing next to Cornwallis. His head was shot off by a cannonball. Benjamin Franklin Stevens, editor, *Clinton-Cornwallis Controversy* (London: privately printed), 2:420. In addition to delays in building the vessels for the flotilla, recruitment was slow. Complicating the task of recruitment was that Barney was competing for recruits with the regular army, the militia, and the U.S. Navy. See Shomette, *Flotilla*, 28–29.

2. Cochrane to Cockburn, April 24, 1814, quoted in Pack, 166–67.

3. Jones to Barney, December 8, 1813, quoted in editor's note in Dudley, 2:398. Also see Shomette, *Flotilla*, 24–27.

4. Cochrane Proclamation, April 2, 1814, PRO, Adm 1/508, 579.

5. Cochrane to Bathurst, July 14, 1814, PRO, War Office 1/141.

6. Cochrane to Cockburn, July 1, 1814, Cochrane Papers 2346, National Library of Scotland, Edinburgh (hereinafter NLS).

7. Lord, 33–37.

8. Cockburn to Cochrane, April 2, 1814, Cochrane Papers 2574, NLS.

9. Cockburn to Cochrane, May 19, 1814, PRO, Adm. 1/507, 59–60.

10. Pack, 166–67. Also plan of Tangier Island, Cochrane Papers 2608, NLS.

11. Shomette, *Flotilla*, 35, and *Tidewater Time Capsule*, 64.

12. Shomette, *Flotilla*, 29.

13. Cockburn to Cochrane, June 25, 1814, Cochrane Papers 2333, NLS.

14. Ibid. Also see Lt. Col. Thomas M. Bayley to Barbour, May 31, 1814, *CVSP*, 10:334–37.

15. Cockburn to Cochrane, June 25, 1814, Cochrane Papers 2333, NLS.

16. Shomette, *Tidewater Time Capsule*, 64.

17. Shomette, *Flotilla*, 36–37.

18. Ibid., 37.

19. Ibid., 37–41.

20. Shomette, *Tidewater Time Capsule*, 67.

21. Ibid., 67–68.

22. Shomette, *Flotilla*, 454–56.

23. Ibid., 49–50.

24. Ibid., 50–52.

25. Ibid.

26. Barney to Jones, June 13, 1814, in Palmer, 2:120.

27. Cockburn to Cochrane, June 25, 1814, Cochrane Papers 2333, NLS.

28. Bathurst to the Duke of Wellington, May 18, 1814, and Lt. Gen. George, Earl of Dalhousie, to Ross, May 29, 1814, in the Duke of Wellington, K.G., ed., *Supplementary Despatches, Correspondence and Memoranda of Field-Marshal Arthur, Duke of Wellington,* 11 vols. (London: John Murray, 1858–72), 9:117.

29. Lord, 36, 313.

30. B. Smythe, *History of the XX Regiment 1688–1888* (London: Simpkin, Marshall & Co., 1889), appendix, "Major-General Robert Ross," 340–50.

31. Ibid., 340–41.

32. Letter of March 12, 1814, from Robert Ross to "Ned" (presumably his brother-in-law Edward Glascock), quoted in Smythe, 342–43.

33. Maj. Gen. G. N. Wood, "Burning Washington: The Lighter Side of Warfare," *Army Quarterly* 104 (1973–4): 352–57.

34. See Christopher T. George, "The Family Papers of Maj. Gen. Robert Ross, the Diary of Col. Arthur Brooke, and the British Attacks on Washington and Baltimore of 1814," *MHM* 88 (Fall 1993): 300–316 (hereinafter, "Brooke diary"); W. A. Maguire, "Major General Ross and the Burning of Washington," *The Irish Sword* 14 (Winter 1980): 117–28.

35. Smith, *Autobiography*, 67–74.

36. Ibid., 187–88. Lt. Gen. Sir Harry Smith ultimately made his reputation in the Sikh War of 1845–46 and in South Africa. The city of Ladysmith, South Africa, is named after Lady Juana Smith.

37. Gleig to Rev. G. R. Gleig, May 14, 1814, Gleig Papers, Ms. 3869, NLS.

38. Smith, *Autobiography*, 191–93.

39. Gleig to Mrs. G. R. Gleig, June 2, 1814, Gleig Papers, Ms. 3869, NLS. Gleig diary quoted in C. R. B. Barrett, ed., *The 85th King's Light Infantry* (London: Spottiswoode & Co., Ltd., 1913), 117.

40. Letters of Capt. Richard Gubbins, June 20 and July 26, 1814, quoted in Barrett, *85th King's Light Infantry,* 117 and 121.

41. Description of Parker as the handsomest man in the British navy, Chamier, 1:202. For biographies of Capt. Sir Peter Parker as well as his grandfather, Adm. Sir Peter Parker, see Sir George Dallas, *A Biographical Memoir of the Late Sir Peter Parker* (London: Longman, Hurst, Rees, Orme, and Brown, 1816).

42. Shomette, *Tidewater Time Capsule,* 28.

43. Madison wrote that after Congress removed to Princeton, the mutineers "betrayed their leaders, the chief of whom proved to be a Mr. Carberry a deranged officer, and a Mr. Sullivan a lieutenant of horse, both of whom made their escape." James Madison, *The Papers of James Madison,* edited by William T. Hutchinson and William M. E. Rachal (Chicago, Ill.: University of Chicago Press, Chicago, 1971) 7:178, 180.

44. Barney to Jones, June 18, 1814, CL 1814, RG45, M124, R64, NARS.

45. Footner, 272–73.

46. Shomette, *Tidewater Time Capsule,* 76–77.

47. Shomette, *Flotilla,* 87–88.

48. Ibid., 88–91.

49. Ibid., 95–97.

50. Ibid.

51. Ibid., 99–100.

52. Pack, 173–74.

53. Gleig diary quoted in Barrett, *85th King's Light Infantry,* 123–24.

54. Lord, 22–24.

55. Lord, 26.

56. Report of Richard M. Johnson, November 16, 1814, in "Report on the Capture of the City of Washington," 525.

57. Shomette, *Flotilla*, 118–23.

58. Cockburn to Cochrane, secret memorandum, July 17, 1814, Cockburn Papers, LC.

59. Ibid.

60. *Daily National Intelligencer*, August 4, 1814. For more on the Cockburn's Potomac raids, see Shomette, *Flotilla*, 124–39.

61. Ibid., 128–29, 133.

62. Capt. James Scott, R.N., *Recollections of a Naval Life*, 3 vols. (London: Richard Bentley, 1834), 3:249, 253, 255, and Brig. Gen. Hungerford to Barbour, August 5, 1814, *CVSP*, 10:367–68.

63. Ibid., 368.

64. Ibid.

65. George R. Gleig, *A Narrative of the Campaigns of the British Army at Washington, Baltimore, and New Orleans under Generals Ross, Pakenham, & Lambert. . .* (Philadelphia: M. Carey & Sons, 1821), 88–89.

66. Shomette, *Flotilla*, 156–57; Chamier, 1:200–202.

67. Smith, *Autobiography*, 1:197.

68. Lord, 55.

69. Smith, *Autobiography*, 1:197.

70. Quoted in Lady Bourchier, ed., *Memoir of the Life of Admiral Sir Edward Codrington with Selections from His Public and Private Correspondence* (London: Longmans, Green, and Co., 1873), 1:315. Other details from Gleig, *Narrative of the Campaigns*, 93–94.

71. Gleig diary quoted in Barrett, *85th King's Light Infantry*, 131.

72. Capt. Harry Smith, "State of the Troops under the command of Major Gen. Robert Ross, Head Quarters, Benedict, 20 Aug. 1814," Cochrane Papers Ms. 2326, NLS. In terms of enlisted men, this accounting shows: 21st Regiment, 884; second battalion of Royal Marines, 687; 4th Regiment, 630; 44th Regiment, 610; 85th Regiment, 516; Royal Artillery, 462; Light Infantry battalions, 329; sailors, 235; first battalion of Royal Marines, 56; Royal Marine artillery, 11. In computing "effectives" account is made, for instance, of the fact that 46 of the 516 men of the 85th Regiment are listed as sick.

73. Gleig diary quoted in Barrett, *85th King's Light Infantry*, 133.

74. Quoted in Bourchier, 1:316.

Chapter Eight

1. Smith, *Autobiography*, 1:198.

2. Lord, 65.

3. Brooke diary, in George, "Family Papers," 305.

4. Ball, 467–68.

5. Lord, 59–60.

6. Wilkinson, 1:740–45.

7. Wilkinson, 1:761.

8. Ibid.

9. Ibid., 762.

10. Smith, *Autobiography*, 1:197.

11. Ross to Mrs. Ross, September 1, 1814, in George, "Family Papers," 308–9, and Lord, 69.

12. Gleig diary quoted in Barrett, *85th King's Light Infantry*, 136–37. The remark about Ross's apparent hesitation is in Gleig, *Narrative of the Campaigns*, 109.

13. Statements of Brig. Gen. William H. Winder, September 26, 1814, and Brig. Gen. Walter Smith, October 16, 1814, in "Capture of the City of Washington," 552–60 and 563–65. The

count of slaves on Benjamin Oden's plantation is from the 1810 U.S. Census for Prince George's County. That census showed that of 20,619 persons in the county, 9,189, or nearly half, were slaves and a further 4,929 were classified as "free persons of colour."

14. Statement of Winder, September 26, 1814, in "Capture of the City of Washington," 552–60.

15. Cockburn to Cochrane, August 22, 1814, Cockburn Papers, LC.

16. Jones to Barney, August 20, 1814, Joshua Barney Papers, Dreer Collection, Pennsylvania Historical Society, Philadelphia.

17. Gleig, *Narrative of the Campaigns*, 111.

18. Caleb Clarke Magruder, Jr., "Dr. William Beanes, the Incidental Cause of the Authorship of the Star-Spangled Banner," *Records of the Columbia Historical Society* 22 (1915): 207–24. See also Sam Meyer, *Paradoxes of Fame: The Francis Scott Key Story* (Annapolis, Md.: Eastwind Publishing, 1995).

19. Lord, 79–81.

20. Ibid., 81–83. President James Madison to Mrs. Madison, August 22, 1814, in Gaillard Hunt, ed., *The Writings of James Madison* (New York: G. P. Putnam's Sons, 1908), 8:293–94.

21. Lord, 83–84.

22. Ibid., 84–85. Also, Thomas L. McKenney, "A Narrative of the Battle of Bladensburg in a Letter [of September 10, 1814] to Henry Banning, Esq.," publisher not known, [Washington, D.C. (?), 1814 (?)].

23. Lord, 86. The quote from Winder and other details are in Thomas L. McKenney, *Memoirs, Official and Personal*, 2 vols. (New York: Paine and Burgess, 1846), 1:45–46.

24. For a contemporary military theorist's views on the inadvisability of night battles, see "Night Operations" in Carl von Clausewitz, *On War*, ed. and trans. by Michael Howard and Peter Paret (Princeton, N.J.: Princeton University Press, 1976), 273–75.

25. Lord, 93–98.

26. Ross to Mrs. Ross, September 1, 1814, in George, "Family Papers," 308–9.

27. Lord, 101–2.

28. Ibid., 104.

29. Ibid., 105.

30. Winder to Armstrong, August 27, 1814, in Palmer, 4:129–31.

31. Brooke diary and Ross to Mrs. Ross, September 1, 1814, in George, "Family Papers," 303, 308–9; Gleig, *Narrative of the Campaigns*, 118. Also statement of Hanson Catlett, Surgeon, 1st Regiment of Infantry, in "Report on the Capture of the City of Washington," 583–85.

32. Statement of Maj. William Pinkney, November 16, 1814, in "Report on the Capture of the City of Washington," 571–74.

33. Lord, 107–8, 114–15.

34. Statement of Pinkney, in "Capture of the City of Washington," 571–74.

35. Lord, 113–14.

36. Ibid., 117.

37. Statement of Pinkney, in "Capture of the City of Washington," 571–74. Also statement of Brig. Gen. Tobias E. Stansbury, November 15, 1814, ibid., 560–62.

38. Lord, 116–17. Also statement of William Simmons, November 28, 1814, in "Capture of the City of Washington," 596–97.

39. James Madison, "Memorandum—Aug. 24, 1814," in Hunt, ed., *The Writings of James Madison*, 8:294–97.

40. Lord, 114.

41. Ibid.

42. Ibid., 120–21. Description of the American positions as given in Brooke diary, in George, "Family Papers," 302.

43. Lord, 120. Also Smith, *Autobiography*, 1:198–99. A question to be answered is how many of the British forded the Eastern Branch. The accounts of Gleig and Brooke seem to indicate that both officers believed all of the British came over the bridge, although the river was fordable at that point. An American school of thought (e.g., Whitehorne, 132–33) holds the Brooke's 44th Regiment crossed the river by way of the ford above the bridge. Brooke's own narrative does not bear this out.

44. Gleig, *Narrative of the Campaigns*, 122.

45. Statements of Stansbury and Pinkney, in "Capture of the City of Washington," 560–62. The positions of the units in the second American line are described by John S. Williams, *History of the Invasion and Capture of Washington* (New York: Harper & Brothers, 1857), 213–14.

46. Lord, 107.

47. Williams, 213, and Ball, 468.

48. Gleig, *Narrative of the Campaigns*, 122.

49. Lord, 125.

50. Statement of Pinkney, in "Capture of the City of Washington," 571–74; Neil H. Swanson, *The Perilous Fight* (New York: Farrar and Rinehart, Inc., 1945), 95–96.

51. Lord, 124.

52. Ibid., 126–27.

53. Statement of Pinkney, in "Capture of the City of Washington," 571–74.

54. Ibid.; Lord, 130.

55. Ibid., 130–35.

56. Ibid.

57. Ball, 468. Statement of Com. Joshua Barney, August 29, 1814, in "Capture of the City of Washington," 579–80. Also Lord, 137–38.

58. Gleig, *Narrative of the Campaigns*, 127. Gleig recorded that the "quickness and precision" with which the sailors had served their guns "astonished their assailants." Also Lord, 137–38.

59. Statement of Brig. Gen. Walter Smith, October 6, 1814, in "Capture of the City of Washington," 563–65.

60. Lord, 138–39, and Shomette, *Flotilla*, 190–91. Also statement of Barney, in "Capture of the City of Washington," 579–80. Barney died in Pittsburgh on December 1, 1818, from bilious fever caused by complications from his wound. The musket-ball was buried so deeply in his thigh that it was not removed in his lifetime. Shomette, *Tidewater Time Capsule*, 94.

61. Lord, 133, 139. The casualty figures are from Hon. J. W. Fortescue, *History of the British Army,* 14 vols. (London: Macmillan and Co., London, 1920), 10:145.

62. Statement of Brig. Gen. Walter Smith, October 6, 1814, in "Capture of the City of Washington," 563–65. Also Lord, 190.

63. Statement of Lt. Col. Jacint Lavall, October 31, 1814, in "Capture of the City of Washington," 569–71.

64. Quote from report of Richard M. Johnson, November 29, 1814, in "Capture of the City of Washington," 529.

65. Statement of Lavall, in "Capture of the City of Washington," 569–71.

66. Ibid.

67. Lord, 146–48, 150.

68. Jacob Barker, *Incidents in the Life of Jacob Barker* (Freeport, N.Y.: Books for Libraries Press, 1970; reprint of 1858 ed.), 121.

Chapter Nine

1. Lord, 158–78; William Seale, *The President's House: A History* (Washington, D.C.: White House Historical Association, 1986), 135–51.

2. Lord, 160–61.

3. Ibid., 161.

4. Lord, 162–63. The original Senate chamber and House of Representatives of the Old Capitol burned by the British can still be seen today, to the north and south of the present Rotunda, side by side with the present-day more spacious chambers. The old House of Representatives is now a halls for statuary. See George C. Hazelton, Jr., *The National Capitol: Its Architecture, Art and History* (New York: J. F. Taylor and Co., 1902), 25–37, 218–37.

5. Hazelton, 35.

6. Lord, 163.

7. Ibid., 163–64.

8. Charles J. Ingersoll, *Historical Sketch of the Second War between the United States and Great Britain. . . ,* 2 vols. (Philadelphia, Pa.: Lea and Blanchard, 1845), 1:200.

9. Ross, otherwise uncharacterized "private letter" quoted in Smythe, 345. Also Gleig, *Narrative of the Campaigns,* 134.

10. Seale, 133–35. In his 1849 history, Ingersoll (2:187) wrote, "Mr. John Sioussa[t], Mr. Madison's porter, a respectable Frenchman, who still survives, pronounces all this account of food, a fable. There was, he says, no preparation for dinner or eating, beyond a small quantity of meat in the kitchen, which he found there after the house was burned, still unconsumed. If there had been food, he says the British would not have eaten it, such was their fear of poison." See appendix 5 for a discussion of alleged American "dirty tricks" including accusations of poisoned liquor and well water.

11. Seale, 135.

12. Lord, 169–71, 176–77.

13. Gleig, *Narrative of the Campaigns,* 132.

14. Smith, *Autobiography,* 1:200–201.

15. Ingersoll, 2:190.

16. Ross to Mrs. Ross, September 1, 1814, in George, "Family Papers," 308–9.

17. Gleig, *Narrative of the Campaigns,* 132–33.

18. Lord, 174.

19. Ibid., 177, 179. Writer John Pendleton Kennedy, a private in the United Volunteers, one of the Baltimore militia units that saw action at Bladensburg, praised the general's moderation: "General Ross is very much esteemed in our army for his kind and generous treatment to our prisoners: we are well assured that no outrages will be permitted while he has the command." John P. Kennedy to Philip C. Pendleton, August 29, 1814, John Pendleton Kennedy Papers, Archives of the Peabody Institute of the Johns Hopkins University, Baltimore, Md.

20. Lord, 180–81.

21. Ibid.

22. Ibid., 181–82.

23. Ibid.

24. Brooke diary, in George, "Family Papers," 303–4.

25. Smith, *Autobiography,* 1:201–2.

26. Statement of Brig. Gen. Tobias E. Stansbury, November 15, 1814, in "Capture of the City of Washington," 560–62.

27. Although the rumors of slave insurrection proved unfounded, some blacks and others took advantage of the chaos in the capital. For example, there was looting by a "rabble" at the president's mansion after the Madisons fled. A slave, Nace Rhodes, later returned some of the president's silver urns, trays, and a candelabra, for which he was rewarded five dollars. See Nace Rhodes, letter to "dear sir," April 24, 1815, District Commissioners' Letters Received, NA.

28. Gleig, *Narrative of the Campaigns,* 148.

29. Lord, 198–99.

30. Maj. Gen. Elers Napier, *The Life and Correspondence of Admiral Sir Charles Napier, from Personal Recollections, Letters, and Official Documents*, 2 vols. (London: Hurst and Blackett, 1862), 77. Scottish-born Capt. Charles Napier (1786–1860) was a cousin of Col. Charles Napier who saw action in the Chesapeake in 1813.

31. Ibid., 79.

32. Ibid., 80.

33. Lord, 197.

34. Ibid., 199.

35. Parker to Cochrane, August 30, 1814, Cochrane Papers, NLS, Ms. 2329.

36. Jeremiah T. Chase to Winder, September 13, 1814, Winder Papers, Ms. 919. MHS.

37. Parker to Cochrane, August 30, 1814, Cochrane Papers, NLS, Ms, 2329.

38. Parker to Cochrane, August 29, 1814, Cochrane Papers, NLS, Ms. 2329.

39. Parker to Cochrane, August 29, 1814, Cochrane Papers, NLS, Ms. 2329.

40. Chamier, 1:141–217. Frederick Chamier (1796–1870) later became a successful writer of naval novels and in 1837 editor of the third edition of James' *Naval History of Great Britain*. It is interesting to note that in editing James' discussion of the war in the Chesapeake, Chamier kept to the official line and did not include the criticisms of Cockburn that mark *The Life of a Sailor*. See P. J. van der Voort, *The Pen and the Quarter-deck: A Study of the Life and Works of Captain Frederick Chamier, R.N.* (Leiden, the Netherlands: Leiden University Press, 1972).

41. Ibid., 1:141–42.

42. Ibid., 1:145.

43. Acting commander Lt. Henry Crease to Cochrane, in Marine, 120–22.

44. See *Niles' Weekly Register*, June 14, 1817, and Marine, 126, and Lt. Col. Philip Reed to Brig. Gen. Benjamin Chambers, September 3, 1814, quoted in Marine, 117–20.

45. Parker to Parker, August 30, 1814, quoted in Dallas, 69.

46. Chamier, 1:207.

47. Marine, 117.

48. Reed to Chambers, quoted in Marine, 117–20.

49. See "Philip Reed of Kent," *Baltimore News*, December 4, 1900, and L. Wethered Barroll, "Remarks On General Philip Reed Beside His Grave At I.U. Church, Kent County, Maryland, September 13, 1959," unidentified newscutting, vertical file, MHS. Reed and 28 men and officers of the 21st Regiment had repulsed a British attempt to burn a vessel in Whorton Creek in July 1813. In Philip Reed, "The Late War," Reed stated that from the inception of the British campaign in spring 1813, he and others "pledged their property to obtain the necessary supplies and provisions . . . for the use and comfort of the troops."

50. Reed to Chambers, quoted in Marine, 117–20.

51. Chamier, 1:209.

52. Ibid.

53. Papenfuse, 151.

54. Reed to Chambers, quoted in Marine, 117–20.

55. Ibid., and Chamier, 1:211.

56. Ibid.

57. Barroll, "Remarks On General Philip Reed." See also oration of William M. Marine, in "Gen. Philip Reed and Caulk's Field," pamphlet PAM 3566, MHS, 44.

58. Napier, *Life and Opinions*, 1:223.

59. Reed to Chambers, quoted in Marine, 117–20.

60. Chamier, 1:211–13.

61. George A. Hanson, M.A., *Old Kent: The Eastern Shore of Maryland, Republished from the Original in the Chestertown Transcript of 1875 and 1876* (Chestertown, Md.: R. H. Collins & Sons, 1936), 110; Lord, 209.

62. Reed to Chambers, quoted in Marine, 117–20.

63. Lord, 207.

64. Ibid.

65. Ibid., 207–8; Napier, *Life and Correspondence of Admiral Sir Charles Napier*, 84.

66. Lord, 208–9; Napier, *Life and Correspondence of Admiral Sir Charles Napier*, 84–85.

67. Lord, 209; Napier, *Life and Correspondence of Admiral Sir Charles Napier*, 85.

68. Lord, 221–23, 239–45.

69. Francis Scott Key to Mrs. Ann Phoebe Charlton Key, September 2, 1814, in Franklin R. Mullaly, ed., "A Forgotten Letter of Francis Scott Key," *MHM* 55 (Dec. 1960): 359–60. Francis Scott Key was born at Terra Rubra, the family home in what is now Carroll County on August 1, 1779. In his later years he served as district attorney for Washington, D.C. He was known as a pacifist and abolitionist. Key died in Baltimore on January 11, 1843. See Victor Weybright, *Spangled Banner: The Story of Francis Scott Key* (New York: Farrar and Rinehart, 1935).

70. Whitehorne, 157, states that "no Eastern Shore regiment reinforced any of Baltimore's or Annapolis's defenders." This is not true. Col. Thomas W. Veazey and militiamen from the 49th Regiment Maryland Militia, who had faced the British at Fredericktown and Georgetown on the Sassafras River in May 1813, were sent to the defense of Baltimore at the end of August 1814. They were added to the First Brigade under Brig. Gen. Thomas M. Forman made up of Harford and Cecil County troops. See bounty land application of Thomas W. Veazey, in F. Edward Wright, *Maryland Militia War of 1812. Vol. 3. Cecil & Harford Counties* (Silver Spring, Md.: Family Line Press, 1980), 70–71.

Chapter Ten

1. Pvt. David Winchester to Brig. Gen. James Winchester, August 25, 1814, James Winchester Papers (hereinafter JWP), Tennessee Historical Society Collection, Tennessee State Library and Archives, Nashville, Tenn.

2. Brig. Gen. Thomas M. Forman to Mrs. Martha B. Forman, September 20, 1814, Forman Papers, Ms. 1277, MHS.

3. Lord, 228–29.

4. Quoted in Marine, 136, and Sheads, *The Rockets' Red Glare*, 61.

5. Howard and Smith exchanged acid words in the senatorial contest of 1798 when Howard accused Smith of "selling out" the United States to France during the XYZ affair. In an anonymous letter, Howard charged that Smith told President John Adams that the American ministers in France should have paid French agents "X, Y, and Z" the bribe they demanded because "it would be cheaper than war." Smith hotly denied the allegation. See Cassell, *Merchant Congressman*, 84–89.

6. Levin Winder to Smith, August 26, 1814, quoted in Lord, 231.

7. Lord, 231–32; Sheads, *The Rockets' Red Glare*, 62.

8. Monroe to General Winder, September 11, 1814, quoted in Sheads, *The Rockets' Red Glare*, 63.

9. Quoted in Marine, 139.

10. Lord, 233.

11. Quoted in Lord, 233.

12. Marine, 406, 410; Lord, 268. For the service of David Poe at North Point, see Mary E. Phillips, *Edgar Allan Poe, the Man*, 2 vols. (Chicago: John C. Winston, 1926), 1:29. Also see listings for Samuel and Uriah Prosser in F. Edward Wright, *Maryland Militia War of 1812, Vol. 2. Baltimore* (Westminster, Md.: Family Line Publications, 1980), 17.

13. Sheads, *The Rockets' Red Glare*, 72–73. Elting (224) ascribes the "very professional line of fortifications to resident French architect, Maximilian Godefroy. . . ." Although Godefroy, the future architect of the city's triumphal Battle Monument (1815–22), did work on the city's defenses, he did not work on them until *after* the Battle of Baltimore, when he helped to strengthen them in case of a feared return by the British. See Robert L. Alexander, *The Architecture of Maximilian Godefroy* (Baltimore: The Johns Hopkins University Press, 1974), 94–99.

14. Minerva Rodgers to Com. John Rodgers, August 25, 1814, Rodgers-Macomb Papers, LC.

15. George Douglass to Henry Wheaton, September 3, 1814, Vertical File, Fort McHenry Library.

16. Smith, *Autobiography*, 1:216–17.

17. Lord, 224, 244–45; Fortescue, 10:149.

18. Gleig diary quoted in Barrett, *85th King's Light Infantry*, 167–68. Lord (245) states that the decision to attack Baltimore was made "early on September 7." However, Gleig's diary entry of September 6 mentioning reinforcement of Ross's army with naval contingents indicates that the decision was made September 6, if not before.

19. Lord, 241–44.

20. Ibid.; Gleig, *Narrative of the Campaigns*, 105.

21. Lord, 243.

22. Ibid. Also John S. Skinner, "Incidents of the War of 1812," Baltimore *Sun*, May 29, 1849, Ms. 1846, MHS.

23. Gen. Robert Ross to John Mason, September 7, 1814, M625, R77, 017, NA.

24. Gleig diary quoted in Barrett, *85th King's Light Infantry*, 168; Lord, 244–47.

25. Gleig, *Narrative of the Campaigns*, 169.

26. Quoted in Lord, 251–52.

27. David Winchester to Brig. Gen. James Winchester, September 11, 1814, JWP.

28. Sheads, *The Rockets' Red Glare*, 82.

29. Ibid., 80.

30. Ibid., 84–85.

31. Ibid. Recruitment for the U.S. Sea Fencibles began in January 1814. Sheads (36) explains that the Sea Fencibles were formed in imitation of the French maritime *garde-côte,* or coast guard. Their duties were, he says, "to keep a vigilant lookout in the harbors by manning gunboats and coastal fortifications."

32. Ibid., 79–80. Although Godefroy was not employed in the physical engineering of the batteries around Fort McHenry, Alexander (95) suggests that it was his suggestion to establish those batteries in support of the fort.

33. Lord, 254–55.

34. Ibid., 252–54.

35. Marine, 147–48. Also, "State of a Division of the troops under the command of Colonel Arthur Brooke, 44th Regiment Foot, Chesapeake, 17th September 1814," LC. This British return lists 4,419 "Total Officers & rank and file" including the four British regiments plus the 2nd and 3rd Battalions of Royal Marines, the Royal Artillery, sappers and miners, and the Royal Marine rocket battery. It does not appear to include the small arms sailors that were added to the force. Cochrane stated in his dispatch to London that the naval brigade comprised six hundred seamen, thus making the total force about five thousand. Cochrane to Croker, September 17, 1814, in Palmer, 4:206–10. General Smith in his report to Acting Secretary of War Monroe asserted that the British landed between seven thousand and eight thousand. See Palmer, 4:187–90. The figure of seven thousand appears to come from a British deserter interrogated before the Battle of Bladensburg. Samuel Smith Papers, LC.

36. Gleig, *Narrative of the Campaigns*, 172; John McHenry to John McHenry, September 20, 1814, McHenry Papers, Ms. 647, MHS. John McHenry (1791–1822), a Calvert Street

merchant, was the second son of Daniel McHenry, brother of Ballymena, Ireland-born James McHenry, George Washington's secretary and secretary of war, for whom Fort McHenry was named.

37. Gleig diary quoted in Barrett, *85th King's Light Infantry*, 168.

38. Brooke diary, in George, "Family Papers," 310.

39. Marine, 150.

40. Brig. Gen. John Stricker to Maj. Gen. Samuel Smith, September 15, 1814, in Marine, 161–66.

41. Gleig, *Narrative of the Campaigns*, 178.

42. Cockburn to Rev. Thomas Ross, September 17, 1814, Public Record Office of Northern Ireland. Also James H. McCulloh, Jr., Garrison Surgeon, U.S. Army, to Smith, September 14, 1814, Samuel Smith Papers, LC.

43. See Marine, 190–94, and "Who Killed Robert Ross? *Or* Wells and McComas: Pro and Con" in Curtis Carroll Davis, *Defenders' Dozen: Some Comments Along the Way at the Halts during the Cavalcade of the Society of the War of 1812 (Maryland)* (Baltimore, Md.: Society of the War of 1812 in the State of Maryland, 1974), 19–21. The two riflemen were reinterred in a special vault in Ashland Square at Monument and Aisquith Streets on September 13, 1858. In 1873, after the raising of subscriptions, a 21-foot obelisk was raised on a 10-foot base. Nowhere on the monument is there mention that the riflemen shot Ross, as if the city fathers acknowledged that there was some doubt. See Jane B. Wilson, *The Very Quiet Baltimoreans: A Guide to the Historic Cemeteries and Burial Sites of Baltimore* (Shippensburg, Pa.: White Mane Publishing Co., 1991), 97–98, 107.

44. Gleig, *Narrative of the Campaigns*, 177–79.

45. Ibid., 179. In his letter to his mother, Gleig did not include this censure of Brooke, stating instead, "Col. Brooks [sic] of the 44th now succeeded to the command, and a fine brave old fellow he is." Gleig to Mrs. G. R. Gleig, September 16, 1814, Gleig Papers, Ms. 3869, NLS.

46. Franklin R. Mullaly, "The Battle of Baltimore," *MHM* 54 (1959): 61–103.

47. Brooke diary, in George, "Family Papers," 310.

48. Ibid.

49. Gleig to Mrs. G. R. Gleig, September 16, 1814, Gleig Papers, Ms. 3869, NLS.

50. Brooke to Bathurst, September 17, 1814, in Palmer, 4:210–13, and Whitehorne, 181–82. The fact that the British 21st Regiment were in column rather than in line explains the high rate of casualties in this unit.

51. Stricker to Smith, September 15, 1814, in Marine, 161–66.

52. Ibid.

53. Ibid.

54. Ibid.

55. John McHenry to John McHenry, September 20, 1814, McHenry papers, Ms. 647, MHS.

56. Gleig to Mrs. G. R. Gleig, September 16, 1814, Gleig Papers, Ms. 3869, NLS; Scott, 3:340.

57. Ibid.

58. Lord, 268. See also L. Frailey, late Brigade Major, 3rd Brigade, Maryland Militia, "List of wounded of the third brigade, at the late engagement at Long Log Lane, September 12, 1814," *Niles' Weekly Register*, December 3, 1814. Frailey makes reference to the inflated claims in Brooke's dispatch: "As the honorable Colonel Brook [sic] has vied with his compatriots in falsifying an *official* report, I beg [the editor to] favor the public with this account. . . . I pledge myself for its correctness." The British casualties are reported in "Return of the killed and wounded, in action with the enemy, near Baltimore on the 12th of September, 1814," PRO, WO 1, and "A return of killed and wounded belonging to the navy, disembarked with the army under Major General Ross, September 12, 1814," PRO, Adm 1, Vol. 507.

59. Gleig, *Narrative of the Campaigns*, 189. On how the rainy conditions caused problems for the troops at Waterloo, see Elizabeth Longford, *Wellington: The Years of the Sword* (New York: Harper & Row, 1969), 379.

60. Gleig, *Narrative of the Campaigns*, 189–91.

61. Lord, 256, 269–70, 277.

62. Quoted in Bourchier, 319–21.

63. Sheads, *The Rockets' Red Glare*, 92–93.

64. Ibid.; Armistead to Monroe, September 24, 1814, quoted in Marine, 167–69.

65. "A Letter Describing the Attack on Fort McHenry," *MHM* 51 (Dec. 1956): 356.

66. Brooke diary, in George, "Family Papers," 311.

67. Smith to Monroe, September 19, 1814, in Palmer, 4: 187–90.

68. Brooke to Cochrane, midnight September 13–14, 1814, Cochrane Papers Ms. 2329, NLS.

69. Clausewitz wrote, "The attacker seldom if ever knows enough about the defence to make up for his lack of visual observation." Quoted in Richard Holmes, *Firing Line* (London: Pimlico, 1994), 122.

70. Diary of Capt. Matthias E. Bartgis, Ms. 1913, MHS.

71. Cochrane letter quoted in Brooke diary, in George, "Family Papers, 311.

72. Brooke diary, in George, "Family Papers, 311.

73. Brooke to Cochrane, midnight September 13–14, 1814, Cochrane Papers Ms. 2329, NLS.

74. Robert V. Remini, *Andrew Jackson* (New York: Perennial Library, Harper & Row, 1969), 72.

75. Gleig to Mrs. G. R. Gleig, September 16, 1814, Gleig Papers Ms. 3869, NLS.

76. Cochrane to Napier, September 13, 1814, Cochrane Papers Ms. 2329, NLS.

77. Account of John A. Webster prepared in July 1853, quoted in Marine, 177–81.

78. Ibid., 179.

79. Ibid., 179–80.

80. Ibid.

81. Ibid.

82. Armistead to Monroe, September 24, 1814, quoted in Marine, 167–69.

83. Ibid.; Sheads, *The Rockets' Red Glare*, 91–103.

84. Ibid., 104–5.

85. Gleig, *Narrative of the Campaigns*, 198.

86. Ibid.

87. Diary of Matthias E. Bartgis, Ms. 1913, MHS. Also "Defense of Baltimore, September 1814," details of participation of Master's Mate Robert Field Stockton in the defense of the city, Ms. 1849, MHS. Stockton, then age 19, served as an aide to Commodore Rodgers.

Epilogue

1. Peter Rowley, ed., "Captain Robert Rowley Helps to Burn Washington, D.C., Part I," *MHM* 82 (Fall 1987): 240–50, and Cochrane to Croker, September 17, 1814, in *Gentleman's Magazine*, December 1814, 583–84. Cochrane wrote, "I considered that an attack on the enemy's strong position [on Hampstead Hill] by the army only, with such a disparity of force, though confident of success, might risk a greater loss than the possession of the town would compensate for."

2. Memoirs of Lt. Gordon Gollie MacDonald, New York Public Library Manuscript Collection, New York, N.Y.

3. Sheads, *The Rockets' Red Glare*, 108–9.

4. James Madison, "Sixth Annual Message [to Congress]," September 20, 1814, in Gaillard Hunt, ed., *The Writings of James Madison*, vol. 8, 1808–19 (New York: G. P. Putnam's Sons, 1908), 306–12.

5. Ibid.
6. Goulburn to Bathurst, October 21, 1814, in Wellington, ed., *Supplementary Despatches,* 9:366.
7. Liverpool to Viscount Castlereagh, October 21, 1814, in Wellington, ed., *Supplementary Despatches,* 9:367.
8. Wellington to Liverpool, November 9, 1814, in Wellington, ed., *Supplementary Despatches,* 9:424–26.
9. Gleig diary quoted in Barrett, *85th King's Light Infantry,* 182.
10. Forman to Forman, September 20, 1814, Forman Papers, Ms. 1277, MHS
11. Whitehorne, 196–97, and Gleig, *Narrative of the Campaigns,* 210.
12. Gleig diary quoted in Barrett, *85th King's Light Infantry,* 187.
13. Cocke to Barbour, December 4, 1814, *CVSP,* 10:404–5.
14. Lord, 317.
15. Robert G. Stewart, "The Battle of the Ice Mound, February 7, 1815," *MHM* 70 (1975): 373–78.
16. Pitch, 236, and Lord, 336–38.
17. *Niles' Weekly Register,* February 18, 1815, and April 15, 1815.

Appendix One

1. Robert Greenhow to Barbour, February 24, 1814, *CVSP,* 10:304–5.
2. Robert J. Barrett, R.N., "Naval Recollections of the Late American War. II.," *United Service Journal* 149 (May 1841): 13–23; Napier, *Life and Opinions,* 1:229.
3. Comte de Las Cases, *Journal of the Private Life and Conversations of the Emperor Napoleon at St. Helena* (Boston: Wells and Lily, 1823), 2(3):34.
4. Chamier, 1:202–5.
5. Morriss, 92.
6. Cockburn, "Memoir of Services," NMM, COC/11, f. 104.
7. Morriss, 92.
8. Cockburn, "Memoir of Services," NMM, COC/11, f. 110.
9. Cockburn to Croker, January 28, 1815, quoted in Morriss, 117.

Appendix Two

1. *Daily National Intelligencer,* August 4, 1814.
2. Shomette, *Flotilla,* 136.
3. See chapter 4 for Havre de Grace events and Brig. Gen. John H. Cocke to Barbour, December 4, 1814, *CVSP,* 10:404–5, for Tappahannock grave desecration.
4. For Havre de Grace allegations, see Swepson Earle, *Chesapeake Bay Country* (Baltimore: Thomsen-Ellis, 1923), 245–48. The allegation that cattle were indiscriminately slaughtered by the British on Specutie Island appears in Marine, 29, but appears not to be supported in a contemporary account. See Wilmer, 10–11.
5. Morriss, 92. Directive from Cockburn to squadron commanders, July 12, 1813, Cockburn Papers, LC.
6. Mobberly to Grassi, October 31, 1814, quoted in Beitzell, *The Jesuit Missions of St. Mary's County, Maryland,* 107–10. In this initial letter, Mobberly was under the false impression that the raiding party was from the brig *Jason* commanded by Captain Watts. He later found out he was mistaken.
7. Dixie to "the Clergymen at St. Inigoes," November 18, 1814, quoted in Beitzell, 114.
8. Quoted in Beitzell, 116.

Appendix Three

1. Napier, *Life and Opinions,* 1:369–70.

Appendix Four

1. "An Appendix Containing an Exposition of Sundry Errors in the Work," in Gleig, *Narrative of the Campaigns*, 383–431.
2. Ibid., 122–23, 125.
3. Ibid., 396.
4. Ibid., 94, 162.
5. George R. Gleig, *A Subaltern in America* (Philadelphia: M. Carey and Hart, 1833).
6. J. A. Every-Clayton, "Who Wrote *A Subaltern in America*?" *Journal of the War of 1812* 3 (Winter 1998): 10–14; Lord, 374; and J. A. Every-Clayton, personal correspondence, September 1998.
7. Gleig, *A Subaltern in America*, 122–23.
8. Gleig, *Narrative of the Campaigns*, 201.

Appendix Five

1. Vice Adm. William Stanhope Lovell, R.N., K.H., *Personal Narrative of Events, from 1799 to 1815*, 2nd edition (London: Wm. Allen & Co., 1879), 164, 169.
2. Napier, *Life and Opinions*, 1:222.
3. Hungerford to Barbour, July 27, 1814, and Lord, 51.
4. Claxton to Hardy, September 16, 1814, Cochrane Papers, Ms. 2329, NLS.

Bibliography

Manuscript Sources

Archives of the Historical Society of Harford County: War of 1812 Papers.

Library of Congress: Cockburn Papers; Thomas Jefferson Papers; James McHenry Papers; Rodgers-Macomb Papers; Samuel Smith Papers.

Maryland Historical Society: Bartgis Diary; McHenry Papers; Stricker Papers; War of 1812 Papers; Winder Papers.

National Archives: Letters Received, District Commissioners; Letters Sent, Office of the Adjutant General; Ross and Mason Correspondence.

National Library of Scotland, Edinburgh: Cochrane Papers; Gleig Papers.

New York Public Library, Manuscripts and Archives Division: Great Britain Navy box.

Peabody Institute of the Johns Hopkins University, Baltimore, Md.: John Pendleton Kennedy Papers.

Pennsylvania Historical Society, Dreer Collection, Philadelphia: Joshua Barney Papers.

Public Record Office, London: Admiralty and War Office Papers, 1813–1814.

Public Record Office of Northern Ireland, Belfast: Ross Papers.

Tennessee Historical Society Collection, Tennessee State Library and Archives, Nashville, Tenn.: James Winchester Papers.

Published Primary Sources

Ball, Charles. *Slavery in the United States: A Narrative of the Life and Adventures of Charles Ball, a Black Man*. Lewistown, Pa.: John S. Tayloe, 1836. Reprint, New York: Negro Universities Press, New York, 1969.

[Barker, Jacob]. *Incidents in the Life of Jacob Barker*. Freeport, N.Y.: Books for Libraries Press, 1970. Reprint of 1858 edition.

[Barrett, Robert J., R.N.]. "Naval Recollections of the Late American War. I." *United Service Journal* 149 (April 1841): 455–67.

Bourchier, Lady Jane, ed. *Memoir of the Life of Admiral Sir Edward Codrington with Selections from His Public and Private Correspondence*. Vol. 1. London: Longmans, Green, and Co., 1873.

Calendar of Virginia State Papers and Other Manuscripts from January 1, 1808 to December 31, 1835; Preserved in the Capitol, at Richmond, Vol. 10. Richmond, Va.: State of Virginia, 1892.

[Chamier, Frederick, R.N.]. *The Life of a Sailor by a Captain in the Navy*. 2 vols. New York: J. & J. Harper, 1833.

Dudley, William S., ed. *The Naval War of 1812: A Documentary History*. 2 vols. Washington, D.C.: Naval Historical Center, Department of the Navy, 1985–92.

[Gleig, George R.]. *Narrative of the Campaigns of the British Army at Washington, Baltimore, and New Orleans, under Generals Ross, Pakenham, & Lambert*. Philadelphia: M. Carey & Sons, 1821.

[Gleig, George R.]. *A Subaltern in America Comprising His Narrative of the Campaigns of the British Army at Baltimore, Washington, &c., &c., During the Late War*. Philadelphia: E. L. Carey & A. Hart, 1833.

"A Letter Describing the Attack on Fort McHenry." *MHM (Maryland Historical Magazine)* 51 (Dec. 1956): 356.

McKenney, Thomas L. *Memoirs, Official and Personal*. Vol. 1. New York: Paine and Burgess, 1846.

[McKenney, Thomas L]. "A Narrative of the Battle of Bladensburg in a Letter [of September 10, 1814] to Henry Banning, Esq." Washington, D.C. (?): Publisher not known, 1814 (?).

Madison, James. *The Writings of James Madison, Volume VIII, 1808–1819*. Edited by Gaillard Hunt. New York: G. P. Putnam's Sons, 1908.

Palmer, T. H., ed. *The Historical Register of the United States. Part II. From the Declaration of War in 1812, to January 1, 1814*. Vol. 2. Washington, D.C.: T. H. Palmer, 1814.

Palmer, T. H., ed. *The Historical Register of the United States, Part II for 1814*. Philadelphia: G. Palmer, 1816.

Rowley, Peter, ed. "Captain Robert Rowley Helps to Burn Washington, D.C., Part 1." *MHM* 82 (Fall 1987): 240–50.

Rowley, Peter, ed. "Captain Rowley Visits Maryland; Part II of a Series." *MHM* 83 (Fall 1988): 247–53.

"Report on the Capture of the City of Washington," *American State Papers*, Military Affairs, Class V, I. Washington, D.C.: Gales and Seaton, Washington, D.C., 1832.

Smith, G. C. Moore, ed. *The Autobiography of Lieutenant-General Sir Harry Smith.* 2 vols. New York: E. P. Dutton & Co., 1902.

Smith, Mrs. Margaret Bayard. *The First Forty Years of Washington Society.* Edited by Gaillard Hunt. New York: Charles Scribner's Sons, 1906.

Van Horne, John C., ed. *The Correspondence and Miscellaneous Papers of Benjamin Henry Latrobe.* 3 vols. New Haven, Ct.: Yale University Press, 1988.

Wellington, Duke of, K.G., ed. *Supplementary Despatches, Correspondence, and Memoranda of Field Marshal Arthur Duke of Wellington, K.G.* Vol. 9. London: John Murray, 1858–72.

Wilkinson, Gen. James. *Memoirs of My Own Times.* Vol. 1. Philadelphia: Abraham Small, 1816.

[Wilmer, James J.]. *Narrative Respecting the Conduct of the British from Their First Landing on Specutia Island Till Their Progress to Havre de Grace ... By a citizen of Havre de Grace.* Baltimore: P. Mauro, 1813.

Newspapers and Periodicals

American & Commercial Daily Advertiser

Federal Republican

Gazette and Publick Leader

Maryland Gazette

National Intelligencer

Naval Chronicle

Niles' Weekly Register

North American Review

Secondary Sources

Alexander, Robert L. *The Architecture of Maximilian Godefroy.* Baltimore, Md.: The Johns Hopkins University Press, 1974.

Babcock, Kendric Charles. *The Rise of American Nationality, 1811–1819.* New York: Haskell House Publishers, 1969. Reprint of 1906 edition.

Barney, Mary, ed. *A Biographical Memoir of the Late Joshua Barney from Autobiographical Notes and Journals in Possession of His Family and Other Authentic Sources.* Boston: Gray and Bowen, 1832.

Barrett, C. R. B., ed. *The 85th King's Light Infantry.* London: Spottiswoode & Co., Ltd., 1913.

Barroll, L. Wethered. "Remarks on General Philip Reed Beside His Grave at I.U. Church, Kent County, Maryland, September 13, 1959." Unidentified newscutting, vertical file, Maryland Historical Society, Baltimore, Md.

Berton, Pierre. *Flames Across the Border: The Canadian-American Tragedy, 1813–1814.* Boston: Little, Brown & Co., 1981.

Brant, Irving. *James Madison, Commander in Chief, 1812–1836*. New York: The Bobbs-Merrill Company, Inc., 1961.

Butler, Colonel Sir William F. *Sir Charles Napier*. London: Macmillan and Co., 1890.

Calderhead, William L. "Naval Innovation in Crisis: War in the Chesapeake, 1813." *American Neptune* 36 (July 1976): 206–21.

Calderhead, William L. "A Strange Career in a Young Navy: Captain Charles Gordon." *MHM* 72 (Fall 1977): 373–86.

Cannon, Richard. *Historical Record of the 21st Foot*. London: William Clowes and Sons, 1849.

Cassell, Frank A. "The Great Baltimore Riot of 1812." *MHM* 70 (Fall 1975): 241–59.

Cassell, Frank A. *Merchant Congressman in the Young Republic: Samuel Smith of Maryland, 1752–1839*. Madison, Wisc.: University of Wisconsin Press, 1971.

Cassell, Frank A. "Slaves of the Chesapeake Bay Area and the War of 1812." *Journal of Negro History* 57 (April 1972): 144–55.

Chappelle, Howard I. *The History of the American Sailing Navy*. New York: W. W. Norton & Co., 1949.

Cranwell, John Philips, and William Bowers Crane. *Men of Marque: A History of Private Armed Vessels Out of Baltimore during the War of 1812*. New York: W. W. Norton & Co., 1940.

Cress, Lawrence D. "The Standing Army, the Militia, and the New Republic: Changing Attitudes toward the Military in American Society." Ph.D. diss., University of Virginia, 1976.

[Dallas, Sir George]. *A Biographical Memoir of the Late Sir Peter Parker*. London: Longman, Hurst, Rees, Orme, and Brown, 1815.

Davis, Curtis Carroll. *Defenders' Dozen: Some Comments Along the Way at the Halts during the Cavalcade of the Society of the War of 1812 (Maryland)*. Baltimore, Md.: Society of the War of 1812 in the State of Maryland, 1974.

Dupuy, Trevor N., Curt Johnson, and David L. Bongard. *The Harper Encyclopedia of Military Biography*. Edison, N.J.: Castle Books, 1995.

Fletcher, Ian. *Wellington's Regiments: The Men and Their Battles from Rolica to Waterloo, 1808–1815*. Staplehurst, Kent: Spellmount Limited, 1994.

Footner, Hulbert. *Sailor of Fortune: The Life and Adventures of Commodore Barney, U.S.N.* New York: Harper & Brothers, 1940. Reprint, Annapolis, Md.: Naval Institute Press, 1998.

Forrest, William S. *Historical and Descriptive Sketches of Norfolk and Vicinity*. Philadelphia: Lindsay and Blakiston, 1853.

Fortescue, Hon. J. W. *History of the British Army*. 14 vols. London: Macmillan and Co., 1920.

"General Nathan Towson, Paymaster-General U.S. Army" in *Sketches of Eminent Americans: Nathan Towson of Maryland*, publisher not known, ca. 1853, pp. 95–136, in the Library of the Maryland Historical Society, Baltimore, Md.

George, Christopher T. "The Family Papers of Maj. Gen. Robert Ross, the Diary of Col. Arthur Brooke, and the British Attacks on Washington and Baltimore of 1814." *MHM* 88 (Fall 1993): 300–316.

George, Christopher T. "Harford County in the War of 1812." *Harford Historical Bulletin* 76 (Spring 1998): 1–61.

George, Christopher T. "Mirage of Freedom: African Americans in the War of 1812." *MHM* 91 (Winter 1996): 426–50.

Gilje, Paul A. "'Le Menu Peuple' in America: Identifying the Mob in the Baltimore Riots of 1812." *MHM* 81 (Spring 1986): 50–66.

Graves, Donald E. *The Battle of Lundy's Lane: On the Niagara in 1814*. Baltimore, Md.: The Nautical & Aviation Publishing Company, 1993.

Graves, Donald E. *Sir William Congreve and the Rocket's Red Glare*. Alexandria Bay, N.Y.: Museum Restoration Service, 1989.

Hallahan, John M. *The Battle of Craney Island: A Matter of Credit*. Portsmouth, Va.: St. Michael's Press, 1986.

Hanson, George A., M.A. *Old Kent: The Eastern Shore of Maryland, Republished from the Original in the Chestertown Transcript of 1875 and 1876*. Chestertown, Md.: R. H. Collins & Sons, 1936.

Hazelton, George C., Jr. *The National Capitol: Its Architecture, Art and History*. New York: J. F. Taylor and Co., 1902.

Hitsman, J. Mackay, and Alice Sorby. "Independent Foreigners or Canadian Chasseurs." *Military Affairs* 25 (Spring 1961): 11–17.

Hopkins, Fred W., Jr. *Tom Boyle, Master Privateer*. Cambridge, Md.: Tidewater Publishers, 1976.

Ingersoll, Charles J. *Historical Sketch of the Second War between the United States and Great Britain. . .* 2 vols. Philadelphia: Lea and Blanchard, 1845.

James, William. *The Naval History of Great Britain from the Declaration of War by France in 1793 to the Accession of George IV*. 6 vols. London: Macmillan and Co., Ltd., 1902.

Jenkins, R. Wheeler, M.D. "The Shots That Saved Baltimore." *MHM* 77(1982): 362–64.

Kohn, Richard H. *Eagle and Sword: The Federalists and the Creation of the Military Establishment in America, 1783–1802*. New York: The Free Press, 1975.

Longford, Elizabeth. *Wellington: The Years of the Sword*. New York: Harper & Row, 1969.

Lord, Walter. *The Dawn's Early Light*. New York: W. W. Norton & Co., 1972.

Lossing, Benson J. *Pictorial Field Book of the War of 1812*. New York: Harper & Brothers, 1869.

McComas, Henry Clay, and Winona McComas. *The McComas Saga: A Family History Down to the Year 1950*, typescript ca. 1950, Library of the Maryland Historical Society, Baltimore, Md.

McKee, Christopher. *A Gentlemanly and Honorable Profession: The Creation of the U.S. Naval Officer Corps, 1794–1815*. Annapolis, Md.: Naval Institute Press, 1991.

Magruder, Caleb Clarke, Jr. "Dr. William Beanes, the Incidental Cause of the Authorship of the Star-Spangled Banner." *Records of the Columbia Historical Society* 22 (1915): 207–24.

Maguire, W. A. "Major General Ross and the Burning of Washington." *The Irish Sword* 14 (Winter 1980): 117–28.

Marine, William M. *The British Invasion of Maryland*. Baltimore, Md.: Society of the War of 1812 in Maryland, 1913.

Maryland: A New Guide to the Old Line State. New York: Oxford University Press, 1948.

Morriss, Roger. *Cockburn and the British Navy in Transition: Admiral Sir George Cockburn, 1772–1853*. Columbia, S.C.: University of South Carolina Press, 1997.

Mullaly, Franklin R. "The Battle of Baltimore." *MHM* 54 (1959): 61–103.

Mullaly, Franklin R., ed. "A Forgotten Letter of Francis Scott Key." *MHM* 55 (Dec. 1960): 359–60.

Napier, Major General Elers. *The Life and Correspondence of Admiral Sir Charles Napier, from Personal Recollections, Letters, and Official Documents*. 2 vols. London: Hurst and Blackett, 1862.

Napier, Lt. Gen. Sir William. *Life and Opinions of General Sir James Napier, G.C.B.* 4 vols. London: John Murray, 1857.

Pack, James. *The Man Who Burned the White House: Admiral Sir George Cockburn, 1772–1853*. Annapolis, Md.: Naval Institute Press, 1987.

Pancake, John S. *Samuel Smith and the Politics of Business: 1752–1839*. Birmingham, Ala.: University of Alabama Press, 1972.

Papenfuse, Edward C., Gregory A. Stiverson, Susan A. Collins, and Lois Green Carr, eds. *Maryland: A New Guide to the Old Line State*. Baltimore, Md.: The Johns Hopkins University Press, 1976.

"Philip Reed of Kent," *Baltimore News*, December 4, 1900.

Pitch, Anthony. *The Burning of Washington: The British Invasion of 1814*. Annapolis, Md.: Naval Institute Press, 1998.

Plummer, Norman H. "Another Look at the Battle of St. Michaels," *The Weather Gauge* 31 (Spring 1995): 10–17.

Quarles, Benjamin. *The Negro in the American Revolution*. New York: W. W. Norton & Co., 1973.

Remini, Robert V. *Andrew Jackson*. New York: Perennial Library, Harper & Row, 1969.

Royster, Charles. *Light-Horse Harry Lee and the Legacy of the American Revolution*. New York: Alfred A. Knopf, 1981.

Scharf, J. Thomas. *The Chronicles of Baltimore*. Baltimore, Md.: Turnbull Brothers, 1874.

——. *History of Baltimore City and County from the Earliest Period to the Present Day: Including Biographical Sketches of Their Representative Men*. Philadelphia: Louis H. Everts, 1881. Reprinted in 2 vols., Baltimore, Md.: Regional Publishing Co., 1971.

Seale, William. *The President's House: A History*. Washington, D.C.: White House Historical Association, 1986.

Sheads, Scott S. "A Black Soldier Defends Fort McHenry, 1814." *Military Collector and Historian* 41 (Spring 1989): 20–21.

——. "Defending Baltimore in the War of 1812: Two Sidelights." *MHM* 84 (Fall 1989): 252–58.

——. *The Rockets' Red Glare: The Maritime Defense of Baltimore in 1814*. Centreville, Md.: Tidewater Publishers, 1986.

Shomette, Donald G. *Flotilla: Battle for the Patuxent*. Solomons, Md.: The Calvert Marine Museum Press, 1981.

——. *Tidewater Time Capsule: History Beneath the Patuxent*. Centreville, Md.: Tidewater Publishers, 1995.

Silver, Albert P. "Lapidum and Its Surroundings. A Sketch Before the Harford County Historical Society, April 28th, 1888," typescript, Archives of the Historical Society of Harford County.

Skeen, C. Edward. *John Armstrong, Jr., 1758–1843: A Biography*. Syracuse, N.Y.: Syracuse University Press, 1981.

Smythe, B. *History of the XX Regiment, 1688–1888*. London: Simpkin, Marshall & Co., 1889. Appendix, "Major-General Robert Ross," 340–50.

Stagg, John C. *Mr. Madison's War: Politics, Diplomacy, and Warfare in the Early American Republic, 1783–1830*. Princeton, N.J.: Princeton University Press, 1983.

Stewart, Robert G. "The Battle of the Ice Mound, February 7, 1815," *MHM* 70 (1975): 373–78.

Swanson, Neil H. *The Perilous Fight*. New York: Farrar and Rinehart, Inc., 1945.

"Walker Keith Armistead," *Professional Memoirs, Corps of Engineers*, U.S. Army, and Engineer Department-at-Large 2 (1910): 392.

Weybright, Victor. *Spangled Banner: The Story of Francis Scott Key*. New York: Farrar and Rinehart, 1935.

Wheeler, Bruce. "Urban Politics in Nature's Republic: The Development of Political Parties in the Seaport Cities in the Federalist Era." Ph.D. diss., University of Virginia, 1967.

Whitehorne, Joseph A. *The Battle for Baltimore 1814*. Baltimore: Nautical & Aviation Publishing Co., 1997.

Wiencek, Henry. *The Smithsonian Guide to Historic America: Virginia and the Capital Region*. New York: Stewart, Tabori, & Chang, 1989.

Williams, John S. *History of the Invasion and Capture of Washington*. New York: Harper & Brothers, New York, 1857.

Williams, T. Harry. *The History of American Wars from 1745 to 1918*. Baton Rouge, La.: Louisiana State University Press, 1985.

Wilson, Jane B. *The Very Quiet Baltimoreans: A Guide to the Historic Cemeteries and Burial Sites of Baltimore*. Shippensburg, Pa.: White Mane Publishing Co., 1991.

Wood, Major General G. N. "Burning Washington: The Lighter Side of Warfare," *Army Quarterly* 104 (1973–74): 352–57.

Index

Carleton College Library
One North College Street
Northfield, MN 55057-4097

WITHDRAWN

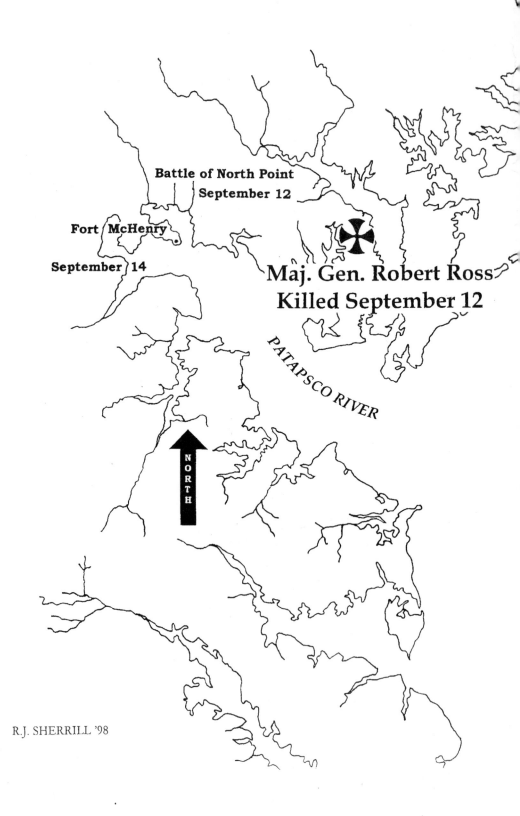

Battle of North Point
September 12

Fort McHenry

September 14

Maj. Gen. Robert Ross
Killed September 12

PATAPSCO RIVER

NORTH

R.J. SHERRILL '98